The Identity of the Church

D1354489

A.T. & R.P.C. HANSON

The Identity of the Church

A Guide to Recognizing the Contemporary Church

SCM PRESS LTD

British Library Cataloguing in Publication Data

Hanson, A. T.
The identity of the church: a guide to
recognizing the contemporary church.
1. Church of England—Doctrines
I. Title II. Hanson, R.P.C.
230'.3   BX5131.2

ISBN 0–334–00683–X

First published 1987
by SCM Press Ltd
26–30 Tottenham Road, London N1

Printed in Great Britain by
Richard Clay Ltd
Bungay, Suffolk

To
The Reverend Michael Hurley SJ
a gallant fellow-soldier in the
ecumenical cause

Contents

Preface

Confusion about the Church

As this preface is being written, many groups of Christians of different traditions are being encouraged to pursue a course of study during the season of Lent, and the title of the course, or of part of it, is 'What Is the Church For?'. Although those who are taking part in this course of study are very likely to benefit from it, still the title is in our view an inappropriate one. You cannot ask what the church is for, as you might ask what the new computer is for or what the Privy Council is for. You might as well ask what is air for or what is the landscape for. The church is there, like the air and the landscape, and you may ask what it is, but to ask what it is for is inappropriate, though perhaps the question is typical of the mechanistic, utilitarian, technologically conditioned spirit of the age. The question is also typical of the confusion surrounding the meaning and use of that word 'church' which prevails today.

To the vast majority of people the word means a building devoted to Christian religious purposes which they never enter except on rare and conventional occasions, and which when they do enter it fills them with an obscure sense of embarrassment. If they were to picture this church it would certainly be in the form of an imitation Gothic building such as our Victorian forefathers delighted to erect with a vast, high nave, an ornate sanctuary separated from the nave by a narrow chancel, and an impressive spire. This building would have been built in imitation of a style which pre-dated the nineteenth century by at least five hundred years and which was devised for functions and purposes which were hardly ever in fact intended or carried out in Victorian churches – those for which medieval cathedrals used to be built. This archetypal church, therefore, this picture which is unconsciously imprinted on the imaginations of the great majority of people in this country

is largely fictitious. If the worshippers in the average church in
England today were to be asked why their church is shaped as it is,
they would have to answer, 'Because a century ago the leaders of
the church liked to indulge in fantasy'. And this fact adds to the
confusion about the church in the minds of people today.

The second most common use of the word 'church' today is to
denote the ministry of any of the denominations. The expression
'he is going into the church' does not mean that the person mentioned is entering a building or is about to be baptized, but that he
is intending to seek ordination in one or other of the Christian
ministries functioning in the country today. This is a mistaken
usage, deriving from the period when the clergy of the medieval
church were much greater in numbers and influence than any
clergy of any denomination are today, and it implies that the church
consists of two bodies, some professional paid Christians called
clergy and some amateur, voluntary Christians called laity. In spite
of its wide prevalence, this expression is misapplied and must subtly
contribute to confusion in the minds of many about the church.

A third use of the word 'church' is that which the great majority
of practising Christians employ today. It means in this sense 'my
denomination'. If we say 'the church needs more support' we never
mean (if we are Anglicans) 'the Methodists across the road need
more support', and even less if we are Roman Catholics do we
mean when we use this phrase 'The Church of England needs
more support'. 'The church' for the vast majority of practising
Christians in this country means 'My church, my denomination'. It
does not even mean the world-wide denomination (far less world-
wide Christianity), but much more often, the local manifestation of
the particular denomination to which the speaker belongs. It is
interesting to note that not one of the uses so far surveyed corre-
sponds to any expression to be found in the New Testament.

When people use the words 'the church' in this very common,
denominational meaning some of them certainly imply, consciously
or unconsciously, that there exists only one genuine church, that is
theirs. Undoubtedly this adds to the confusion prevailing today on
the subject of the church. A recent convert to the Orthodox Church
in this country on leaving the Church of England declared to the
press that he was joining the true church. It would have been
relevant to ask him, 'Which true church?' Those who attended a

recent meeting of the Anglicans and Orthodox were present at a reception which included many members of the Roman Catholic Church as well as the Orthodox representatives. On this occasion an Orthodox archbishop, welcoming the guests, thought it suitable to remark that the Orthodox Church was the only true church. Anglicans who at this point found themselves in the company of two bodies of people each representing a large Christian community, both of which claimed to be the only true church, must be pardoned if they felt a certain sense of irony.

There are those in the Church of England who hold that their church is represented wholly and without remainder in the acts and decisions of the General Synod. There are those who believe that the Church of England is in some genuine sense represented in the Houses of Parliament, not only in the Upper House, in which some of the bishops of the Church of England sit as of right, but also in the Lower, which they regard as holding a kind of watching brief over the church. There are those who take very seriously the position of the Queen as Supreme Governor of the Church of England and Defender of the Faith. There are those who believe that the church is virtually constituted by the bishops; there are those who appear to think that when a man is consecrated as a bishop of the Church of England he becomes by some strange process what he was not before – a sworn betrayer of orthodoxy and underminder of traditional liturgy determined to introduce heresy in order to mislead ordinary decent people. These diverse opinions certainly add to contemporary confusion about the church.

In this preface therefore we must make clear what we are intending to do in this book. We will discuss and make as clear as we can what, in our view, the church is, what are its limits, what should be its doctrine, what is the status of its ministry and the nature of its sacraments, how in the present state of disunion, confusion and uncertainty we can conceive that the church of Jesus Christ exists. We are in fact attempting to give a theology of the church, in formal language what is called an ecclesiology. We think that this task is particularly necessary for Anglicans today, and perhaps most for members of the Church of England, who have every reason to be particularly confused and uncertain on this point. The fact that we live in a period when ecumenical co-operation and dialogue are being practised as they never have been in the history of Christianity since denominations developed makes the necessity for being clear on this subject all the greater. But the authors must insist that they are not here proposing to deal with the many ethical, social, political and even economic issues and choices which face the church (however it be defined) today. There will be places in which some of these issues will necessarily be referred to, but they will only appear as far as they are strictly necessary to a theological analysis of the church. Nor are we directly setting out a blueprint for the church of the future, though we may indulge in a little prediction at the end of the book. But this is not an attempt to remodel the shape and structure of the church, though it certainly will involve a good deal of criticism of one sort or another. This warning should obviate that particularly exasperating type of criticism which blames authors not for what they have written but for what the reviewer thinks they should have written. This book is a strictly theological exercise.

This book is, it must be understood, intended as a sequel to that work in which the two authors first joined forces, *Reasonable Belief* (1980). The reader must therefore expect that we shall quite often refer to that book, leaving subjects which we might have tackled here to the discussion of them in the earlier work. Joint authorship of this type entails (at least for these authors) that both take responsibility for whatever is said in the book, which both have approved, whichever of them may have originally written it. It also means that occasionally both speak of what only one has experienced; e.g. only one of us has lived in India and only one visited Russia, but we speak as if both have. This might be termed by grammarians the didymean (or geminian) plural.

1

The Doctrine of the Church: A Historical Survey

1. The Church in the New Testament

For the last hundred and fifty years the doctrine of the church has been a subject of keen debate among Christians in the West. In the nineteenth century the rise of the Oxford Movement in the Church of England, and the event of the First Vatican Council in the Roman Catholic Church occasioned impassioned disputes among Christians of these two communions. Since then the growth of the ecumenical movement, and the very significant meeting of the Second Vatican Council, have kept the topic of the church in the foreground. The extension of the Christian church to the third world, and the fact that in many countries today the church is facing government discrimination and even persecution, have also influenced Christian thinking about the nature of the church.

This work is written from the standpoint of two Anglican theologians living during the closing decades of the twentieth century; we have suggested that Anglicans, at least members of the Church of England, are in a state of confusion today about what they should hold concerning the nature of the church. From about 1889 (when *Lux Mundi* was published)[1] until roughly the end of the Second World War there was something like an agreed doctrine of the church among Anglo-Catholics. This was largely due to the outstanding intellectual leadership of Charles Gore. Since that time Gore's doctrine of the church has been severely shaken both by the influence of the ecumenical movement and by the progress of New Testament scholarship. It is still true to say that in so far as there is an agreed doctrine of the church among Anglo-Catholics it is that of Charles Gore, but it is probably only held in its original form by those who have not kept abreast with either biblical or theological scholarship (a group, it seems, which is still quite numerous). Other Anglicans simply do not seem to have a doctrine of the church and perhaps do not see the need of one.

But surely this is an era in which of all times Anglicans ought to have some sort of an idea as to what doctrine of the church they hold. In some ways it might seem to be the era of the *via media*. Thanks to the new atmosphere inside the Roman Catholic Church inaugurated by Pope John XXIII many of the best informed Roman Catholic theologians are beginning to reformulate some of their basic doctrines. Among these the doctrine of the ministry and the nature of the priesthood certainly find a place. The other reformed churches on the other hand, partly through experience in the church of the third world, and partly through their membership of the World Council of Churches, are modifying some of their more rigidly anti-catholic attitudes. Very often we hear from both these camps formulations of doctrine which sound surprisingly like what Anglicans have regarded as their traditional beliefs. It is not that everybody is becoming more Anglican, but that the Anglican appeal to early tradition and to the Bible as interpreted by the church of the first few centuries is being widely recognied as the best way forward for the divided denominations. In these circumstances it would be very unfortunate if Anglican theologians were to find themselves unable to put forward any ideas as to the nature of the church or of the ordained ministry. In the past hundred years Anglican scholars and theologians have contributed much that is of value in this area. There is every reason why they should continue to do so now.

This work is therefore an attempt to formulate a credible doctrine of the church today. That word 'credible' has been carefully chosen because in the past both Anglicans and some Christians of other traditions have formulated doctrines of the church which have not been credible. The main reason for this has been that they have formulated doctrines which unchurch vast numbers of perfectly good Christians. Any doctrine of the church that includes the assumption that millions of Christians, either now or in the past, must be judged not to be real members of the church at all refutes itself. An example of this would be the claim made by Pope Boniface VIII in 1302 that only those Christians who acknowledged the jurisdiction of the Bishop of Rome could be saved; or the claim made by some Anglicans that confirmation by episcopal laying on of hands was an essential part of the process of entering the Christian church; or the belief that Christians belonging to non-episcopal denominations were not really part of the church at all and were incapable of celebrating the eucharist; or the tenet cherished still by extreme Protestants in Northern Ireland, that Roman Catholics are so far gone in doctrinal error that they may not be regarded as Christians at all; or the view, which is certainly defended by some Eastern Orthodox Christians, that since the schism between the Eastern and the Western Churches in 1054 there has been no legitimate Bishop of Rome and consequently that the papal throne has been vacant for more than nine hundred years. All such doctrines of the church are strictly incredible because they deny what are easily verifiable facts of religious experience or historical reality.

There is another sense in which not only the doctrine of the church but the church itself can become incredible. If the church's manner of life conflicts too violently with its professed beliefs people will cease to believe in it. This is a sphere of which the church has become much more conscious during the last generation under the influence of Marxist thought and practice. If, for example, Anglicans resolutely insist that episcopal government must be included in any reunion scheme to which they are a party, they render themselves incredible when their own system of episcopal government is so bureaucratic that the average worshipper never meets his diocesan bishop. Or if the Bishop of Rome styles himself 'the servant of the servants of God', but makes autocratic claims to the unquestioning obedience of all Christians, he becomes incredible. If any church claims to be the area in which is to be found Jesus Christ, who came 'not to be ministered to but to minister', it loses its credibility as long as it ignores the plight of those in its midst who are poor, helpless, or oppressed. We are faced therefore with the question: what can we say about the nature of the church today that is consistent with the witness of scripture, the evidence of history, and the experience of Christians?

We begin, as we must, with the doctrine of the church in the New Testament. At the outset we must make one observation that has great significance for how we interpret the evidence. We can no longer assume that the two great 'captivity epistles' Colossians and Ephesians are authentically Pauline. We must even more

emphatically reject the Pauline authorship of the Pastoral Epistles –
I and II Timothy and Titus. These are conclusions which have
been accepted by scholars on the Continent ever since the turn of
the century, but have only just begun to penetrate the consciousness
of those who are interested in the doctrine of the church in England.
The reasons for these conclusions cannot be given here; but it can
be said with confidence that the Pauline authorship of Ephesians is
defended by few scholars today. The question of Colossians is
more complicated; it is difficult to deny that Colossians 4 has a
thoroughly Pauline ring; but other features in the first three chapters seem to link the letter closely with Ephesians. Certainly as far
as the doctrine of the church is concerned it is closer to Ephesians
than it is to the universally acknowledged Paulines. As for the
Pastorals, almost every New Testament scholar has given up the
attempt to defend the Pauline authorship. The great majority of
scholars would put them at least a generation after Paul's death. A
date early in the second century seems the most likely.

These are not idle speculations. If Colossians and Ephesians are
not Pauline then we do not have to try to harmonize their account
of the church as the body of Christ with what Paul says in I
Corinthians and Romans about the church as the body of Christ.
This is probably a gain since the two figures, though obviously
connected, are not identical and do not convey exactly the same
relationship. The dating of the Pastorals is even more important for
our topic: if Paul did not write the Pastorals but they in fact reflect
the state of the church at the end of the first century, then in Paul's
day we cannot claim that there was either a fixed ministry with
graded orders, or a regular ceremony of ordination, or strong
emphasis on the deposit of belief. As we have seen, only in very
recent times have Anglican ecclesiologists begun to accept these
critical conclusions. It may therefore be a good moment for Anglicans to reassess their doctrine of both church and ministry.

Did Jesus found the church? This claim is often made, particularly perhaps by those who also hold that he foresaw a long history
for his church and that he therefore provided it with a duly authorized ministry. But it is a misleading statement; it conjures up a
picture of Jesus at some point cutting a white tape and saying: 'I
hereby declare the Christian church to be open'. Or at least it
suggests that Jesus founded the church in the way that Alexander

the Great founded Alexandria, or the way that W.B. Yeats and Lady Gregory founded the Abbey Theatre. We must say that Jesus did not found the Christian church in any of these senses. When Jesus came the church was there already. Even Charles Gore, who held very definite opinions about Jesus' intentions for his church, wrote in old age that one should not think of Jesus as 'founding' the church: 'The church is in the first instance the holy people of God'.[2] Karl Barth well points out that there is not in the New Testament any formal institution or founding of the church as there is of the eucharist because the account of Jesus in the New Testament is the account of the renewed people of God.[3] We thus encounter one of the two most important descriptions of the church in the New Testament, the church as the people of God.

But what does the word 'church' mean. It translates of course a Greek word, *ekklēsia*. In profane Greek usage it does not carry any necessarily religious overtones. It is not a cultic word. The same can be said for all the words used in the New Testament to denote those who undertake ministry in the church, a profoundly significant fact for the doctrine of the ministry. It first occurs in Paul's letters and is obviously a fully accepted term which Paul himself did not introduce. It means literally the assembly of those who are 'called out', but there is no evidence that New Testament writers make any capital out of this. They never use the verb *ekkalein* 'to call out' or the noun *ekklētoi* 'those called out'.[4] The LXX uses the word *ekklēsia* to render the Hebrew word *qāhāl* or 'assembly', usually of the assembly of Israel in the wilderness. But it also uses *sunagōgē* to translate the same Hebrew word. Schmidt surmises that the word *ekklēsia* may have been adopted by Greek speaking Jewish Christians to designate the Christian church in distinction to the synagogue.[5] Paul normally uses the word for the local church. He can write of 'all the *ekklēsiai* (churches) of Christ' in Rom. 16.16. There seems to be a consensus among scholars that he can occasionally use *ekklēsia* for the universal church and that he does so in I Cor. 12.28.

Only twice in the Gospels is Jesus represented as using the word *ekklēsia*, Matt. 16.18 and 18.17. The first of these passages relates the promise of Peter that on this rock Jesus would build his church, and in the second passage Jesus tells his disciples to bring the case of a recalcitrant brother before the church. If these are authentic sayings of Jesus it is very unlikely that they were originally uttered in Greek, so we are driven to look for a Hebrew or Aramaic equivalent for *ekklēsia*. Schmidt[6] points out that in the first passage *ekklēsia* refers to the universal church and in the second to the local church, so we must look for a Semitic word that can bear both meanings, by no means a simple task. Schmidt assumes that Jesus normally spoke in Aramaic to his disciples. If so the word we seek is unlikely to be *q'hālā*, the Aramaic equivalent of the Hebrew *qāhāl*, since that word is very rare in rabbinic literature. An alternative is *'ēdāh*, a word used in the Hebrew Bible for the congregation of Israel, frequently translated by the LXX with *sunagōgē*. This word is used by the Qumran community for their sect. A more likely candidate is the Aramaic *k'nisitā'*, the same word as is used today for the parliament in modern Israel. This word is used to render *ekklēsia* in the Syriac versions of the New Testament. Schmidt conjectures that this word may have been used by Jews to describe the earliest Christian community, which would of course be in their eyes a nonconformist sect.[7] But there must be the very gravest doubt as to whether these two Matthaean passages give us anything like Jesus' authentic words. We do not find that in the rest of the New Testament Peter holds the key position that Matt. 16.16f. suggests; and the second passage looks very much as if it reflects the situation of the early church rather than the circumstances of Jesus' own life.

The fundamental and oldest account of the church in the New Testament is that it is the people of God. Just as Israel was God's people under the old dispensation so the Christian church is God's people under the new. But this in itself implies an all-important modification of this statement: the Christian church is the people of God in the messianic age. In other words, the doctrine of the church in the New Testament is thoroughly eschatological; the people of God are living in the last time, between the coming of the Messiah in the flesh and his *parousia* at the end of history.

Bultmann puts this clearly when he writes that the *ekklēsia* is 'the eschatological congregation, and hence its existence belongs to the eschatological salvation-occurrence'.[8] Conzelman[9] calls the church 'the eschatological people of God', and Ridderbos 'the messianic congregation of the great end-time'.[10] Though Paul, as we shall see, uses another description as well, he is just as familiar as any other writer of the New Testament with the concept of the church as the people of God. The difficult middle chapters of Romans, chapters 9–11, are entirely taken up with making sense of this transfer of God's election from old Israel to new church; and the detailed analogy from the experience of Israel in the wilderness period which we find in I Cor. 10.1–11 is wholly dependent on this assumption. It is indeed echoed in every other part of the New Testament. See for example Stephen's speech in Acts 7; I Peter 1.1; 2.1–10; James 1.1. Indeed we must describe this as the normative and essential description of the church in the New Testament.

Whiteley quoting Fridischen writes 'Each community represents on the spot the one and indivisible Christian church', but he rejects the claim that 'the whole church is present in each congregation'.[11] Alan Richardson in his *Introduction to the Theology of the New Testament* has the distinction of devoting proper attention to the unity of the church in the New Testament: 'Men did not found the church', he writes, 'nor can they found a new church', and he adds that the only words in the vocabulary of the New Testament by which our modern denominations could be indicated would be *schismata* or *haireseis*, 'schisms' or 'sects'. The New Testament writers would have written no doubt 'The British Council of Schisms'! He concludes: 'men cannot create church unity, and (let us thank God for it) they cannot destroy it'.[12]

There are literally dozens of figures used for the church in the New Testament; bride of Christ, building, plant, priesthood, race, temple. But one stands out above the rest, both because it is used rather more and because it has been far more influential in the tradition of the church. This is the figure of the church as the body of Christ. Behind this figure lies the belief that is at the root of all Paul's christology. For Paul the sufferings, death, and resurrection of Jesus Christ were not merely historical events. They were also cosmic events. Consequently Christ's disciples must in some sense reproduce these events in their lives: Christians must suffer with Christ, die with Christ (in baptism), and rise with Christ. This is because, owing to the cosmic act of salvation which God has accomplished through him, all Christians are 'in Christ'. Indeed, since the term 'Christian' had probably not been invented in Paul's day, this is his description of a Christian, one who is 'in Christ'. Bultmann calls this phrase 'an ecclesiological formula'.[13] Both he

and Kümmel[14] believe that the concept of dying and rising with
Christ was borrowed by the very earliest Christians (not by Paul)
from the mystery religions. This is debatable. The concept may
have come to Paul through the apocalyptic tradition in Judaism.
Alan Richardson is right when he says: 'The Pauline conception of
the church as the new-created humanity in Christ is a thoroughly
eschatological conception'. [15]

We should be clear as to what exactly it is that Paul says about
the church as the body of Christ in I Corinthians and Romans, the
only letters in which he uses the concept. What he writes in I Cor.
12.27 is 'you are a body in Christ'. [16] We could almost paraphrase it
'a space for Christ to develop'. E. Schweizer in his article on *sōma*
in the *Theological Dictionary of the New Testament* says that the body
of Christ is the area in which the church lives. [17] Mersch rightly
adds that Paul never says that the members of the church **are** the
Spirit.[18] We must conclude, though this would not be Mersch's
view, that Paul does not mean the members of the church *are*
Christ. By *sōma* (body), says Bultmann, Paul normally means the
whole person.[19] This is where what Paul says in I Corinthians and
Romans differs from what is said in Colossians and Ephesians. In
Romans and I Corinthians the church is the whole body of Christ.
In Colossians and Ephesians Christ is the head of which the church
is the body in the sense of the trunk. Elsewhere, Bultmann points
out that Paul does not say Christ and the believer share the same
supernatural substance, but that they share the same life-situation.[20]

Before we decide how literally the concept 'body of Christ'
should be understood, it is as well to point out that this figure is just
as eschatological as is the concept of the church as the people of
God. Alan Richardson writes: 'not till "the day of Christ" will the
church of redeemed sinners be in actuality what it is now eschato-
logically, the perfect manhood of Christ'.[21] When Paul exclaims
'Shall I therefore take the members of Christ and make them
members of a prostitute' (I Cor. 6.15), he does not mean that this
could literally happen. He is protesting at the idea that those who
are called to be members of Christ should make themselves members of prostitutes.[22] The church is destined to be the sphere of
Christ's unhindered activity, and is partly so already, but will only
be wholly so at the *parousia*, when all the faithful will live fully in the
dimension of the Spirit.

There is, however, one tradition of exegesis that takes the concept of the church as the body of Christ with full seriousness. The Catholic tradition generally has tended to deny that we are here dealing with a figure, and to press the phrase almost to the extreme of literalness. This is indeed the theme of Emil Mersch's well known book *The Whole Christ*.[23] But this tradition has its champions among Anglicans also. Lionel Thornton; for example, can write: 'We are members of that body which was nailed to the cross, laid in the tomb, and raised to life on the third day'.[24] This is a sentence which has a fine rhetorical ring about it but which encounters overwhelming semantic difficulties if one wishes to translate it into language intelligible to an educated person today. Even Alan Richardson, who is no reductionist in this area of thought, demurs at this language.[25] The sort of interpretation defended by Thornton was, however, given a new lease of life by an influential book by J.A.T. Robinson published in 1952 called *The Body*.[26] In this work Robinson, relying to a large extent on the evidence of Colossians, which he took to be authentically Pauline, argued that Paul viewed the members of the church as literally constituting Christ's risen body. On the whole subsequent scholarship has tended to reject this theory. Ridderbos in particular refutes it in detail:[27] he points out that such a theory requires that it was the church who appeared to Paul on the Damascus Road. J.A.T. Robinson had claimed that the essential transition is made at I Cor. 10.16-17: the bread is made the body of Christ; we eat it and so we become the body of Christ. Ridderbos replies (*a*) 'body' and 'blood' here are not a general description of Christ but indicate his sacrificial death. We are given a share in that death by eating and drinking. (*b*) The church therefore cannot be identified with the sacrificial death of Christ. Paul is saying that the unity of the church consists in its sharing in the body and the blood. (*c*) We must accordingly regard 'body of Christ' as a metaphor. (*d*) Both sacraments represent the unity achieved by Christ's death. He adds that the metaphor cannot be pressed in Col. 2.19 and Eph. 4.15-16 (both of which passages Robinson took to be Pauline): 'Christ cannot be thought of as a subordinate part of his own body which is involved in the process of growth towards adulthood, and which as part of the body must itself consequently be "in Christ"'.[28] Whiteley reaches very similar conclusions when he writes: 'the eucharistic body of Christ is not to be identified either with the church or with the resurrection body; but it is a link between the two'.[29]

Naturally there has been much speculation as to the origin of Paul's figure of the church as the body of Christ: did it come from Jewish apocalyptic (Albert Schweitzer), rabbinic speculation about the primal man Adam (W.D. Davies), Stoic philosophy (W.L. Knox), or incipient Gnosticism (Bultmann)? We cannot give a confident answer. But one might venture a guess that Paul believed he had scriptural justification for his doctrine, even though we cannot trace where in scripture he found it. We can see, however, why Paul felt it necessary to elaborate the figure: the traditional apocalyptic programme associated the resurrection of at least the faithful with the coming of the Messiah and the inauguration of the messianic age. The Messiah had come and had even become 'the firstborn from the dead'. Why had the rest of the faithful not also been granted this resurrection, especially those who had died as believers? The concept of the church as the body of Christ went some way towards solving this problem.

This figure is, we have insisted, eschatological. It depends on the assumption that the *parousia* is coming soon. But the *parousia* did not come and nearly two thousand years later shows no sign of coming. What difference does this make? A good deal undoubtedly. Perhaps the eucharist is to some extent a substitute for the *parousia;* at the eucharist the church is sacramentally apprehensible as the body of Christ. But the non-arrival of the *parousia* must serve us as a constant warning against the danger of identifying the church *tout court* with the body of Christ. Such an identification has led in the past to megalomania on the part of church leaders. There is always an element of 'not yet' in the being of the church. The Christian moral imperative is 'be what you are'. Or as Ridderbos puts it 'What the church is in Christ it is more and more to become'.[30]

In the two letters Colossians and Ephesians the 'body' figure is modified. The church is the body of which Christ is the head. This probably represents a simplification of what was at best a very difficult doctrine. The author of the Pastorals, no profound theologian, ignores it altogether. But this modified presentation of the metaphor is complicated in Ephesians by the desire of the author to allow for continuous growth in the church. Schmidt rightly says that it is illogical that Christ should be both the head of the church and the bridegroom (see Eph. 5.21–23); and the notion of the body (or house) growing is not consistent with the view of the authentic Paul.[31]

One gains the impression that in Colossians-Ephesians the universal church is more clearly and more closely identified with Christ ('the new man') than is the case in the authentic Pauline epistles. This is perhaps part of the process of simplifying Paul's obscure doctrine in the light of the realization that the *parousia* was not to be expected immediately. But it also represents a certain idealization of the church; the church of Colossians-Ephesians is more like the form that the church is destined (or at least called) to grow into. We do not find here a realistic existential description of the church as it is in any given moment in history. For a full account of this see Stig Hanson, *The Unity of the Church in the New Testament*.[32]

There is something like the doctrine of the church as the body of Christ in the Fourth Gospel. The implication of John's comment in 2.21 is that the church, the place where God is to be worshipped in Christ, is Christ's risen body: 'But he spoke of the temple of his body.' The figure of the vine in John 15. 1–8 points in a similar direction. We are only part of the vine in so far as we abide in Christ. We also find in John 17 and in Ephesians 3.10 a clear concept of the universal church, but it is not hierarchically structured: in the list of unities given in Eph. 4.3–6 we have 'one body' and 'one baptism' but not 'one eucharist' or 'one ministry'. At the very end of the New Testament period we encounter in the Pastoral Epistles two new features: a regularly ordained ministry and something like a rival church (see also I John 2.18–19). But this we will examine later.

Bultmann has an illuminating comment on the development of the doctrine of the church during the New Testament period. Paul, he says, knew how to unify the idea of the body of Christ with the idea of the Israel of God, since for him the body of Christ was precisely the eschatological congregation. But in later times the eschatological element and the emphasis on the people of God fade out and an ontological interpretation of the body figure fills the foreground. Christians forgot that they were living in the end times 'and the church changed from being a fellowship of salvation to being an institution of salvation'.[33] We may sum up the situation by saying that in the New Testament the church is constituted by worship and life. It is liturgical and sacramental, but not hierarchical or sacerdotal.

2. The 'Catholic' View

Before we pursue the history of the doctrine of the church down to our own day, we ought to give some attention to a quite different interpretation of the New Testament evidence which is probably held by a majority of Christians today. This is the 'Catholic' theory of the origin of the church. It is closely bound up with the doctrine of the origin of the ministry, so we will have to look at this also, though we reserve a fuller treatment of the doctrine of the ministry until later.

We begin with the Roman Catholic view. We shall confine ourselves to Mersch and to the two ecclesiological documents of Vatican II. This is because we are looking for something like officially approved doctrine. We could certainly find very different views about both church and ministry in the works of a mumber of outstanding Roman Catholic theologians who are *au fait* with biblical scholarship, such as Raymond Brown, Edward Schillebeeckx, and R.J. Daly. But their conclusions have not yet received anything like official acceptance.

Emil Mersch SJ, as we have already noted, wrote a very influential work between the wars on the doctrine of the mystical body. He certainly represented the official position in his day. Indeed at that time in the history of the Roman Catholic Church no other view could easily have found expression. Mersch identifies the church *tout court* with the Roman Catholic Church, leaving no room for any other form of church. He is therefore faced with the problem of defining the status of those claiming to be Christians who do not accept the authority of the Pope. He has in fact left himself with very little room for manoeuvre if he wishes to avoid the simple but unacceptable solution that all non-Roman Catholic Christians have the status of pagans. He gets pretty close to this position, it is true: 'Apart from unity (sc. with the Roman Catholic Church) charity is false, the martyr dies in vain, and miracles are a deception'.[34] But schismatics, he allows, may have some good in them; if so, this because of 'the hidden bond that still unites (the sect's) adherents with the parent stem'.[35] They seem in fact to be anonymous Catholics. Towards the end of his work he tries to answer the question: who are members of the mystical body? The answer seems to be: all living members of the Roman Catholic Church, the blessed departed, catechumens, and the souls in purgatory. No room is left for anyone, alive or dead, who is not a member of the Roman Catholic Church.[36] He crowns his work by the statement 'The Church is Christ'.[37] Fr Mersch's doctrine has the merit of simplicity, but it must surely come under the category of 'incredible' mentioned above. We can here appropriately quote Avery Dulles SJ: 'the idea that most of mankind would be eternally damned for not being Catholics is incredible and theologically intolerable'.[38]

From Mersch we turn to the Second Vatican Council. This, like its predecessor was very much concerned with ecclesiology and it provides an account of how the church was founded. We begin with a statement from *Lumen Gentium*, the Dogmatic Constitution on the Church. After his resurrection Christ 'handed over (the church) to Peter to be shepherded (John 21.17), commissioning him and the other apostles to propagate and govern her ... This church, constituted and organised in the world as a society, subsists in the Catholic Church, which is ruled by the successor of Peter, and by the bishops in union with that successor, although many elements of sanctification and truth can be found outside her visible structure. These elements, however, as gifts properly belonging to the church of Christ, possess an inner dynamism towards Catholic unity'.[39] Here is Mersch's claim reasserted but modified. Those outside the Roman Catholic Church are not completely disqualified. Mersch would have said that the church founded by our Lord consists of the Roman Catholic Church; 'subsists in' is a notable concession. A further modification comes when, speaking of those who are not Roman Catholics, the document says: 'we can say that in some real way they are joined with us in the Holy Spirit'.[40]

Then we hear of 'a sacred teaching authority'.[41] And later comes a full-blooded theory of apostolic succession: 'Jesus Christ ... established his holy Church by sending forth the apostles ... He willed that their successors, namely the bishops, should be shepherds in his Church even to the consummation of the world ... He placed Peter over the other apostles, and instituted in him a permanent and visible source and foundation in unity and fellowship'.[42]

'The apostles took care to appoint successors in this hierarchically structured society.'[43] The bishops are successors to the apostles: 'he who hears them hears Christ while he who rejects them rejects Christ '.[44] Episcopal consecration, it seems, confers the grace of teaching.[45] But the episcopal body has no authority without the Pope, who has 'full, supreme, and universal power over the church'.[46] Everyone is under obligation to accept the teaching of the Pope even when he is not speaking *ex cathedra*: 'Although the individual bishops do not enjoy the prerogative of infallibility, they can nevertheless proclaim Christ's faith infallibly'.[47] The Pope's definitions 'of themselves, and not from the consent of the church, are justly styled irreformable'.[48] The faithful in a diocese are described as the bishop's subjects.[49] Later on we read: 'With ready Christian obedience laymen as well as all disciples of Christ should accept whatever their sacred pastors, as representatives of Christ, decree in their role as teachers and rulers of the church'.[50]

We now turn to the *Decree on Ecumenism*, where we certainly find a genuine desire to concede as much to those who are not Roman Catholics as the principles expressed in *Lumen Gentium* can allow. We learn that those born into divided churches cannot be blamed for their divisions: 'men who believe in Christ and have been truly baptised are in real communion with the Catholic Church even though this communion is imperfect'.[51] 'All those who have been justified by faith in baptism are members of Christ's body'.[52] Again 'The Holy Spirit has used separated churches and communities ... as means of salvation whose efficacy comes from the grace and truth which in all its fullness has been entrusted to the Catholic Church'. But they add 'We believe that our Lord entrusted all the blessings of the new covenant to none others than the apostolic college of which St. Peter is the head'.[53] We also learn that the Eastern churches possess 'true sacraments and above all by apostolic succession the priesthood and the eucharist'.[54] This admission must further complicate the ecclesiology of the Roman Catholic Church. We end with a warning note: 'ecclesial communities which are separated from us lack the fullness of unity with us which should flow from baptism ... we believe that especially because of the absence of the sacrament of Orders they have not preserved the genuine and total reality of the eucharistic mystery.'[55]

About this presentation of the Roman Catholic doctrine of the church both before and at the Second Vatican Council we must remark first that it shows no sign whatever of the influence of New Testament criticism: texts are quoted without any consideration of their relation to the New Testament as a whole. Statements are made about the transmission of authority from Christ through the apostles to the first bishops which could not possibly stand up to strict historical scrutiny. The figure of Peter is seen in the light of later tradition rather than of what can actually be learned about him from the New Testament. In the same vein really nothing is abated from the full papal claims of Vatican I. We are still presented with a Pope who is an autocrat demanding unquestioning obedience. But to this has now been added a genuine consciousness of the exist-ence of Christians, and even of 'ecclesial communities', outside the Roman Catholic Church. More than that, it seems that valid orders and real sacraments may exist outside this communion. Little or no attempt is made to reconcile these two positions. In fact they are irreconcilable. Logically Mersch holds a far stronger position. But these concessions are of immense significance: they provided a foothold for those theologians inside the Roman Catholic Church who wished to develop a much more optimistic view of Christian communities outside the Roman Catholic Church. These concess-ions and modifications of the old-fashioned rigorist view must be understood not as the last word that can be uttered in the way of concession, but rather as the starting point for the working-out of a drastically altered doctrine of the church which will take account of both biblical criticism and the ecumenical movement.

Just as we chose a semi-official apologist and two official docu-ments to illustrate the Roman Catholic doctrine of the church, so we shall now have recourse to the most influential Anglican theo-logian of the period 1890-1940 as our representative of the Anglo-Catholic doctrine of the church. Anglicanism does not have a 'magisterium'; it does not issue official teaching from a single authority, and does not demand from the laity unquestioning obedience to the word of the hierarchy. But Charles Gore was in his day by far the most influential church leader in the Anglican Communion. As we have had occasion to remark already, in as far as modern Anglo-Catholics have a distinctive doctrine of the church and ministry, it comes from Charles Gore. It will be instructive therefore both to examine his doctrine of the church and to indicate where it seems no longer to be capable of being defended.

Unlike the authors of the documents of Vatican II, Charles Gore cites evidence and argues his case. In 1886 he published a book called *The Church and the Ministry*. It went through several editions, the latest of which in 1936 incorporated Gore's latest thoughts on the subject (Gore died in 1932). It is from this edition that we quote. Gore always held the Pauline authorship of both Colossians and Ephesians, and originally of the Pastoral Epistles as well. By the latest edition he obviously had some doubts about the Pastorals: 'I think myself that the Pastoral Epistles must have been written under St Paul's superintendence, but not in the main by his hand'.[56] This is of course the well known 'secretary hypothesis', still defended by a few scholars. A once-for-all delivered faith (a phrase from the Pastorals of course) suits a once-for-all delivered ministry, he suggests.[57] He assumes that Jesus planned a church in order to contain 'the inestimable treasures of redemptive truth and grace'.[58] He refers to the organization mentioned in Eph.4.11 as 'a visible hierarchy' and of course he attempts to identify at least some of the functions mentioned in that passage with the three orders of the traditional ministry.[59] Later on he writes: 'there have always ... existed in the Church ministers, who, besides the ordinary exercise of their ministry, possess the power of transmitting it'.[60] He is therefore faced of course with the problem of defining the status of non-episcopal ministries: 'Now, what heresy is in the sphere of truth, a violation of the apostolic succession is in the tradition of the ministry'.[61] Again 'No ministry except such as has been received by episcopal ordination can be legitimately or validly exercised in the Church'.[62] The church in the time of the apostles is described as 'a great spiritual hierarchy of graduated orders'.[63] He has to suppose an ordination for Apollos for which there is no evidence in the New Testament, because Paul classes him as one of the stewards of the mysteries of God, whom he wishes to identify as authorized office-holders (I Cor. 4.1–6). Moving on to the time of Ignatius of Antioch, he quotes J.B. Lightfoot to the effect that Ignatius presents us with the spectacle of an episcopal ministry that is 'firmly rooted' and 'completely beyond dispute'.[64] This is pressing the evidence very hard indeed: if it is completely beyond dispute why does Ignatius emphasize and defend it so violently? And how to explain the fact that there appears to be no monepiscopacy in either Rome or Philippi when Ignatius writes to these churches? Gore sums up the situation by saying that Jesus Christ 'founded a society to be the depository of his truth'.[65] We will permit ourselves one more quotation, this time from a later book of Gore's, *The Reconstruction of Belief*: 'St. Paul regarded himself certainly as an officer of the church'.[66]

We must now briefly explain why Gore's position is untenable today and in doing so we will of course be criticizing the position of *Lumen Gentium* as well. Perhaps we can sum it up most succinctly under six heads:

1. Gore does not take the full humanity of Jesus with sufficient seriousness. He represents Jesus as conscious that his movement would have to survive through many centuries of turbulent history, and therefore as deliberately planning a church to safeguard and transmit his teachings and a ministry to rule that church. The evidence that Jesus had any such intentions is flimsy in the extreme, and is mostly drawn from those parts of the Fourth Gospel which are least likely to be historical.

2. As long as one holds that the Pastorals are authentically Pauline one can plausibly argue that an ordained ministry was a feature of church life in Paul's day. Once put them a generation later and you have a 'tunnel period'. Gore had just begun to doubt the full authenticity of the Pastoral Epistles, but could not afford wholly to dissociate them from Paul. Most scholars today put them at the end of the century. If so, there is a tunnel period during which we have no evidence of the transmission of authority.

3. Gore assumes not only that the apostles were the nucleus of the church (which no doubt they were), but also that they were appointed as officers of the church. The evidence for this is not very convincing. For example John, though he represents Jesus as giving authority to the disciples, never calls them apostles and indeed evinces a marked lack of interest in the ordained ministry. The twelve (with James the brother of the Lord) certainly had an authority which Paul respects. But it was an authority that came from their being the nucleus of the church in Jerusalem and from their having been witnesses of the Lord's resurrection. On Gore's premises James the brother of the Lord should have been an

original apostle. In addition to this there is virtually no evidence that any of the original twelve transmitted authority to anyone else. In fact in the New Testament we never find an original apostle doing anything like transmitting authority to a successor.

4. There are people in the Pauline churches who have the duty of pastoral oversight; cf. I Cor. 16.15–16; Phil. 1.1; I Thess. 5.12–13. But we are never told that these people had been commissioned (far less ordained) by Paul or by anyone else. They do not look like the ordained clergy of a generation later.

5. By the time of I Peter and the Pastorals an ordained ministry has developed, perhaps in some places even an incohate episcopate. But the evidence suggests that it developed locally. It does not seem to have been authorized from some central authority, least of all from the original apostles. Even in the Pastorals themselves there is no concept of apostolic succession in the sense in which Gore understands it. There is a deep concern for the deposit of faith, a concern which Gore unjustifiably reads back into the mind of Jesus himself.

6. Until the end of the first century the church is neither clerical-ized, hierarchical nor sacerdotal. In the Pastorals we perceive the growth of clerical order and at least a two-tier hierarchy, with perhaps the hint of a third tier. But the ordained ministry is not at all sacerdotal. It is never explicitly associated with the eucharist.

We may sum up our conclusions in three propositions: Jesus did not institute a ministry for the church; the apostles did not transmit authority to any successors: the ordained ministry in the traditional sense only appears on a local scale at the end of the century. It would not be going too far to claim that the great majority of New Testament scholars of all traditions in the West today would accept the truth of these propositions.

3. The Later Church

In order to understand the full significance of the ecumenical movement we must append a brief sketch of the doctrine of the church as it developed up to the end of the nineteenth century. By the end of the first century a structured ministry had emerged consisting of presbyter-bishops and deacons. Very soon after this, by the time of Ignatius (ob. 113) in Asia Minor there had developed a threefold ministry of bishops, presbyters and deacons. We should note this had apparently taken place in and through the church community. The ministry did not descend by a line of authority direct from Jesus through the apostles.

This clerical order proceeded to take over most of the functions which in the Pauline churches at any rate had belonged to the local church as a whole. This process of clericalization can be seen even in the Pastoral Epistles: the sort of advice about doctrine and discipline which Paul in his authentic letters gives to the local church as a whole is given in the Pastorals to the representatives of the ordained ministry.

In the ensuing two centuries the struggle with Gnosticism on the one hand and with Montanism on the other tended to emphasize the church as an institution. No doubt the persecution to which the rulers of the Roman Empire spasmodically subjected the church tended in this direction also. By the year 325 the Christian church consisted of the institution now spread out all over Europe, governed by bishops, who met occasionally in local synods. There were, it is true, schisms, notably in North Africa. But except for North Africa these were on a small scale.

Then came the Constantinian revolution whereby the Empire instead of persecuting the church first granted it liberty, then began to show it favour, and finally adopted it as the state religion obligatory on virtually all subjects of the emperor. This was not an instantaneous, but a very rapid process. It naturally had the effect of greatly increasing the institutional aspect of the church. In the Eastern Empire the church became something like a department of state, and until that Empire fell in 1453 church and state continued to operate in the very closest harmony. Not that there were not conflicts, witness the Iconoclastic controversy. But nobody imagined that the church should be independent of the state.

In the West the course of affairs was different because there the structures of state actually began to collapse. The consequence was that the church had in effect to take over the running of society; church and society became so closely identified that to belong to the one implied belonging to the other. By the end of the Dark Ages (which are usually reckoned to have lasted from about AD 500 to 1000), bishops had become barons (in some parts of

Germany they became independent princes), canon law and secular law were closely integrated, the civil service was staffed by the
clergy, the papacy was in process of becoming a minor European
power. In these circumstances opposition to the church became
treason and was punished by the state. In the East after the fall of
Constantinople the church became a beleaguered citadel, closely
associated as a political unit with its members, so that the very
survival of the community depended on the survival of the church.
One might almost say that from 1453 onwards the Eastern Orthodox Church has spent most of its time in a state of siege, first by
Islam and now by Communism.

The Reformation in the West produced the spectacle of schism
on a grand scale: within the course of one generation the medieval
Catholic Church lost a third of its adherents in Europe, and in the
course of the ensuing three centuries this division was extended
into the new world. But the Protestants did not secede in one body.
As a matter of fact none of the great leaders of the Reformation
explicitly intended to found a new church. When, in 1534, Henry
VIII compelled parliament and the convocations to repudiate the
authority of the Pope, he had no idea that he was inaugurating a
new way of being a Christian. Even the Calvinists, though they
certainly believed that the church needed reformation from the
foundation up, were not consciously forming a sect. They hoped in
fact to capture the whole church, and they succeeded in doing so in
Scotland and elsewhere. In some places, notably the Scandinavian
countries, the entire church turned Lutheran almost overnight.
There was almost no Catholic remnant left. Only the radical reformers (Anabaptists and Mennonites) contemplated the possibility of
a formal break with the state.

The unreformed Catholic Church immediately unchurched the
breakaway groups. This meant that the reformed churches had to
work out an ecclesiology for themselves. Each tradition did this for
itself. The temptation of course was to fall back on a doctrine of an
invisible church: the true church was made up of real Christians
known only to God. But this ecclesiology was no help to church
leaders responsible for the organization and discipline of large
churches numbering millions. On the whole Lutherans and
Calvinists defined the church in terms of correct doctrine and
practice: the church is where the true word of God is preached and

the sacraments rightly celebrated. The Church of England in its Articles adopted this definition (see Article XIX). But since the theory was that everyone in England belonged to the Church of England, Church of England apologists tended to say that everyone in the country ought to belong to the national church. Nonconformists, whether Romanists or Calvinists, were unreasonable people to whom attention need only be paid in as far as they had any political influence.

After the wars of religion in the seventeenth century, Europe settled down into a situation of *cuius regio eius religio*; but mutual tolerance did not come until the nineteenth century. Until then it was almost impossible to be a Protestant with full civil rights in a Catholic country, and difficult to be a Catholic with full civil rights in a Protestant country. Protestants on the whole showed no great desire completely to unchurch Catholics. In the meantime the Protestant churches had suffered a series of schisms, notably the emergence of a strong Methodist church in Britain. In America fissiparous sectarianism flourished. The Church of England had an ambiguous attitude towards Protestants: it regarded them as unnecessary and embarrassing in England, but was prepared to treat them as fellow-Christians on the continent.

There were two important developments in ecclesiology during the nineteenth century: the Roman Catholic Church, threatened by the loss or diminution of its traditional state support in France, Spain, and Austria, rallied round the Pope, adopting a centralizing policy and enforcing ever more complete uniformity in worship. This naturally increased its exclusiveness; the First Vatican Council (1870) defined the infallibility of the Pope. In 1896, in his bull *Apostolicae Curae*, Leo XIII declared Anglican orders to be null and void. In the meantime the rise of the Oxford Movement in the Church of England had begun to swing Anglicanism in a Catholic direction. The hands of those Anglicans were greatly strengthened who believed non-episcopal orders to be invalid and who questioned the status of reformed bodies as parts of the church. The Church of England, now further than ever from unity with a more and more intransigent Rome, seemed permanently inhibited from moving any closer to the rest of Protestantism.

No one in the West knew exactly what to make of the Eastern Orthodox churches. The Council of Trent ignored them. They for their part were equally puzzled by Western Christianity, often feeling themselves as much alienated by its Catholic as by its Protestant forms. A few brave prophets like Solovyov in Russia boldly maintained that in God's eyes the church was not divided, but to most people living at the turn of the century it must have seemed that Christendom was permanently divided into mutually exclusive sects.

2

The Ecumenical Experience

1. The Origins of Ecumenism

The ecumenical movement is an attempt, to be found within all denominations, to remove the barriers between the churches which have grown up through the centuries, with the ultimate aim of recovering a united church. It is usually dated from the Edinburgh Conference of 1910, but of course its roots go much farther back. It has today begun to affect all traditions on an increasing scale. It is probably the most significant movement in the Western church since the Reformation.

Why, we may ask, did Christians suddenly begin to be concerned about the divided church round about the year 1900? They had been divided for long enough. We can distinguish three main causes for this relatively sudden concern:

1. Far-seeing Christians realized that the Constantinian era in church history was coming to an end. In country after country in Europe church and state were moving apart. This was as true of Catholicism as of Protestantism. As each denomination found itself deprived of the support of the state it was natural that it should look towards fellow Christians of other denominations. This feeling did not begin to affect the Roman Catholic Church until well into the twentieth century. The first effect of lack of state support on that church was, as we have seen, to make it adopt a centralizing, exclusive policy. But by half way through the century many of the best minds in the Roman Catholic Church were beginning to realize that they could not for ever ignore the existence of Protestants especially as it was Protestant scholars who were exploiting the relatively new critical approach to the Bible. This realization first

made itself felt on an impressive scale at the Second Vatican Council (1959–63).

2. A marked feature of church life during the nineteenth century was the growth of overseas missions undertaken by all major denominations in the West. These met with varying fortunes; but in some parts of Asia and in many parts of Africa strong indigenous churches began to appear. At first these Asian and African churches seemed to be mere reproductions of Western-style church life in an exotic setting: Gothic buildings such as Western Christians were used to sprang up amid the palm trees of South India; Zulu candidates for the priesthood were expected to take their training in Latin; Lutheran converts in China were sedulously taught the Augsburg Confession. Gradually, however, indigenous church leaders began to emerge. As some of them went to the West for their training they began to realize that a great deal of what they were taught as essential theology was heavily conditioned by Western church history, and much of it was quite irrelevant to their church situation. Moreover they also began to recognize that the Western missionaries who had founded their churches had in fact only transmitted to them part of the total Christian heritage. They could see that it was possible to be a Christian in more ways than one, and they wondered whether what the other denominations offered might not be worth having. In addition in many places they were living among a huge non-Christian population. In such circumstances Western denominational divisions seem an expensive luxury. Consequently there arose an increasing demand for unity from missionaries and church leaders of the third world.

3. Biblical criticism began to have its effect on the thinking of Western theologians. Much of the exclusive claims of the Catholic tradition appeared to be based on very flimsy historical foundations. The original leaders of the Oxford Movement, for instance, could quite genuinely believe in the apostolic succession. But their descendants of one or two generations later, if they had received an up to date biblical and theological training, could maintain no such innocence. They knew, or at least suspected, that the 'apostolical succession' as understood by their fathers and grandfathers was a myth. This inevitably affected their attitude towards those whom they had unchurched on the ground that they did not possess that authority which (they had believed) our Lord had entrusted to the

rulers of his church. Such a shift of opinion seemed for a long time to have left the Roman Catholic Church unaffected. But this was only because a series of Popes, beginning with Leo XIII (Pope from 1878 till 1903) and his successor, Pius X (1903–14) had imposed a rigid censorship upon the church with the aim of preventing any Roman Catholic from adopting (and if possible even studying) the methods of biblical criticism. Such an attempt to suppress free thought and research could not last for ever. By the time that the Second Vatican Council met in 1959 it had been virtually abandoned.

2. The Effects of Ecumenism on Ecclesiology

We must now come to terms with the ecumenical movement ourselves. Our contention is that the ecumenical movement is more than an idea or an ideal; it is an experience, and it is possible to some extent to describe that experience. The first step consists in meeting one's fellow Christians of other traditions and making the discovery that they are perfectly good Christians. They are good Christians not *despite* their being Roman Catholics or Anglicans or Presbyterians, but because of it. As one comes to know one's fellow-Christian and discusses with him or her one's problems as a Christian, one becomes aware that we all have very much the same problems to face, and if we are honest, we confess that we share the same doubts. After a certain amount of this sort of personal contact the 'shop window' attitude which every Christian is tempted to take about his own denomination begins to relax. At first when one finds oneself among Christians of other traditions one's natural tendency is to defend one's own tradition. After all it is one's own and it enshrines certain beliefs and practices that mean much to those who share it. The Catholic emphasizes the complete orthodoxy and harmony of belief in his church; the Protestant points to the freedom and democratic spirit of his; and so on.

But gradually as familiarity and intimacy increase among Christians of different traditions this defensive attitude passes away. Each person is able to admit the weaknesses in his own church; he is even able to laugh at them. There is no longer any need for the 'shop window' attitude. Honesty may prevail. At this point there is general agreement that as Christians we are all in much the same predicament, all trying to cope with much the same problems with the equipment with which we have been furnished, all subject to similar weaknesses, and all sharing in a common belief, though perhaps at this stage it has still to be explored.

This is the point perhaps where the ecumenical conversion may take place. The conversion consists in the transition from a position of recognizing that your fellow Christian of another tradition *is* a fellow Christian in a similar situation to yours to a position of actually liking and admiring the tradition which he represents. This is an experience very difficult to convey; indeed it is almost impossible to translate it into cold print. But it happens. The best one can do is to give some examples of it from one's own experience.

The first missionaries to return to the West after serving for some time in the newly united Church of South India were faced with this problem (*experto crede*). In the Church of South India we had discovered that our various traditions were not necessarily opposed but could actually be complementary. We had come to have a genuine appreciation and admiration for the traditions other than our own that went to make up that church. We had even in some degree begun to see what it felt like to be a Christian of some other tradition. But how to convey this to those at home who had had no such experience? We met with polite (or not so polite) incredulity. 'The traditions of which you speak so warmly do not appear like that here at home. Either they become different when they are transplanted to India or you are mistaken.' That was the prevailing reaction.

I believe that a similar experience was encountered by those who wrote the first ARCIC report on the doctrine of the eucharist and of the ministry as agreed between Anglicans and Roman Catholics. I witnessed an Anglican member of that ARCIC group defending that report before a number of Anglican theologians. They pointed out that, if one were to accept the words of the report in their strict sense, Anglicans had made a number of concessions towards the Roman Catholic claims concerning the papacy which would probably not be acceptable to many Anglicans. The champion of the report replied that the group of Anglican and Roman Catholic theologians who drew up the report simply had not thought in terms of concessions and claims. When they first met, he said, they were very strange and even suspicious of one another. Some members of the group knew very little about the other tradition. But as they continued to meet and to explore each other's minds there grew up a mutual respect and affection, so that by the end some of them admitted that they had come to have a completely new understanding of the other tradition. Their findings therefore were a genuine product of minds that had effected a real meeting. As I listened to his defence of the report I realized that he and his colleagues had indeed enjoyed the ecumenical experience.

The third and last stage of the ecumenical experience is perhaps the most fruitful one: it consists of a sharing of experience, a free interchange of ideas, a going forward to new formulations, new areas of understanding on the basis of what has already been achieved. Now one is no longer, let us say, the Anglican coming into contact with Roman Catholics and Protestants. One is an ecumenical Christian with the task of remoulding the entire church nearer the ideal of unity. One has set out on a campaign in which one's fellow-workers are all Christians of any tradition who have shared the ecumenical experience, and the rest of the church as yet unconverted is one's parish. It is emphatically not that one has abandoned all one's convictions in return for a vague undenominational creed. On the contrary, one retains everything that one values in one's own tradition; but now one shares them with everyone else. Above all this stage requires shared ecumenical activity. This is where the proof of the ecumenical experience comes.

Naturally, the sort of ecumenical activity which is possible varies immensely with the circumstances. It may only consist in running a 'hunger lunch'. It may mean founding a new ecumenical institute. Whatever it is, it has the effect of ranging all the ecumenical workers on one side, bringing them together in one fellowship which transcends denominational barriers, giving them in fact a foretaste of what a united church of the future might be, and, most important of all, convincing them that such a church is a real possibility.

This ecumenical experience and ecumenical activity sooner or later demands a theological justification. Everyone enters the ecumenical experience with the ecclesiology of his own tradition, but that ecclesiology cannot remain unaffected by the ecumenical experience. One simply cannot go on indefinitely working with one's fellow Christian, facing theological problems, discussing theological issues at a deep level, and continue to regard him as a very doubtful candidate for membership of the church. If he is an ordained minister of another tradition, it is at least very difficult indeed to go on with all this joint ecumenical work while still reminding oneself that he is not a genuine minister at all but strictly speaking a schismatic layman. This is not merely a question of politeness; one comes actually in practice to recognize that he has a commission.

There are various ways of avoiding this conclusion, some resorted to by Catholics, some by Protestants. The Catholic may stoutly maintain his exclusive view, but admit to himself that somehow his Anglican or Protestant friends are exceptions. Another half-way stage that is sometimes encountered is to show the utmost friendliness to one's Protestant friends and colleagues, but to omit no opportunity of pointing out how many converts from Protestantism one's own church is gaining. This is, I suppose, a sort of compensation process: 'strictly speaking I should not be so friendly with these people, who are after all heretics and schismatics; but I will make up for it by constantly suggesting that their sects are declining while the true church is increasing.' The Protestant on the other hand compensates himself by treating the Roman Catholic, however friendly and cordial he be, as essentially an alien and exotic species: 'I know you have these extraordinary practices which no doubt mean something to you, but do not expect me ever to make the smallest effort to understand them.' The great repugnance is to admitting the truth: we are all on the same level ecclesiologically and stand in equal need of each other.

Thus genuine ecumenical experience and activity require a new basis for ecclesiology. We have discovered that we are all brothers and sisters in Christ; we share a great deal of the same faith, and would probably find that we share more if we explored it further. We are all in the same predicament. We cannot any longer regard our separated brethren as second-class citizens or even innocent schismatics. We are driven to conclude that in fact we are all equally members of the same church. God does not recognize our divisions, even the most hallowed and ancient of them. If there is schism in the church, it is internal schism and we are all guilty of it. Despite our strenuous efforts through the centuries, we have not succeeded in dividing the church ontologically (in its being). It is still one in God's eyes. Nor can any one denomination, however large, claim to be that church to the exclusion of everyone else.

3. Counter-Arguments Met

We have been taking a lot for granted in the foregoing pages. In particular we have assumed that everyone is open to the ecumenical experience. In fact however, the great majority of active Christians is still largely untouched by the ecumenical spirit, certainly as far as personal experience is concerned. When one estimates in cold blood what the ecumenical experience demands it must be admitted that it is not the sort of thing which the ordinary church-goer could be expected to take in his stride. It means in effect going back in some respects on four hundred and fifty years of history. It does not mean undoing the Reformation but it certainly means transcending it. For all Christians, reformed and unreformed alike, this can be a traumatic experience. For Catholics the heretics and schismatics of yesterday must now be regarded as the beloved separated brethren. For Protestants the benighted bigot and the sheepstealing cleric of yesterday must be welcomed as friends, fellow Christians and fellow workers. It is true that both the Roman Catholic and the Anglican communions respectively have during the last generation asked for a still more remarkable leap into the past on the part of their faithful in the sphere of eucharistic worship; they have asked them to return to a state of affairs which has not existed in the church for sixteen hundred years. But that change has not required new personal contacts, altered relationships with those previously regarded as alien, which is exactly what the ecumenical movement demands.

We must try then to face the arguments that are produced against the ecumenical movement, or at least against pushing it to the extreme which we have outlined above. These arguments seem to be reducible to five in number. Let us consider them in order:

1. 'The ecumenical movement is only a phase or fashion; we shall soon be back where we were before.' This argument is often used by those who do not want to face the considerable change of attitude which the ecumenical experience brings about. They are usually those who were quite satisfied with the relation of the

denominations in the pre-ecumenical period. There may be some
who have a vested interest in the *status quo*; wherever in any
denomination there is anything like an establishment those who
benefit from being members of it naturally oppose change. In
addition there are those (often converts from one tradition to
another) who have what may be called a psychological vested
interest. Some people, for example, join the Roman Catholic
Church apparently because it seems to give them a respectable
reason for disliking or despising their fellow Christians of other
traditions. At the other end of the scale are those whose Protestantism is of a strongly negative character. Their religion seems to
consist in believing and doing exactly the opposite of what Roman
Catholics believe and do. Their *raison d'être* as Christians consists
in a protest against what they regard as the errors of Catholicism.
When the Roman Catholic Church appears to be accepting many
of the principles of the Reformers, they are appalled. Their *raison
d'être* is disappearing before their eyes.

To this argument we must reply that the ecumenical movement
is not simply a passing fashion. It will not just go away if ignored. It
has already effected irreversible changes, especially in the Roman
Catholic Church. Relations between Christians can never be the
same as they were before. Biblical criticism and the progress of
theological thought outside the Eastern Orthodox Church are now
being conducted on an ecumenical scale. Neither can again be
reduced to the position it was in before. To take a simple example:
it was possible in the early years of the century for Pope Leo XIII to
compel all Roman Catholic clergy at least to accept the Mosaic
authorship of the Pentateuch, or at any rate not to deny it in public.
This was one of the conclusions of the Biblical Commission which
he set up and which he commended to the faithful as providing
reliable and officially commended solutions to all questions concerning the Bible. Such a thing would not be possible now, even if a
Pope were foolish enough to try to enforce it. For more than a
generation Roman Catholic scholars have been using the methods
and accepting the conclusions of modern biblical criticism. No
Pope could compel them to disavow this.

More than this: the experience of working closely with Roman
Catholics, clergy, religious, and laity, must convince anyone who
has enjoyed it that their participation in ecumenical activity is

sincere and that a bond has been formed which cannot be broken. There can be no question of any authority in the Roman Catholic Church calling back into a pre-Vatican II situation those of its members who have committed themselves to ecumenical co-operation.

But this applies also to Anglicans and Protestants. For Anglicans who are not mere obscurantists there can be no going back to the position of Charles Gore of fifty years ago. Talk about 'the apostolic ministry' and 'Catholic order' will go on of course. But when it is challenged, examined, when credentials and evidence are asked for, it will not prove to be the Gore position that is defended. Well informed Anglo-Catholics know that they cannot fall back on such arguments.

And what of the Protestants? Do they stand by as a sort of *tertius gaudens* seeing all the arguments against the historical plausibility of the 'apostolic succession' that they have been using for years triumphantly vindicated? They have their own measure of reassessment to do. The traditional Protestant appeal to *sola scriptura* is no longer tenable. It is now clear from the researches of biblical scholars that there never has been a time when scripture was not accompanied by some form of traditional interpretation. Scholars have explored the methods of scripture interpretation used by the authors of the New Testament itself, and have found that they took for granted much of the tradition of Jewish exegesis in which they had grown up. In other words, if it comes to a choice between scripture alone and scripture and tradition, we must opt for scripture and tradition. In this respect the Catholics have been right. This does not mean that any old tradition can be justified. On the contrary, modern historical research has shown that a great many hallowed traditions hitherto treated as undoubted fact must be regarded as unhistorical. The mere claim that a belief has been held for centuries in Christian tradition tells us nothing as to its historical foundation. But scripture without a tradition of interpretation simply falls to pieces. It is not self-interpreting. Indeed, a great task that now awaits Christian theologians in the West, one that should be undertaken on an ecumenical and not a denominational basis, is to decide the exact nature of the Christian tradition of interpreting scripture.

2. 'In order to take part in the ecumenical movement in the way

which has been set out above it is necessary to compromise one's principles. We must not be asked to come to terms with error.' I have heard this argument very recently from a Roman Catholic monk and an Anglican bishop. It is very similar indeed to that which Ian Paisley in Northern Ireland would use as a justification for his denunciation of the ecumenical movement, except that he would speak of 'Reformation principles' instead of 'church principles'. We shall concern ourselves with two sorts of principles here, what are called 'church principles' and doctrinal principles.

'Church principles' usually signifies the belief that the episcopal order, or the episcopal order in unity with the Pope, is essential for the existence of the church, and that those bodies of Christians who do not possess it are so gravely defective that communion with them should be prohibited. Later on in this work we shall be discussing episcopacy more fully. As will be seen, we are very far from dismissing it or despising it. But here it must be firmly asserted that using episcopacy in order to unchurch those who do not have it is not justified on historical grounds. There was a time in the very early history of the church when there was no episcopacy and no substitute for it which might connect the first bishops with the apostles. Episcopacy therefore must not be made a *sine qua non* of church order. We certainly hold the view that it is extremely desirable that episcopal order be extended to those who do not have it. But this should not be attempted by means of making unjustifiable claims on its behalf.

In this context it might be worth while examining that word 'compromise'. If you compromise yourself, you do so in the eyes of someone else. Now suppose for the sake of argument that the Catholic side of the church were to extend communion to all Christians baptized in the name of the Trinity, in whose eyes would they be compromised? Not in their own: one cannot be compromised in one's own eyes. Not in the eyes of those to whom they extend communion, for they do not hold these 'church principles'. The answer can only be: they would compromise themselves in God's eyes. But God has already compromised himself in this respect in as much as he has extended his grace to these non-episcopal Christians. His Holy Spirit is at work among them. Our Lord is not absent from their eucharists. (What this means for the traditional concept of validity we explore later in this work.) The truth is that this language of 'compromising church principles' only makes sense as long as traditional denominational barriers are regarded as sacrosanct. Once admit that God does not respect these barriers and these sacred principles begin to look vulnerable.

There is, however, another sense in which the Catholic wing might seem to be compromising itself in entering into close relations with other Christians. They might be compromising their doctrinal purity. The other day I was present at an ecumenical conference during which a Benedictine monk explained why the Roman Catholic Church cannot enter into communion with Anglicans and Protestants. 'We are sure', he said, 'that we possess doctrinal orthodoxy. We have every reason to suspect that you have not. We must not enter into communion with those whom we suspect to be heretics.'

This was a standard argument before Vatican II. It depends on the assumption that doctrinal orthodoxy can be exactly expressed, defended, and checked by reference to credal and confessional formulae. This assumption has been in fact discredited by the progress of biblical and historical research. It is now widely recognized, not least by leading Roman Catholic scholars, that doctrinal formulae from the past, though valuable as markers and milestones, cannot be treated as unalterable expressions of the truth and need reformulation and often reassessment from time to time. In addition a good deal that was taken to be established fact even as recently as a hundred years ago must now be regarded as legend – a very simple and uncontroversial example is the story of the magi in Matthew 2, which most modern scholars would agree is legend and not history. Doctrinal orthodoxy therefore cannot be neatly measured by credal or other traditional formulae. The whole Christian faith on its intellectual side is undergoing a thorough reassessment in the light of modern knowledge in a number of different areas of thought. In this process Roman Catholic scholars are taking a full part. A claim to possess complete doctrinal orthodoxy on the part of any one tradition is simply an indication that the claimant has not kept abreast with the progress of Christian scholarship. We are all, Catholics and Protestants alike, caught up in the same situation of having to reformulate and reassess our belief. We are more likely to carry through this reassessment successfully if we undertake it together. In such circumstances accusations of heresy are very often beside the point.

It should hardly be necessary to add that Anglicans who accuse Protestant churches of heresy are in an even worse position to justify the accusation than are Roman Catholics. The latter can, if they think it worth while doing so, claim that their church has never officially abandoned a position of the most rigid orthodoxy as far as formulae are concerned, and has indeed until recently shown itself most prolific in producing new formulae for the faithful to accept – not to mention the fact that up to the present moment despite the ecumenical movement it has shown itself still capable of disciplining and restraining those who do not satisfy these formulae. But Anglicanism in general and the Church of England in particular is hopelessly 'compromised', if this means failing to discipline those who deviate from confessional orthodoxy. Not only its layfolk, but its ordained priests can profess and publish views totally at variance with traditional Christianity, or indeed with any recognizable form of Christianity whatever, without the church authorities lifting a finger or doing anything whatever to dissociate his views formally with those of the rest of the church. Such being the situation, for an Anglican to accuse the Protestant churches of heresy is sheer hypocrisy.

3. There is the argument put forward so amusingly by Ronald Knox in *Reunion All Round*: 'Where do you stop? Are you willing to work together with *anyone* for the reunion of the church?' This is perhaps the most serious of the objections. The Christian church is so seriously divided that it is impossible to draw a hard line between those who must be regarded as Christians and those who are so far astray in what they believe and practise as Christians that they cannot well be regarded as Christians. To say this is to admit that it is possible to be a heretic and that there are limits within which Christian orthodoxy can be discerned. They are much wider limits than have traditionally been observed. But we must say that Mormons for example, and probably the Watch Tower Sect, are not Christians and should not be treated as such. Africa is full of various 'independent churches'. Some of these are very little different from the main line churches. Others are forms of traditional African religion thinly disguised as Christianity. How are we to distinguish? Where are we to draw the line?

Perhaps the best solution to a problem to which there is no ideal response is that proposed but not adopted by the World Council of

Churches. It requires a profession of Trinitarian belief from any body of Christians applying for membership. This would exclude professedly Unitarian churches. Even here however, we must distinguish, because some apparently Unitarian churches only refuse a profession of Trinitarian belief on the grounds that they do not approve the use of formal creeds at all. There are Unitarian ministers who firmly believe in the doctrine of the Trinity.

There is also the problem of those who do not believe in the practice of baptism at all, notably in this country the Society of Friends and the Salvation Army. Genuine as is one's admiration for both these bodies, they can hardly be reckoned as 'ecclesial communities', to borrow the useful phrase coined at Vatican II. Their function is really that which religious orders serve in the Roman Catholic Church. If the Church of England in the seventeenth and nineteenth centuries had not been weak and partly paralysed by its connection with the ruling class, they would have been contained as movements within the national church. May one not very respectfully call them noble parasites? They are parasitic only in the sense that they flourish only where there is already a Christian community that practises baptism. On the whole they do not attempt to found churches in non-Christian societies. In such circumstances (a non-Christian society) baptism is essential as an initiatory rite. Without it Christianity would long ago have been absorbed by the surrounding majority religion.

In the long run perhaps this problem may solve itself. Extreme evangelical Protestantism has in itself a fissiparous, centrifugal tendency which would inhibit it from desiring reunion in any circumstances. Extreme fundamentalism runs out into lunatic deviations, witness the British Israel movement.

4. 'Why bother with attempts to reunite the denominations? Why not continue as we are, except that we all accept one another into communion? Mankind is diverse, so very diverse forms of Christianity should be encouraged.' Certainly it would be better that we should all be in intercommunion as we are than that we should continue as we are out of communion with each other. But there are considerable objections to simple communion all round as a solution to our divisions. The main objection is that it provides no means by which the riches of the church, now divided among the separate denominations, can be shared among all. If God has given

some special gifts to each denomination he must wish them to be shared among all his children, not confined to those of one tradition. The only way by which this can be done is by a closer, more integrated form of union than mere federation. Certainly we as Anglicans should wish to share whatever is good in the peculiarly Anglican tradition with everyone else. And we should surely desire to share the peculiar treasures of many other traditions, not least the Roman Catholic and Eastern Orthodox.

Another objection to this solution is that it would only work in the West, where in most places there is a full array of denominations – though even in the West there are many country areas in which virtually only one tradition of Christianity is available. In many (indeed most) parts of the church in the third world the local Christian has no choice of denominations: he must be a member of the local church, whatever its tradition, for there is no other. This was brought vividly home to my mind on one occasion in South India: upon formation of the united church, a theological college had been formed on the site of an already existing Anglican one. This meant bringing in members of the other uniting traditions on to the staff. Since the site was in an ex-Anglican area there was on it a fine cathedral in which the daily recitation of the Prayer Book office of Morning and Evening Prayer took place. A member of the staff of the newly formed college was an Indian ex-Congregationalist. He had been converted from Hinduism as a young man and had joined the local church, which in his area was Congregationalist. Now, thanks to union, he encountered for the first time regular liturgical worship. He was delighted with it, but after some experience of it he protested: 'Why were we not told of this before?' Why indeed? We have exported to the third world a church in which God's gifts are divided among mutually exclusive denominations. We owe it to Christians in the third world to give them a church in which all God's gifts are available to all.

The objections to the federal solution to reunion have been very clearly put by Bishop Lesslie Newbigin in his book *The Household of God*. Federation, he writes, 'demands no death and resurrection as the price of unity';[1] and again 'The disastrous error in the idea of federation is that it offers us reunion without repentance'.[2] These words, coming from one who has had extensive experience of life within the Church of South India, must carry weight.

5. Another more recent and quite potent objection to the ecumenical movement can often be heard today, especially among younger people. They say that the ecumenical movement has now shot its bolt and has become a mere useless talking-shop. A great sense of disillusionment about all official union schemes and world assemblies has overtaken many people, especially in England. Twice within the last few years the Church of England has been asked to enter seriously into a scheme for reunion with other denominations: there has been both the Anglican-Methodist reunion scheme and the more recent scheme which included most of the Free Churches in England. Twice in the highest organ of the Church of England's self-expression, its General Synod, these schemes have failed to win sufficient approval to make them viable. Inevitably many people have relapsed into a despairing sense that no formal official scheme of reunion will ever succeed against such indifference and hostility. They suggest that we concentrate on developing the best possible relations and co-operation with other denominations at the local level and give up trying to establish an officially recognized common ministry and common administration of sacraments and common ecclesiastical structures.

It is hard to struggle against mindless prejudice and the powerful forces of inertia and conservatism. One can sympathize strongly with Christians in the English Free Churches if they conclude that the Church of England is beyond the influence of reason, beyond being impressed by even the greatest concessions and sacrifices made by non-episcopally governed Christians in the interest of unity. But the question must be asked of those who are disillusioned with the ecumenical movement, what is the alternative? It is indeed true that many cases have recently occurred of individual denominations entering into discussions with each other with the result that they have found a surprising measure of agreement even on questions which had been thought to be controversial, e.g. Roman Catholics with Anglicans, Anglicans with Methodists, Roman Catholics with Methodists. And such conversations as these have mostly been set up independently of the ecumenical movement as formally organized. But it would be absurd to claim that this movement has not prepared the way for such conversations, that the conversations would have been conceivably possible unless the movement had completely changed the atmosphere of inter-church relations. These conversations are the fruits of the ecumenical movement; they are a sign that the movement is active, alive, and effective. It may be that we are at the moment in a phase when conversations between individual denominations are the best way of expressing that movement. These conversations are not in fact in the proper sense 'ecumenical'. 'Ecumenical' means including the whole church. Sooner or later these conversations if they are to have success must lead the churches involved to relating themselves to the whole Christian body, and to speaking about common ministry, sacraments, and structure. The establishment of such a relationship is precisely what the ecumenical movement is for.

Perhaps a word might here be said about what might be called the practice of ecclesiological blackmail. Blackmail is levied in ecclesiastical circles when any minority within a church threatens to break off from the majority and either form a separate body or join some other already existing body if something takes place within that church to which the minority is opposed, e.g. the ordination of women or the introduction of the office of bishop. A milder form of the same blackmail can be seen among those who say (for instance) that the Church of England should not ordain women priests because this would gravely prejudice its character or status in the eyes of the Roman Catholic or of the Orthodox Church. The first sort of blackmail should be met in the way in which all blackmail should be met, by refusing to give in to it. This is not a refusal to make concessions to the weaker brethren. People who threaten to leave the church are not weaker brethren, but men and women who are prepared to divide the church for the sake of gaining their ends. The milder form of blackmail must also be resisted. The susceptibilities of other Christian bodies must of course be respected, but not to the extent of our refraining from doing what we think it is our duty before God to do. Anyway, as far as the Roman Catholic Church is concerned it is unrealistic to behave as if the questions and decisions which beset us are not also reflected among them. The question of the ordination of women is the subject of a lively debate within the Roman Catholic Church itself. That church is in many parts of the world so drastically short of candidates for the priesthood that not only a married priesthood but also the possibility of women becoming priests is a likely option in the future, and there are plenty of people within that communion to remind the authorities of this.

About the ecumenical movement there is in fact a certain historical inevitability, as there was about the Reformation. As we have indicated above,[3] from the end of the eighteenth century and the beginning of the nineteenth century onwards the main churches of Europe began to loosen the bonds which had ever since the Reformation tied them tightly to the authority of the state, whether the state was Catholic or Protestant. The initiative for this came both from the state and from the church. As the nineteenth century went on many European movements were directed towards helping the church to identify itself as a distinct entity in contrast to the state. There was the Ultramontane Movement in the Roman Catholic Church, whereby the church was drastically centralized so that all the threads of power were put into the hands of the Pope. In England there was the Oxford Movement, whose original motive was to distinguish the existence, authority, and identity of the church from those of the state. There was the Great Disruption in Scotland, the origin of which was the desire of local congregations to appoint their own ministers instead of having them chosen by unrepresentative patrons. Not dissimilar movements could be discerned in the Danish Lutheran Church. The Anglican Communion in Ireland was in 1869 disestablished and dissociated entirely from the government of Ireland. For Christians who recognized that the church had an authority and existence distinct from the state in which it lived the next logical step was to recognize that in matters religious they had more in common with Christians in other states than they had with their own state or society. The form which this logical step took was the ecumenical movement. There is no alternative to this movement, defective and unsatisfactory though it may be in many ways, except despair and isolation.

In short, every responsible Christian should now ask himself or herself: Can I not have the Catholic experience without becoming a *Roman* Catholic? Can I not have all that is best in Anglicanism without calling myself an Anglican? Can I not enter into the Methodist heritage without labelling myself a Methodist? Nothing but a thoroughgoing sharing of our traditions in a church where there is one ministry and no denominational barriers will make it possible for that to happen.

3

An Ecclesiology for Today

1. Definition of the Church

We should now be in a position to outline a doctrine of the church that is credible in the modern world. Since we do not regard the ordained ministry as constitutive of the church, we can leave the doctrine of the ministry to a later point. But first we should make some preliminary observations in order to clear away some misconceptions that might arise.

First, we must not identify the church with Christ. We have seen that this is the conclusion of one tradition in Roman Catholic ecclesiology. It comes from taking too literally and in too metaphysical a sense the Pauline doctrine of the church as the body of Christ. As Karl Barth writes of the church: 'Even in its invisible essence, it is not Christ nor a second Christ, nor a kind of extension of the one Christ'.[1] Barth does however say later on:[2] 'The being of the Christian community is a predicate or a dimension of the being of Jesus Christ himself', though he is careful to add that this does not mean that Christ exists only as the church exists. We certainly need this admirable reformed emphasis on the danger of divinizing the church. This divinizing is what Barth very appropriately calls *sacro egoismo*.[3] One can be betrayed into making all sorts of claims for the church as a visible institution that one would not make for any individual: 'it is infallible, completely holy, immune from the need of reform, etc'. Our doctrine of the church must preserve a becoming modesty: the church must no more regard itself as in secure possession of righteousness and orthodoxy than the individual should. It is just as easy for the church to sin as it is for the individual, and the church needs repentance and forgiveness as much as the individual does. Lesslie Newbigin expresses this admirably: 'The moment the Church begins to think that it possesses the fullness of divine grace, it has fallen from that grace',[4] and he goes on to say very profoundly: 'we must abandon the attempt to define the Church's *esse* in terms of something that it has and is'.[5]

Next we must consider the question of the visibility of the church. What we must certainly not do is to take refuge in the doctrine of an invisible church. It is true of course that part of the church is invisible, the greater part in fact, the part that consists of those who have died and are now in the presence of God. But the church on earth must not be regarded as an invisible body, whose membership and location is known only to God. If this were the case, there would be no point in bothering about reunion at all, since we would have no assurance that the divided body, even if it were to be united, is in fact the church. For all we know, the invisible church might be wholly united. In any case, we will not treat the church on earth as invisible as long as we follow the guidance of St Paul. He always assumed when he was writing to the Christians in Corinth or Rome or anywhere else that he was writing to the church there. We must be able to have some idea of who are members of the church militant here on earth; otherwise there can be no assurance of Christian fellowship. Barth rightly insists that 'it is not improper but proper to the Christian community to be visible'.[6] He even accepts Bossuet's famous claim that the Catholic Church was as visible as is the kingdom of France or the republic of Venice. What is invisible in the church, he says, is the presence and activity of Jesus Christ, and that is what has to be made outward and visible.

At the same time, Barth very properly warns us against too much reliance on the institutional element in the church. The church is people, not organizations, still less buildings. Hence we must work for the church as the people of God, but not necessarily for the institution whose headquarters are in the Vatican or in Church House, Westminster, or in George Street, Edinburgh. Once more we quote Karl Barth; 'God in Jesus Christ became a man ... and he did what he did *propter nos homines*. Hence the smallest sigh or laugh of a man is surely more important to him than the support of the most important institutions, the construction and working of the most marvellous apparatus, the development of the most holy and profound ideas'.[7] If we could always bear this in mind, we would avoid those unpleasant situations which have certainly occurred from time to time in the history of the church, when the policy of church leaders, though sincerely undertaken from a belief that it is for the good of the church, results in inhuman or sub-Christian treatment of persons; where methods are employed that would be regarded as dishonest or unworthy were they to be used in any other context. Indeed, one might very well find a rule of safety for church policy here; wherever the policy of the church falls below the standards of decency and honesty of the world outside the ecclesial institution, something has gone wrong. The alleged needs of the institution have been given precedence over the needs of the person. The 'holy egoism' of the organization has been allowed to take control. This can happen in any tradition, whether it is the Scots ministers badgering Montrose on the scaffold with their unwanted ministrations; or the Jesuit authorities treating George Tyrrell with a degree of underhandedness and injustice that no English court of law would have allowed; or the contemporary Church of England allotting to the women in its employment a status and prospects that would be considered completely unacceptable in any profession in contemporary Western society.

Perhaps the danger of institutionalism in church life is all the greater today because we have largely lost the dimension of eschatology. During most of the New Testament period this dimension was able to play a full part because the earliest Christians believed that the *parousia* really was going to take place soon. We have, not unnaturally, lost that conviction today, and the element of eschatology is not to be regained by an artificial excitement based on the expectation that an event which has been just about to happen for two thousand years really is just about to happen at the end of the second millennium of our era. The element of eschatology must rather be preserved by a constant preservation of the openness of the church to the future. The church is not a closed corporation whose structure and organization is immutably fixed till the end of history. The effect of eschatology on the church today should be seen in openness to the future, in a refusal to settle down, in a constant remembrance that we are the pilgrim people of God.

The continuity of the church therefore must consist basically in the continuity of the people of God. This is not to play down the value of ministerial continuity. No denomination that has a ministry at all fails to take careful steps to see that it is continually transmitted. But it is not the continuity of the ministry that constitutes the church, but the continuity of the members of the church themselves. Dillistone in his book *The Structure of the Divine Society* sees this clearly enough, but seems to go rather too far in the opposite direction from ministerial continuity when he writes: 'God cannot in any way be limited by natural or historical forms.... The only continuities are the continuities of Jesus Christ and his Spirit. There are no continuities in natural or historical forms'.[8] If this means that no form of church organization is sacrosanct in the sense that without it the church cannot exist, we must agree. But Dillistone's language gives one the impression that the church itself on earth does not seem to be continuous; as if it was a sporadic phenomenon, appearing now here now there, and disappearing as easily. This is not the impression we gain from the New Testament. Paul and others write to the church in Corinth or wherever under the conviction that the church is a continuing entity, not a temporary phenomenon. And when the author of Ephesians writes about the universal church, he plainly regards it as something that will last through history and be identifiable as such. Karl Barth has sometimes been accused of holding this sort of 'Cheshire cat' ecclesiology, though it must be said that a study of the last volume of his *Church Dogmatics*, where he is dealing with the doctrine of the church, does not really substantiate this accusation. The truth is that God in Christ has chosen to call and save actual historical men and women, and therefore the church in any age is made up of actual historical men and women, and it is in them primarily that the continuity of the church consists. If this seems to be limiting God's action, we must conclude that he chooses so to be limited.

Consequently we can now identify the church militant here on earth. The church consists of the totality of the denominations. If we want to speak in biblical terms we will say that the church *is* the people of God and that it is called to be the body of Christ. This is why such practices as infant baptism are defensible (though not necessarily contemporary baptismal practice). A child of Christian parents can be treated as capable of becoming a member of the people of God, of making up part of the body of Christ. The calling only becomes effective as understanding develops.

The church therefore is one and undivided in God's eyes. We must accustom ourselves to seeing our denominational divisions as man-made barriers which obscure the essential unity of the church from the eyes of the outside world. There is a valid analogy here with the life of the Christian believer. The believer has been redeemed by God in Christ, may be said to be 'in Christ', can be called a member of 'the holy ones' and 'the saints'. But all through his life he has to strive to make this redemption which is his more real and more obvious, so that even at the end of a life of commitment to Christ he must still be regarded as a sinner as well as a saint. As Pascal once observed: all mankind is divided into two groups: sinners who think that they are righteous, and saints who know that they are sinners. So with the unity of the church: God has purchased for himself a holy church by the blood of his dear Son. That church which exists on earth can only be one. Our divisions therefore have not succeeded in producing two churches or a hundred churches. They have only succeeded in obscuring the unity of the church to the outside world, in the same way that the sin of the individual Christian obscures to the outside world the fact of his redemption in Christ.[9]

Although it is true that we have not succeeded in dividing the church in God's eyes, we must pursue the analogy with the redemption of the individual Christian to its logical conclusion and add that the real unity of the church is not complete until the *parousia*. Just as the individual Christian's redemption is not complete until at least his death (and even then perhaps requires a period of development), so the church is not complete until the consummation, and no doubt its unity is an element in its completeness. In his book, *The Unity of the Church in the New Testament*, Stig Hanson has shown that the thought of the church growing up into Christ is a distinctive element in the ecclesiology of Colossians-Ephesians. In this process of growth, growth in unity must have a place. But this is no justification whatever for our denominational divisions. Even were all our denominations to disappear into one organically united church there would still be plenty of scope for growth in unity.

2 Internal Schism

If this is a true account of what the church actually is, then our divided condition is a disgrace. Newbigin writes that the spectacle of parallel bodies of Christians not admitting any obligations to each other is disgraceful.[10] Only slowly are we waking up to the disgraceful nature of this situation. A hundred years ago most Christians took our divisions for granted as the most natural thing in the world, just as a hundred years ago most people took for granted the poverty and social oppression of the industrialized West as part of the natural order of things. Nor can we evade our responsibility by maintaining that our denomination is the true church and that all others are either schismatics who have broken away from the true church, or heretics who have lost the true gospel. Once more we quote Newbigin: 'far from saying as Streeter did between the wars "all have won and all shall have prizes", a more appropriate motto would be "they have all turned aside, they have altogether become unprofitable"'.[11] We are all guilty of dividing the church. Because we all of us together go to make up the being of the church in the world, none of us can escape responsibility for the state of internal schism in which we exist.

Newbigin defines the church thus:[12] 'the Church itself is the visible company of those who have been called (by God) into the fellowship of his Son'. I do not think we can improve on this as a definition of the church militant. This is not to suggest that the epithets 'catholic' and 'apostolic' have no relevance to the being of the church: 'I believe in one, holy, catholic, and apostolic church' says the Nicene Creed. We have maintained that the church is one, though its unity is marred and obscured by sin. The church is called to be holy, must be constantly striving to grow in holiness, and, if it ever lost the character of holiness altogether, would cease to be the church. It is called to be catholic, and is catholic only in as far as it is universal, has room for all varieties of people, and shares throughout its members those institutions and practices which it has found most valuable to its life during its long history. The catholicity of the church is marred and hindered by its disunity. As long as the church is divided it cannot be completely catholic. The church is apostolic in as far as it adheres to the gospel which the apostles preached, and continues its apostolic mission to the world. There is no such thing as an 'apostolic ministry' in the church which can claim divine justification over against any other forms of ministry, still less is there an 'apostolic see' that can make claims to jurisdiction on the basis of being apostolic. Any form of ministry in the church can be called apostolic to the extent to which it carries out the purposes for which the ordained ministry was originally established, that is the preaching of the gospel and the mediation of God's redemption in Christ. Hence, if we commend any one form of ministry above others (as we do later on), it can only be on the grounds that it is more likely to be effective in carrying out the apostolic task of ministry.

Karl Barth defines a Christian as one who confesses Jesus as Lord.[13] This is hardly satisfactory for our purpose. We ought to be able to use a common baptism as the basis for our ecclesiology. Vatican II showed some signs of doing this, and there is plenty of justification for it in the New Testament. After all, there is the 'one baptism' of Eph. 4.5. Karl Barth later on in his last volume[14] insists that the question as to whether a man is a Christian does not depend on his conversion experience, but on whether he has heard and tried to obey the call. It is this truth that baptism safeguards. In baptism God issues the call, makes his claim on us, admits us to his church. Our membership does not depend on the extent of our obedience, though if we do not obey our membership is dormant and may at the end become completely ineffective. Just as our being forgiven depends on God's act of forgiveness, but we cannot be forgiven if we do not ask for forgiveness, so with our membership of the church: we are baptized into membership of the church and are therefore called to obey God in Christ. So we may perhaps amend Barth's definition of the Christian so as to read: a Christian is one who has been baptized into the fellowship of the church and who is therefore called to obey God in Christ.

This does, it is true, raise the question of those bodies of Christians who do not practise baptism at all (as opposed to Baptists, who refuse baptism to small children). We must not unchurch them. It would be outrageous to deny that members of the Society of Friends or of the Salvation Army are Christians. But we must repeat that the existence of these bodies of Christians is in a hidden way dependent on the practice of baptism by other Christians. We must therefore accept members of these bodies as our fellow-Christians, but look forward to the time when in one undivided church all that they have to contribute has been included in the life of the church. Then perhaps the protest against the wrong use of sacraments in which their movements originated will no longer be needed.

Besides the two bodies we have already mentioned there also exist a number of other unattached Christian groups, most of which do not have any relation to the World Council of Churches, and many of which would not desire it. It is not quite fair to classify all these under the heading 'sects'. We must distinguish as follows:

1. The Western-type sect: here we find the self-supporting 'Evangelical Church', the 'Holiness Church', the fundamentalist breakaway from the main line churches, such as Ian Paisley's 'Free Presbyterian Church' in Ulster, or the Evangelical Anglican Church in South Africa, originally a protest against the Anglo-Catholic tendencies of the Anglican Church in South Africa. These are essentially Western-type bodies, since they think in terms of Western theology and protest against Western developments, such as biblical criticism or the Tractarian Movement. They have their counterparts of course in the third world. Anyone with a few thousand rupees to spend can form a church like this in South India, which will last at least until the Western money runs out.

2. The African Independent Churches: these are breakaways from the main-line churches (Roman Catholic as well as the others) in Western, Eastern, and Southern Africa. They vary enormously in organization, doctrine, and stability. Their beliefs range from relative orthodoxy to a thinly veiled version of some traditional African cult. Some of them are mere one-man or one-woman affairs, which collapse with the death of their founder. Others are formidable organizations which even the government of the Republic of South Africa must respect. What they all have in common is an indigenous leadership, emphasis on specifically African elements such as healing and dream interpretation, and a remarkable absence of Western-style education as far as concerns both leadership and rank and file.

3. Unattached communities of persons wishing to live the Christian life without any adherence to an institution. This is a relatively recent phenomenon and occurs both in the West and in the third world. Often many members of these communities are unbaptized and do not want baptism. One hears for example of groups of people in India who say that they wish to be Christians but have no desire to accept baptism or to join an Indian church that appears to them to be over-Westernized and over-institution-

alized. In the West there are similar groups who are attempting to contract out of society in the name of Christ.

We must regard the great majority of people in all these classes as members of the church. There are probably some in class 2 who are so close to traditional African religion and so far from anything recognizable as traditional Christianity that their membership of the church must be doubtful. And perhaps there are some in class 3 who have no serious commitment to Christianity. But we have no justification for relegating all those who are not in the main-line churches to an area of outer darkness. The edges of the Church Militant are necessarily blurred. There is no litmus paper test for church membership. We may make more detailed comments about each of these classes.

Class 1: These we will have always with us. There is a type of temperament which prefers the small body where everyone knows everyone else and all are united in opposition to some principle or organization. The 'holiness' type of sect acts on the principle that one cannot be described as a real Christian unless one exhibits one particular type of sanctity and perhaps shares one particular type of experience. Such a sect must be fissiparous in its very essence because in the last analysis one can only have certainty about one's own holiness. The paradoxical situation is that if one is convinced of one's own holiness one has thereby become exactly the type of person whom Jesus denounced most vigorously. There will always be the possibility of the Western type sect being formed where there is a semi-educated mass of Christians, a charismatic leader, and a sleepy or over-institutionalized main-line church. Very often the sect will not survive the death of the charismatic leader. Sermons and prayers conducted by non-charismatic semi-educated ministers tend to be very dull.

Class 2: These must be regarded as a completely different phenomenon. They are primarily an expression of African national feeling. Indeed in the Republic of South Africa they are almost the only legal means of expression for this. The African Christian often feels himself at a great disadvantage over against the Western missionary; he is lacking in Western technology, Western education based on a long tradition of written records, Western experience of highly organized church structures which the missionary has imposed upon the African church. To make a very broad generalization, the Western denominations in Africa have held on to leadership in their churches for too long. Even today, for example, the Roman Catholic Church in many parts of Africa is heavily dependent on expatriates for providing its ordained ministry. At the other end of the scale fundamentalist Christianity seems quite unconscious of the danger of missionary imperialism. The emergence of the African Independent churches is a serious judgment upon the way in which all the main-line churches have conducted their missionary work. At the same time there is something pathetic in the spectacle of the independent churches tending to reproduce some of the least desirable features of Western Christianity, high-sounding titles for church leaders, Westernized clerical dress that is often obsolete in the West, even a clerical caste, or at least an in-group leadership. The most striking instance of the African Independent churches is the Kimbanguist Church in the Congo. It numbers its members in millions and is regarded by some as a most hopeful instance of indigenous Christianity and by others as a semi-Christian reaction to brutal Belgian imperialism. One must not condemn the leaders of the African Independent churches, but one cannot refrain from deploring them. They are a sort of caricature of Western denominationalism and like all good caricatures reproduces quite faithfully some of the less attractive features of the original. In some parts of Nigeria there seem to be as many denominations as congregations: a large part of the church exists in a condition of permanent fissiparous internal schism. Efforts are now being made on the part of the main-line churches to come to terms with the independent churches, chiefly by offering a better education to their ministers. This will no doubt bear good fruit in years to come.

Class 3: These groups are not only a protest against the highly institutionalized churches of the West, but also against the church's involvement in, and compromise with, society. Not a small part of the protest is directed against the churches' acceptance of nuclear armaments. Such groups are like the Friends and the Salvation Army in that they exist by virtue of the churches and they would not continue in existence if they were not replenished by discontented members of the main-line churches. They are of themselves ephemeral but they should be treated with seriousness and respect. They are at the very least a reminder to the church of the perils involved in a connection with society which cannot be avoided if the church is to have any impact on the milieu in which it exists.

The doctrine we have outlined above carries the implication that the great majority of schisms in the history of the church have been internal schisms, in the sense that, though new bodies of Christians have been formed, this has not meant that the church in reality in the eyes of God has been divided. Those who separated themselves have not in fact left the church. It would seem in fact that schism as such, in the sense of a division among Christians which does not necessarily carry with it a fatal deviation in doctrine, must necessarily be internal schism. A schism that carried a body of Christians outside the church altogether would have to be a schism accompanied by a very drastic deviation in belief or practice. Thus when in the course of time almost the entire North African Church became Muslim, that was not really schism so much as apostasy. Or suppose that a body of Christians somewhere in the world were to declare that people with black skins are an inferior race and may not be admitted to membership of the church, that would be such a serious deviation from Christian practice as to raise the question of apostasy.

This conclusion does not mean that there is no such thing as schism or that unjustified and wilful schism is not a very serious sin. We can all imagine circumstances in which an act of schism is totally unjustifiable. Imagine for example a parish in which a layman with a certain gift of leadership quarrels with the vicar on unjustifiable grounds and sets up his own little sect. That would be schism and schism very much to be condemned. Even the most justifiable schisms carry with them unpleasant consequences. Lesslie Newbigin points out that when someone breaks away from a larger body on a point of genuine principle (as may happen sometimes), that principle becomes constitutive of the new body which is set up and something is lost of the fullness of the fellowship.[15] This is obviously true of the churches of the Reformation. However justifiable their action in breaking away, they lost much that the medieval church, for all its corruption, contained. Their church life was impoverished. But we can go further, and say that schism can have undesirable effects on the body from which the dissidents break away. Because the chief issue on which the reformed churches broke away was the authority of the papacy, the continuing Roman Catholic Church was led to over-emphasize the position of the Pope. As some Roman Catholic historians and theologians are pointing out today, the centralization of everything on the Pope, and the personality cult of the 'Holy Father' are indirect consequences of the Reformation, and are not characteristic of the life of the Western church through all the centuries. In this respect perhaps the Eastern Orthodox Church has something to teach all us Westerners. Because it has not experienced a really traumatic schism for centuries, it is hard to find any one principle that it has over-emphasized. Schism therefore, though it does not succeed in ultimately dividing the church, is an evil to be avoided except in the most extreme and urgent circumstances.

Before concluding this section, we must point out some relevant consequences of the ecclesiology which we had adopted (apart from its consequences for the doctrine of the ministry, which we treat separately). One consequence is that there can be no degrees of churchliness. We must not try to maintain that, although all who are Christians in the sense which we have defined are members of the church, because of the denomination to which they belong some of them are less fully members of the church than others. Newbigin rightly repudiates the idea that 'there are degrees of membership of the church, some churches being in the centre and possessing all the plenitude of "churchliness" and others at varying distances, until on the far horizon one discerns presumably the Quakers, the Salvation Army, and the Plymouth Brethren'.[16] This is of course precisely what Vatican II does, even suggesting by its language that one can grade non-Roman Catholic bodies in degrees of approximation to the true church, with the Eastern Orthodox coming by far the nearest to the real thing, and Anglicans perhaps just perceptibly less distant than the rest of Protestantism. But, as we have suggested, this will prove in the long run a very difficult doctrine to defend. Far more defensible from the logical point of view is Mersch's forthright relegation of all who are not Roman Catholics to the area of outer darkness. It suffers from the disadvantage of being quite incredible today. To their credit be it said, modern Roman Catholics do not want to regard all Christians who do not belong to their Communion as little different from heathen. Hence their difficulties. But we will explore this question more fully later when we consider the subject of validity.

Some Anglicans would very much like to put non-episcopal Christians into the same category as Roman Catholics put all other Christians. And one must do them the justice to add that, like modern Roman Catholics, they do not want to put them virtually on a level with heathen. But of course they encounter exactly the same difficulties as do Roman Catholics in defining what exactly is the ecclesial status of such Christians and what the nature of the grace which they receive. And they do not even have the satisfaction granted to Roman Catholics of being able to point to official church statements and confessions which un-church all 'non-catholic' Christians. Anglicanism never has unequivocally claimed that its retention of the threefold ministry has put itself on the 'catholic' side of Christianity so far as to embolden it to declare all non-episcopal Christians as not possessing full membership of the church.

Together with the repudiation of degrees of churchliness, we must also reject attempts to define how far individual Christians belong to the church. Karl Barth has well written: 'There is no cleavage of the community into qualified and unqualified members. We are all qualified and all unqualified'.[17] And he adds later: 'The statement "I am a mere layman; I am no theologian" is evidence not of humility but of indolence'.[18] He has no doubt in mind the distinction made in the Roman Catholic Church between the teaching church and the learning church. The teaching church consists of the hierarchy and the clergy from the Pope downwards, and the learning church of everyone else. Despite its generally progressive tone, this distinction is sedulously observed in the Vatican II document *Lumen Gentium*. Nowhere in it is there any suggestion that lay people should have anything to do with either expounding doctrine or ruling the church. In this sense it is still a profoundly clericalized document. We may well quote Avery Dulles in criticism of this view: 'the Church is compared to a school-master – except that unlike most schoolmasters, the Church teaches by the authority of office, rather than by giving evidence for what it says'.[19]

But this distinction never has been absolute, and makes very little sense today. We shall be talking about the authority of the ministry later, but here we may certainly insist that authority in matters of doctrine must depend on competence, ability, learning and not on office alone. In the West at the moment hundreds of women every year are becoming qualified in theology, biblical studies and related subjects. Most of them emerge from the university with better qualifications in these subjects than are possessed by most of the clergy. They will not presumably, in the Catholic tradition anyway, be admitted to holy orders, and yet they are better qualified to teach and expound the faith than are many of the clergy. In these circumstances to maintain that only the clergy are entitled to teach the faith is absurd. The possession of gifts for the benefit of the church does not depend on being ordained. Equally to be rejected is the medieval idea that the religious life, or the life of the priest, is a higher form of Christian life, nearer the life of Christ. But such ideas are much less frequently voiced nowadays.

Finally, just a word on the familiar tag '*extra ecclesiam nulla salus*', there is no salvation outside the church. To be fair, the documents of Vatican II do not accept this principle. On the contrary, they make it plain that those who have never heard of Christianity are not without hope. But it might be worth while noticing how a distinguished Anglican theologian of the inter-war period, Lionel Thornton, takes it. In his book *The Common Life in the Body of Christ* he writes as follows: 'What is common to all must be shared. What is shared cannot be had in isolation. This is the truth summarized in the familiar words: *Extra ecclesiam nulla salus*'.[20] Thornton is in fact contending against a form of individualistic, pietistic Christianity, quite alien to the spirit of the New Testament, that only concerns itself with the salvation of the individual. But surely we may legitimately apply Lionel Thornton's words to the ecumenical movement as a whole: 'What is common to all must be shared.' God has given to every tradition of Christianity certain gifts which he means to be shared by all Christians. 'What is shared cannot be had in isolation.' If we jealously hug our own traditions and refuse either to share them with others or to receive what others have to give us, we shall find eventually that our gifts have disappeared. God does not will that his church should permanently appear divided to the outside world. If we will not or cannot do anything effective to end our divisions, God's left hand, visible in the processes of history, will bring it about that we either unite despite ourselves or perish.

3. A Theology of the Church

We still have to make a final theological estimate of the account of the church which has been given in these pages. If everyone who has been baptized belongs to the church, how are we to envisage the church and its structures theologically? In theological text-books it is usual at this point to list what are called 'the notes of the church', i.e. that the church is One, Holy, Catholic, and Apostolic, and then to explain that they apply to one denomination (naturally that of the writer) or group of denominations, but not to others. On our premises we cannot do that. Certain principles must first be laid down:

1. The church is not created by man but given by God. We do not organize or convert or decree the church by our own efforts. That is why it is called Holy. The church is not simply an organization as the Salvation Army, or the Society of Jesus, or the Mothers' Union is an organization. The church is created by its relationship to Christ, and we do not invent, manipulate, or produce Christ. In one aspect the church is divine, *given*, not achieved by human effort. This is one reason why those who boast of the converts they have made resemble too closely for comfort Red Indian braves boasting of the scalps which they have collected. We do not convert people. The Holy Spirit enables them to have faith. The sacrament of baptism has, among other virtues, this great advantage. We do not bring water out of our minds, distil it from our spiritual experience. It reaches us from outside, and by no stretch of the imagination can we dupe ourselves into thinking that it is anything but an obstinate brute fact, objective and independent of ourselves. That is why sacraments are not merely a means of conveying grace. They are also a pledge, a reassuring sign that what is happening is not invented in the depth of our subtle minds, not affected by our almost infinite capacity for self-deception. In 1652 two London tailors, John Reeve and Lodovic Muggleton, independently underwent impressive religious experiences which convinced them that God was speaking directly to them and revealing that they were the

two prophets of Revelation 11.1–14. Out of this experience sprang the sect of the Muggletonians, Muggleton taking over from Reeve who died early. It neglected all sacraments, all ministry, and denied that God answered prayer or showed any concern for his people beyond endowing his prophet Muggleton with infallibility. It appears now that within the last few years the very last Muggletonian has died so that we may pronounce the sect's epitaph. Muggleton had some virtues and some flashes of insight, but on the whole he was an example of religious self-deception from which the use of sacraments should deliver us. It is not advisable to call the church a sacrament, but it has that objectivity, that givenness which sacraments also share. We are not free to control, or manipulate the church any more than we are free to control or manipulate the other gifts of God.

2. Jesus Christ does not reach his people in varying degrees of authenticity. It is ridiculous, if not actually offensive to God, to suggest that there is, for instance, a Catholic or Orthodox Christ who is the genuine article, in contrast to Protestant Christs who may vary extensively in their reality or genuineness. Jesus Christ is the same yesterday and today and for ever (Heb. 13.8). He does not come to us in a utility or second-class form. Roman Catholics are by training and inherited prejudice much inclined to make some such assumptions about Protestants, usually without any spiteful intention. They are genuinely surprised to find that Protestants are positively convinced that their own ministries are valid and their sacraments effective. Roman Catholics have been bought up to regard Protestants as well-meaning but second-class Christians who lack that Catholic something which authenticates their Christianity. But if we believe (as the Roman Catholic Church now says that it believes) that baptized and believing Christians in any tradition are actually united to Christ, then the conviction that non-Catholic Christians are in some sense less Christian, less closely related to Christ, than Catholic Christians is impossible to hold. There is only one Christ. From the point of view of sacramental efficacy you are either united with him or you are not. Of course the individual's response to Christ may vary indefinitely and may be affected by all sorts of factors such as the kind of doctrine which you have learned, your own moral character, the kind of society in which you are living, and so on. But this applies to any Christian in

any denomination. A non-practising baptized Roman Catholic can hardly be said to be more authentically Christian than a fervently believing Baptist who has received adult baptism. Those who are united to Christ are united to the same, unvarying, one Christ.

3. When therefore St Paul wrote 'Is Christ divided?' (I Cor. 1.13), he was asking a question which expected the answer 'No'. His point was that Christ *cannot* be divided; Corinthian Christians who were separated into parties taking as their labels various outstanding personalities, Paul, Peter, Apollos, could be divided (though they ought not to be). But Christ is not divided. The church therefore in a certain sense is already indivisibly one in such a way that men and women cannot divide it. Now, if we accept this point the temptation arises to identify this church, one and indivisible, with one or other of the existing denominations, probably the Roman Catholic or the Orthodox. This is a blindingly simple solution which has been much favoured through the centuries of Christian history, and it carries with it the advantage that it enables its proponents to enjoy a strong sense of self-righteousness and complacency, because they always identify the single true church with their own denomination. The Orthodox declare that they are quite sure that their church is the true church, but cannot be sure about any other, even the Roman Catholic Church. They are safe in the ark. Whether the unfortunates who did not gain admission to the ark are sinking or swimming, they really do not know. The Roman Catholics are equally confident that theirs is the one true church, and are searching for ways in which they can detect elements of a church in other less fortunate denominations; they are, so to speak, looking round for life rafts with which other Christians are to be provided. The same mentality can show itself in much smaller bodies than these two. The Muggletonians, for instance, whose membership was confined to a very few thousands in the British Isles and a scattering in the USA, were convinced that they, and they alone, endowed with the teaching of the prophet Muggleton, were the true church. The church here is reduced to the size of a canoe.

People who think like this should first ask themselves, where in such a situation would you expect Jesus Christ to stand? With the secure, complacent, well-authenticated party, or with the outcast, the unqualified, the deprived (as all non-Catholics are on this view)? There can be only one answer. Jesus was crucified by the conventional, established, correctly religious authorities, and he spent much of his time associating with the outcast and the socially disreputable, and incurred some odium thereby. Next, it is worth asking, Is it not insulting to God thus to monopolize him for one denomination? If God wished it to be known that there is only one true church which can be wholly identified with one denomination, why has he so manifestly blessed the missionary activities (for instance) of a wide variety of denominations? The only two answers to these questions return us to the same position as before: you can say that the sacraments of the inauthentic churches and their ministries are somehow faulty and defective, or (a characteristic Anglican variety) simply non-U, in spite of all appearances to the contrary; you are then faced with the impossible task of explaining *how* sacraments and ministry are inauthentic. Or you can begin again to qualify the exclusiveness of your own body by making various concessions to others: they have elements of correctness, or they are effective but irregular, and so on. The Orthodox attitude of simply refusing to pronounce upon the Catholicity of others while being completely confident of their own is only a polite form of uncharitableness. Pilate was a good deal politer than Caiaphas. But the actions of both men tended in the same direction in the last analysis. We conclude therefore that the church of Christ as given to us by God is one, but that we cannot identify this church exclusively with any existing denomination. Indeed we must resist doing so, recognizing this tendency as a temptation similar to the temptation which Jesus met in the wilderness.

We can envisage the relationship of the existing, empirical church divided into denominations on the analogy of St Paul's doctrine of justification by faith. In Paul's account, God has already given us all that we need for salvation (I Cor. 3.21–23); he has given us status as his children, access in grace to him, peace, joy, forgiveness, wholeness, for he has given us Christ. But we are by this very gift called so to respond as to make what God has given real in our own lives, in our daily decisions, in our characters and minds and behaviour. We must 'become what we are', answer in existential reality to what God has given us in heavenly reality. So with the church. God has given us Christ and has thereby brought us into the 'heavenly Jerusalem ... the assembly of the first-born who are enrolled in heaven', the number of his elect, his chosen people (Heb. 12.22–23). We must now as a community, as a church, respond by making real and living in empirical experience what already exists for us in God's truth. We must become the church which we are. And just as no individual can claim that he is perfect, entirely conformed to God's calling, beyond the reach of sin, so no denomination has the right to claim that it alone is exclusively the true church, that it alone is 'without spot or wrinkle or any such thing' (Eph. 5.27). This does not mean that the church is a kind of unattainable ideal, a castle in the air, a star to which we can hitch our wagon, any more than it means that Christ is out of our reach, imprisoned in some inaccessible perfection. The incarnation is a contradiction of this idea. The church is *there*, given. But we must realize it in our ecclesiastical structures. As long as division exists anywhere among Christians, the church is not wholly realized. As long as Christians are content to exist in a divided state from each other, each divided body claiming to be the true church, or a true church, the church is not fully, properly realized, and we are all, Catholic and Protestants, evangelicals, charismatics, conservatives, and liberals, curialists and conciliarists, under an equal obligation to work towards greater unity, not only of the spirit, but also (because we believe in the incarnation) of structure, of ministry, of sacraments, of wholehearted agreement in fundamentals.

'Man is born free', said Rousseau, 'but I see him everywhere in chains'; God has made the church one; we see it everywhere divided. And if we are arrogant enough to imagine that our church is a secure ark in which we can traverse the dangerous seas of ecclesiology, then Christ is outside that ark, drowning with the rest of the unchurched multitude.

4. But are there no limits to this universal, heterogeneous assemblage of Christians which we have defined as the church? As far as formal limits go, we can only set the limit of baptism. If a body of Christians practises Christian baptism in the traditional manner, then we have no right to say they are not in the church. The matter is taken out of our hands. Christ is not divided. But just as individual baptized Christians can have very different relationships to Christ in accordance with the responses to him which they can and do make, so different Christian communities can have, within the limits of the church, different relationships, as communi-

ties, to Christ. One of the most obvious qualifications of this
relationship is provided by how they behave as Christian
communities. If, for instance, two Christian communities are now
engaged and have long been engaged in violent strife with each
other without making any very obvious effort to settle their differences and live together in Christian brotherhood, the authenticity
of their membership of the church must become suspect, no matter
what high claims they may make to either Catholicity or orthodoxy.
In Northern Ireland, for example, all the denominations (with the
honourable exception of the Non-Subscribing Presbyterians and
the Society of Friends, both of which communities would be
regarded by the rest as suspect in order and doctrine), have for long
been engaged in bitter communal strife based on denominational
differences and are still so engaged. It is not simply that individual
members of these denominations frequently indulge in vilification
and occasionally in murder of their rivals. Even the most respectable and law-abiding members of these Christian bodies are in
effect, and usually in intention also, involved in a conspiracy to
perpetuate religious disunion and strife. For some of them this is
the very meaning of Christianity. In such a situation we must say
that the credibility of their membership of the church is called
drastically in question. While each side is maintaining vociferously
that it has all the marks of authentic Christianity, whereas the
Christianity of the other side is doubtful or non-existent, we may
legitimately ask whether any of them are Christian, whether they
have not reached a point where they are no longer recognizable as
the Christian church, whether their candlestick is any longer in its
place. The same may be said of the credibility of several Christian
denominations in Lebanon. Christian denominations, no matter
how correct their doctrine, how traditional their liturgy, how burning their evangelistic zeal, which allow themselves to become the
pretext for communal violence and civil war may well fear to hear
the terrible words of Christ 'Truly I say to you, I do not know you'
(Matt. 25.12).

The other qualification which must be applied to membership of
the church is a doctrinal one. Intense desire in a church for
doctrinal correctness is of course a pathological condition which is
to be avoided. But there must be a limit beyond which doctrinal
deviation becomes alienation from the membership of the church.

This truth has in the past history of the church been grossly exploited and distorted, but this is no reason why we should assume that any or every doctrine is acceptable as long as it is sincerely held. Violent distortion of the Christian tradition of doctrine, or gross over-emphasis upon one doctrine at the expense of the others, or the introduction into Christian doctrine of ideas which are alien to it or even contradictory of it, must affect the status among God's people of communities which err in this way.

Christians ultimately claim to know the truth and to be entrusted with the duty of spreading it. That is why the church is called Catholic and Apostolic. We must not ignore this fact.[21]

5. But, we must ask finally, what about the structures of the church? Sacraments, ministry, Bible, worship, not to mention bishops and archdeacons and archpriests and cardinals, and elders and conferences and synods and Popes, do these make no difference to membership of the church? We have already expressed our opinion of baptism. We regard it as necessary to the existence of the church in as far as, while we do not deny that Christian bodies who do not practise baptism belong to the church and deserve the name of Christian, we believe that they ought to recognize that they exist, so to speak, on the spiritual capital of the other Christians, not by courtesy of the rest of Christendom but by reason of it. The eucharist too is necessary for the existence of the church, for it is by the eucharist that the church sustains and feeds its continuing life in Christ. We do not believe that the ministry is essential to the very existence of the church, though a realistic appraisal of Christianity will confess that it is difficult to conceive of the Christian church continuing in existence through history without a ministry. The emergence of an official ministry very early in the second century was a development manifestly blessed and guided by the Holy Spirit. That the Bible is necessary for the functioning, indeed for the life, of the church few people will doubt; and this entails the continuous expounding, publishing, and distribution of the Bible. All other structures must be judged on their merits, and the criterion to use in judging them is, how far do they assist the maintenance and expansion of the gospel of Jesus Christ, and how far do they contribute to the life of Christ's people in the Holy Spirit? To take this attitude is certainly not to condemn all ecclesiastical structures and institutions. Precisely how to evaluate them and how

to determine what structures are useful and valuable and what not is the task of those who are engaged in the ecumenical movement, which is to say, in our view, those who take responsibly their calling to serve God in Christ through his church.

This account of the church may seem to some to be altogether too vague. It leaves us with an all-embracing church, one from which it would not be easy to exclude very many who call themselves Christians. To some the church must be a readily identifiable institution whose membership is clear and recognizable, and equally an institution which can make it quite clear who are those who do not belong to it. One can see the advantage of this, but, quite apart from the grave theological objections to defining the church in this sort of specific way, a survey of the history of the church suggests that a too readily identifiable church will almost inevitably offer temptations to its leaders to act despotically. Few leaders can resist such temptation; few can refuse the opportunity of behaving like the Inquisitor in Dostoevsky's great parable as related in *The Brothers Karamazov*.

Dostoevsky's Inquisitor was imaginary, but we do not need to go back hundreds of years, as he did in that passage, to find despotic churchmen and a despotic church. The Church of England in the sixteenth and seventeenth centuries, in the period when it enjoyed the support of the state, fell to the temptation of acting despotically. The Orthodox Church in Greece today acts despotically when it is given an opportunity to do so. But for most Western Europeans the prime example of a despotic church, still quite fresh in the memory of many, will probably be the Roman Catholic Church in the recent past. Until quite recently in countries where it commanded the allegiance of the majority of the population the Church of Rome exercised an ecclesiastical despotism. Anglicans in Ireland and Orthodox in Poland could tell of unhappy experiences under such a régime. Irish Anglicans will remember not without bitterness the policy pursued rigorously by Charles McQuaide, Roman Catholic Archbishop of Dublin in the forties and fifties of this century. Non-Roman Catholics were as far as possible excluded from influence in public affairs. Successive governments of the Republic of Ireland were subjected to pressure from the Archbishop to induce them to conform to the ecclesiastical empire which he was building. Every effort was made to ensure that social and welfare services were run by the Roman Church and not by the state. Criticism of any kind within his diocese was discouraged or suppressed. He really believed that he could run a significant part of Ireland on the principles of the scholastic theologians of the thirteenth century, whom he admired, by means of an autocracy of which he was the autocrat. Enforced retirement, the advent of the Second Vatican Council, and finally the Great Reaper himself mercifully put an end to this enterprise. But those who endured it, and those who have heard about it, should never forget the danger it presented. It represented one ugly end-result of the system of centralized and papal despotism encouraged by Pope Pius IX and fostered and deepened by Leo XIII and Pius X. Even in England, where Roman Catholicism has not been in a position to influence the government since the middle of the sixteenth century, under the rule of Cardinal Vaughan at the end of the nineteenth century Roman Catholics at least were given the impression that Christian doctrine consisted of pronouncements of the Pope which were actually or virtually infallible and were to be accepted by the faithful uncritically without any attempt to analyse or modify them. In Italy itself, home of the papacy, owing to the political history of that country, the Roman Catholic church was unable to exercise an effective despotism over its people. But readers of that admirable book *Church and State in Fascist Italy,*[22] by that distinguished and versatile scholar Dr D.A. Binchy, will perhaps be pardoned if they draw the conclusion that Pope Pius XI (in some ways the hero of the book) in his frequent protests against the arbitrary acts of Mussolini's government was in effect saying: 'Catholics, do not be influenced by the autocratic totalitarian Fascist régime; accept instead my (autocratic totalitarian) régime'. This Pope certainly had no use for democracy, in spite of his undoubted courage in opposing Fascism. Indeed he appeared to have little respect for political liberty of any sort.

We must therefore beware of the temptation to absolutize and divinize the human, fallible, provisional aspect of Christ's church. We must beware of what Roman Catholics themselves have recently begun to call 'triumphalism'. This marks a healthy and welcome revulsion from the phase of despotism through which their church has recently passed and which most Roman Catholics now regard as over. If we conclude that no existing institution has the right to regard itself solely and exclusively as the true church, in contrast to all others which are to a greater or lesser degree inauthentic, we shall possess a good remedy against this particular ecclesiastical malady.

On the other side, however, in strong contrast to the church which tries to dominate or even absorb society is the church which allows itself to be used or manipulated by society. That the church in Europe and elsewhere has in the past allowed itself to be used for its own ends by feudal society and by capitalist society can hardly be doubted. The church in many parts of the world is today paying the price for this surrender to the dominant elements in society. Today, however, a new and startling attitude to the role of the church in society has emerged in some countries. It is called liberation theology.

Liberation theology is a Christian reaction to the predominant system of thought in our day, Marxism. It has originated in an area of the world, Central and Southern America, where there is a combination of gross social oppression and a church which has been in a position of influence for a long time and has been very much associated with the ruling classes. This has produced a revolutionary situation which is being exploited by Marxists. Christians who sympathize with the revolutionary movement are naturally influenced in their thinking by their Marxist fellow-travellers. Liberation theologians criticize traditional ecclesiology on three counts:

First, they maintain that throughout the church's history ecclesiology, in common with all other branches of theology, has been unconsciously conditioned, if not determined, by the class structure of the society in which it originated. Thus, when the Roman Empire decided to patronize the church instead of persecuting it, the form of the church became adapted to that of the Empire, The church began to be regarded as the spiritual or religious aspect of the Empire. The structures of the church began to resemble those of the Empire (the very word 'diocese' originally applied to an administrative division of the Empire). Similarly in the Middle Ages the church integrated itself into the feudal system which prevailed in the West. The liberation theologians draw the conclusion that, because of its close connection with the ruling class, the church has never been free to criticize the social system, denounce social oppression, or join in the struggle for social justice.

Secondly, liberation theologians draw inspiration for their theology from a particular interpretation of the career of Jesus Christ. They tend to portray him as a social revolutionary, or at least as a social reformer. They point to the undoubted fact that he deliberately associated with those who were on the fringes of society, and they maintain that he found God among these people rather than among the rich, the powerful, and the devout. They give special emphasis to Jesus' teaching about the poor, and suggest that the coming of the kingdom of heaven carried definite social implications, and even that Jesus had a programme for social reform. They claim that he was put to death by the ruling authorities because he was regarded as a threat to their régime.

Thirdly, liberation theology maintains that practice is the proof of doctrine. In this respect they are very close to the Marxist doctrine of praxis. They are not just saying that faith without works is vain. They claim that God can only be found among the poor and oppressed, and that the only way of knowing God in Christ, or at least the only adequate way, is by joining in the struggle for social justice. The Christian life and the struggle for social justice are in effect identified. The church is thus according to them intended to be the place where the poor find vindication and the oppressed are encouraged and enabled to resist oppression. A church which takes no notice of the struggle for social justice has, according to them, ceased to be part of the church.

This is a serious challenge which cannot be brushed off by a few scornful words about student revolutionaries. It must be considered carefully and, if there is any truth in it, that truth must be acknowledged and acted upon. We take first the charge that the doctrine and structure of the church is socially conditioned and always has been throughout the church's history.

It is perfectly true that the doctrine of the church has been much influenced by the social conditions in which the church exists in any age or place. But we say 'conditioned' not determined. If our theology were *determined* by social conditions, we could never be conscious of this determination. We would be so wholly determined by our environment that we could not get sufficiently far away from it to criticize it. The very fact that we can put forward a theory about the social conditioning of the church shows that we are not wholly determined by our social situation. It is inevitable that the church will take its colouring from the society in which it exists. Our task must be to become aware of this and to be constantly on the alert to judge the church's being and life by the standard of the gospel. We must point out moreover that liberation theology itself is just as much conditioned by the social circumstances in which it originated as is any other theology . We must not claim for liberation theology that phony quality of being 'scientific' which is the very questionable means by which Marxists attempt to escape from the *'tu quoque'* argument. However, we may be grateful to the liberation theologians for pointing out the extent to which our ecclesiology is conditioned by the social circumstances in which it is formed. We must not assume that the version of the church which we enjoy in our age is normative for all time. Those who are familiar with the well-known nineteenth-century novel *Quo Vadis?* by Henryk Sienkiewicz about Christians in Rome under Nero will remember the absurdity of the way in which the author represents Peter as being addressed by his fellow-Christians in very much the same terms as Roman Catholics would have addressed Pius IX or Leo XIII.

At the same time we must also refuse to be bullied by the arguments from the sociology of thought which consist in claiming that our thought is so much socially conditioned as to be actually invalid. One meets in some writers today the epithet 'bourgeois' as applied to an argument or a doctrine. In his recent book on the Trinity[23] Jürgen Moltmann is not wholly guiltless of this form of sociological damnation. Forms of Trinitarian theology which he rejects are stigmatized as 'bourgeois'. The assumption behind such reasoning is that the critic knows the true motivation behind the argument of his opponent better than the opponent does himself: 'You imagine you know why you hold this doctrine, but I have access to your true motivation.' The fatal objection to this form of debate is that it is two-edged. If my doctrine is to be stigmatized as 'bourgeois', I can with equal justification describe yours as 'proletarian'. (Indeed one wonders whether Moltmann would not be proud to champion a proletarian doctrine of the Trinity.) If you believe you can invalidate my argument by suggesting it is merely the product of my bourgeois environment, I can invalidate yours just as effectively by explaining it as the product of your proletarian background. We end up all square and the debate has not progressed an inch.

This sociological blackmail is widely used by Marxists. As we have indicated above, they give themselves a special exemption from the influence of social circumstances on their own thinking, because their philosophy is supposed to be scientific. This fond belief in a scientific philosophy has long ago been exploded by modern thinkers. It represents in Marxism the preservation for ideological reasons of a long-discredited strain of positivism. It should have no place in honest theological thinking today.

We return therefore to the second ingredient in liberation theology, its interpretation of Jesus as a social revolutionary, or at least a social reformer. It is true that a marked feature of Jesus' ministry was his association with those who were on the fringes of society and his denunciation of those who prided themselves on their piety. But this association with 'sinners' was not primarily motivated by a desire to alter the system that had produced these outcasts. They appealed to him precisely because they did not make any claim to piety or devotion, and therefore were more open to the challenge of the kingdom. The imminence of the kingdom of God which Jesus proclaimed meant that all Israel was thrown into the position of a sinner. The coming of the kingdom brought judgment for all; all needed to repent. Therefore those who had never imagined that they were anything but sinners had a natural advantage. There is no evidence that Jesus planned to alter society; the coming of the kingdom made that irrelevant. Nor did he have any programme of social reform. So the picture of Jesus the revolutionary leader or Jesus the social reformer is a purely imaginary one.

When we turn to the rest of the New Testament we find even less to substantiate the case for liberation theology. Most of the writers of the New Testament are sublimely unconscious of the need for social reform. Even what appears to us to be the monstrous social evil of slavery is calmly accepted by them. The only writer in the New Testament who appears to have anything like a social conscience is the author of the Epistle of James, and he does not support his condemnation of the rich by referring to Jesus' teaching.

All this of course does not mean that Christians need have no social conscience, nor that Christianity has nothing to say in the realm of social ethics. But our convictions about social justice and the social order are drawn either from the Hebrew prophets, who had much to say on this topic, or from our apprehension of the revelation of God's nature in Jesus Christ. The God so revealed is not one who is indifferent to social injustice. We do not need to misrepresent Jesus as a social reformer in order to find material for a Christian critique of society.

Thirdly, we must not identify the struggle for social justice with the Christian life. When this happens, the Christian element in the struggle disappears, and Christian revolutionaries soon become indistinguishable from any other revolutionaries. It is perfectly true that the church in the past has frequently been compromised in its witness and activity by its association with the state and with society. But the relation of the church to the state varies immensely from age to age and from place to place, just as the amount of social injustice to be fought varies from age to age and from place to place. At this very moment the situation of the church in various parts of the world varies from that of triumphalism[24] to that of outright persecution by the state. It is probably fair to say that the peculiar relation of the Church of England to the state has meant that within its walls criticism of the state has been muted. Indeed it is only just passing out of a situation in which everyone assumed that the established church must always be on the side of the ruling classes. In addition it must be conceded that the strongly middle-class membership of the Church of England influences its attitude towards social issues. But a strongly proletarian church would be just as much conditioned by its proletarian membership: compare, for example, the way in which the Roman Catholic Church in Ulster reflects the political views of Roman Catholics there (and the same could just as well be said of the Protestant churches in that area).

Where there is gross social oppression the church must take the side of the oppressed at the peril of its life. It is doing so today to some extent in South Africa and to an increasing extent in Central and South America. But where it cannot honestly be said that there is at the moment gross social oppression, as is the case with most of the countries in the industrialized West, the church is not to blame if it is not always actively seeking social causes with which to associate itself. The issue of nuclear arms does not come under the description of social oppression. It is, however, an urgent and important political issue on which Christians are divided. If the church ignored it altogether it would be very much to blame. But this is not the case. There is one area of the world, the subcontinent of India, where there is gross social injustice and hardship and still, it must be said, a good deal of social oppression. The Christian church here is very much in a minority and for that reason perhaps has not distinguished itself as a leader in the struggle for social justice, though it has done, and still is doing, a great deal in the way of social betterment.

Should Christians as Christians be more sensitive to the need for social justice? Probably they ought to be. So far in this century it is Marxists who have stood out as the champions of social justice – until the revolution has taken place. Then for the most part they become apologists for social tyranny. But Christians know that even after the revolution the same questions about the church's relation to society will come up to be answered, only now all the more urgently because the state is now demanding an uncritical admiration from the church. Christians also know that the revolution does not change human nature, and that those who hold power after the revolution are just as liable to the corruption of power as were their predecessors before the revolution.

The Christian church is always called to be critical of society in the name of Christ, as it is to be critical of itself. The church must always protest against social oppression and fight against it with such weapons as are available and appropriate. But it must do so without the hatred, bitterness, and unscrupulousness of Communism. In a revolutionary situation the Christian will seem 'soft' to the Marxist. If he did not, he would not really be a Christian. So the challenge of liberation theology is a real one, motivated by the best intentions. But it must be faced and overcome.

4

Orthodoxy

1. The Present Situation

To judge by the strenuous regularity with which clergy deny that
they know anything about or have any use for theology, one could
well conclude that theology has no effect at all on the church. But
in fact even the loose intellectual permissiveness of the Church of
England can be seen to be affected by theology in the long run. The
art of our stained-glass windows, the manner in which we furnish
and decorate our churches, even the choice of hymns which we
sing, are ultimately determined by the kind of theology which
theologians were at one time teaching. New churches are not built
in the same style as the old were. We no longer attempt to reproduce the Gothic, nor even to make our churches look from the
outside like jam-factories, as we did in the 1920s and 1930s. The
epitaphs on memorials in churches are eloquent witnesses to the
changing theology of those who erected them. In the eighteenth
century the epitaph would proclaim that the deceased was, in the
well-known example, 'A devoted mother, an affectionate wife, a
benefactress of the poor, and a cousin of the earl of Cork, and of
such are the kingdom of heaven'. In the nineteenth century the
memorial would wax eloquent about the reliance of the deceased on
the redeeming blood of his or her Saviour. In our day the memorial
would be more likely to carry some such terse but unmistakably
vulgar and this-worldly message as 'Good-bye, mum!'. Of the influence of theology, not only on church furnishing but even on what is
said and thought in church, we must pronounce, *'Eppur si muove'*. It
moves indeed, and in the Anglican communion at least in recent
years it has been moving at an accelerated pace because of our
liturgical reforms. A new *Book of Common Prayer* ultimately changes
the theology of the congregation using it more effectively than all

the parson's sermons, all the efforts of Sunday School teachers and confirmation classes, and all the books on the church bookstall.

But the effect of theological change is a delayed effect. It takes a considerable time for new theology to filter or seep down from the lecture-room to the pew. In some ways it might be said that in spite of all appearances and talk of our living in a period of rapid social change, the period between the appearance of any new theological current and its becoming visible at the grass roots is longer than it used to be. The 'Tracts for the Times' a century and a half ago, for instance, appear to have had an almost instantaneous impact. Within a very few years there was a solid mass of Tractarian opinion in the Church of England. But today it seems to take longer for the new ideas to be assimilated. In the first decade of this century Friedrich von Hügel wrote as if very soon all intelligent Christians would accept that the Fourth Gospel was not written by the apostle John and that the discourses ascribed in it to Jesus Christ would be recognized as not representing the Lord's *ipsissima verba*. But how many educated church-going Christians today accept these conclusions? How many clergy accept them and allow such acceptance to appear in their teaching? Only a very small number.

The reasons for the delay between the scholars' work and the churchman's ideas which is so evident today are varied. One is that in relation to the educational level of the rest of the population the average priest is less advanced than he used to be. The parish priest a hundred years ago was quite often the only well educated person, or among the few well-educated people, in his parish. Now quite often there will be a great many lay people in his congregation who are better educated than he, and sometimes he will number among his parishioners one or two people who have had a better theological education than he, and – bitterest humiliation of all! – one of them may be a woman! He will probably not know Latin and is on the whole unlikely to be able to read the New Testament in Greek with any fluency; he is most unlikely to know Hebrew. We do not know what proportion of clergy of all the denominations possess a degree from a reputable university or equivalent institution. Is it fifty per cent? We greatly doubt if it is as much.

Another reason for this gap between lecture-room and pew is the confusion, complexity and specialization of contemporary scholarship. Scholars are indecisive animals, but preachers desire certain, clear and lasting conclusions. As well expect a scientist to be competent in all branches of science today as expect a clergyman to be up to date in all branches of theology. There are of course quite a lot of writers who are publicists in theology rather than specialists, who mediate new ideas and currents of scholarship to the clergy and the teachers. But there are not enough of them, and they face a peculiarly difficult task. The tendency to fragmentation in contemporary schools of theology or religion does not help either. In short, a large number of clergy today have not had a proper theological education and in spite of all increases in our institutions of higher education have not been given the tools for serious theological study.

The difference between the attitude to the Christian faith of anybody who today is a competent theologian and the man or woman in the pew or the average tenant of a pulpit is most marked. Their whole approach to the Bible, to the history of doctrine, to concepts such as revelation, miracle, or God's activity in history will be quite different. What is one to do or say if a faithful churchgoer asks one to describe as far as one can from one's scholarly knowledge the crossing of the Red Sea by Moses and the turning of water into wine by Jesus at Cana of Galilee? 'My dear man (or woman), the one is a legend surrounded by the mists of early history, and I doubt very much if the other happened'? Or what reply are we to make to the earnest, uninstructed but intelligent lay person who points out that Jesus certainly accepted the view, common to all the writers of the New Testament, that David predicted the coming of the Messiah in his Psalms and recorded what God was saying about this event, as in Psalm 110, 'The Lord said unto my Lord, Thou art my son, this day have I begotten thee'? We live in a world where a totally different attitude to these subjects from the traditional one is not only taken for granted but is simply unavoidable. The lay person and the average minister of religion has either never entered that world or has forgotten it. Life in that world comes naturally to us; we have breathed its air for forty years. It would need a revolution to enable that air to blow through the pews.

We happen by the providence of God to live in a period when theology and scholarship are governed by a spirit of fragmentation, a centrifugal impulse, in an era of what might be called theological dissipation. The great system-builders of our youth have passed away – Barth, Maritain, Brunner, Tillich, Niebuhr. There are some systematic theologians on the Continent, Küng, Schillebeeckx, Pannenberg, Moltmann. Notice that they are almost all Germans. We can import German theology; we have done so in the past and we still could do so today. But contemporary German theologians are not as powerful, as attractive, as the German theologians of our youth, and nobody can say that their influence is very visible in the parishes. There is a certain cult of Bonhoeffer, but it does not impress us greatly. German theologians take as little notice of Bonhoeffer, in spite of British admiration of him, as British take of Thomas Carlyle, in spite of German admiration for him. We certainly are producing no systematic theology of home-growth whatever. What is happening, however, is a notable movement to dismantle traditional dogma. The work of Hick, Wiles, Cupitt, Lampe, of Nineham, and of several less eminent names calls us in different voices and for rather different reasons to abandon the doctrine of the Incarnation and the doctrine of the Trinity, to disembarrass ourselves of traditional theological baggage and in its place to produce – what? At this point their voices die out into faint speculation or a babble of uncertain conjectures. And on their side the scholars of the New Testament can give us little comfort. In spite of a strenuous search lasting at least thirty years they have been quite unable to find a criterion whereby we can distinguish between the authentic and the inauthentic records of the words and deeds of Jesus. They can, and do, however, conclude confidently that we must abandon any idea that there is a theology of the New Testament. One can see why recent years have been marked in religious circles by a rising tide of fundamentalism and frightened conservatism.

But it is futile simply to deplore the growth of conservatism defended by no new arguments. It is the fault of the theologians that this conservatism has arisen. Those of us who are concerned with doctrine or systematic theology have given the purveyors of theology at the grass roots very little to work on.

We cannot and dare not return to fundamentalism, nor to the situation where Popes or Doctrinal Commissions of the Curia or bishops produced authoritatively and arbitrarily doctrine as from an unquestioned oracle whose meaning and matter it is the theologians' task meekly and assiduously to expound and justify. The days of the unquestionably authoritative Bible and the unquestionably authoritative hierarchy are over. Intense rearguard actions may be fought, but it must be clear to all intelligent people that to revive either is to fight for a lost cause. For our own part, our conscience simply forbids us to defend fundamentalism. We know according to all the criteria whereby we can test truth that it is wrong, and we cannot and dare not follow untruth with our eyes open, not even for the sake of sparing the consciences of the faithful.

On the other hand we perceive very well the folly of deliberately abandoning the search for orthodoxy. We realize what, it seems to us, not enough Protestant scholars have realized, that the church and the Bible are inseparably bound up together. Protestants are very ready to adopt the perfectly true slogan, 'No Bible, No church', but too often they fail to see that the converse applies, 'No church, No Bible'. The very concept of a Bible, of a New Testament, implies and demands a church to interpret and to teach the collection of documents which the church itself has set apart to be at once the raw material and the norm of its doctrine. From this there follows by inexorable logic the necessity of orthodoxy. To reduce Christian doctrine to the individual interpretations, insights and whims of each theologian, and finally of each individual Christian or arbitrary group of Christians, which is the logical outcome of much contemporary theology, is in fact to dissolve Christianity. We cannot agree to the dismantling and abandonment of the dogmas which the church in the first four centuries of its existence painfully achieved after a laborious process of trial and error. We cannot embrace the kind of pious nihilism to which Don Cupitt appears to be calling us. We cannot jettison the historical circumstances of the career of Jesus as, at least at one point in one of his books, Maurice Wiles appears to advocate. We cannot cease to believe in Jesus as mediator, which is what Geoffrey Lampe explicitly suggests at one point in his *God As Spirit*[1] and implicitly argues in many other parts of it. We cannot follow Dennis Nineham in his positively gleeful call to sink the whole of Christian tradition on the grounds that it is irrecoverable or incomprehensible or both.

We must therefore respect, recover, seek for orthodoxy. But it must be a *critical* orthodoxy. It must be an orthodoxy much more flexible, readier to make concessions to the advances of scholar-

ship, less arrogant and strident, more tentative and sensitive and
chastened than ever before. We must not be ashamed of openly
seeking to be orthodox. We must not allow sneers that we are
simply supporting the Establishment nor taking refuge in nostalgic
archaism to divert us from professing that we want to be orthodox.
But we must realize that orthodoxy is something that has to be
created, toiled for, discovered only after much exercise of sound
scholarship and honest thought. The task in the present situation is
a formidable one, whether we consider the condition of contemporary philosophy or biblical scholarship, or the thorny but unavoidable subject of the development of Christian doctrine. It is
made more difficult by the barriers which Christians have erected
between each other by their historical divisions. But it is a task
which must be attempted and to which we must devote all the
resources which we possess. It is not enough that we all study the
Bible, quote the Bible, include texts from the Bible in our prayers
and our liturgies. It is not the Bible that unites Christians, but the
church's tradition in interpreting the Bible, as the history of the
ecumenical movement has shown. What we need is agreement on
doctrine, on what we teach when we are not just repeating the words
of the Bible. Indeed it might be an advantage if, without abandoning the Bible as a source for our doctrine, we were, taking for once
Professor Nineham's advice, to distance ourselves a little from the
Bible, to keep, so to speak, the whole wood in mind without being
distracted by the individual trees.

What we have been saying seems a far cry from the teaching of
Christianity in pulpit and classroom. But in fact it is not. In the first
place, our argument rests upon the assumption that doctrine will be
made in an ecumenical enterprise. And this is a very relevant
consideration in the present situation. We are convinced that as
theological scholarship is now inter-confessional, so doctrine, and
the doctrine which is taught at grass-roots level, must be inter-
confessional. This does not mean boiling down our doctrine to a
colourless and insipid lowest common denominator, but that
theologians of all denominations ought to be consciously co-
operating to achieve common doctrine, common orthodoxy, not by
each simply defending his confessional tradition in the last ditch
but by creating a new understanding of orthodoxy in the light of
modern conditions and of modern critical scholarship. We are the

more encouraged to attempt this seemingly impossible task because we realize through what we have been able to study during the last forty years of the history of doctrine that this process is one that in one sense or another has always been happening. The history of theology is the history of the theologians and ultimately the faithful adapting and altering, shifting and developing the tradition which they inherited in face of the demands and needs of their generation, its pressures, discoveries, tensions and currents of thought. We may well be conscious of the needs of adaptation. But we must not forget what we are adapting, the orthodox Christian faith, which must be both faithful to the original revelation and continually changing.

In this difficult enterprise which we have set before our readers we have one great advantage, in addition to the quite new opportunities for ecumenical co-operation which exist today. Theology is no longer the preserve of the clergy; all over the country there are laymen and laywomen who, through the work of the schools of theology in our state-supported universities and colleges, have received as good a theological education as most of our clergy, in fact probably better. They are capable of becoming the teachers of both clergy and laity if their potential were properly realized and organized. Many of them teach in schools already. There is no reason why they should not teach in church. They could become in God's providence the means of rescuing us from our present state of doctrinal fragmentation, dissipation and ossification into a more constructive, creative and comprehensive presentation of the Christian faith in school and church.

Perhaps what we most need is simply faith, trust. Catholic must trust Protestant and Protestant Catholic. We must have faith in God that we can together discover, recreate, orthodoxy not in spite of critical scholarship and pressing theological problems, but because of them.

2. The Limits of Orthodoxy

There are still people who believe that there is something noble and courageous in being heretical, that is to say in holding views that are contradictory to and destructive of the traditional doctrines of the Christian faith, and that theologians are people who are gravely shocked at encountering any deviation from traditional orthodoxy, who would like to excommunicate and ostracize holders of deviant views, if they had the power. The truth is that theologians have often met far more radical versions of heresy than those who think they shall shock them have ever heard of, and have long ago learnt never to be shocked at any viewpoint. The days when heterodoxy was liable to land the holder of it in trouble are long past; even the Roman Catholic Church is much more tolerant of deviation than it used to be. But somehow, for many people, the word 'orthodoxy' still conjures up the smell of fire and the picture of the rack. We are still suffering from the horrible and disgraceful behaviour of our ancestors in the days of persecution for doctrinal deviation. Not that there is any shortage of Inquisitors in the twentieth century, but in many countries secular ideologies, such as Marxism, have taken over the role of the Inquisitor from the churchmen. Many conventional Christians do not seem to realize this.

There is nothing in itself creditable or courageous in differing widely from the traditional doctrines of the Christian church, though there is nothing morally wrong in doing so honestly either. There have, of course, been periods when the defiance of the church as a whole, by a courageous and lonely individual, can be recognized in the light of history as right and noble, as we can see in the case of Athanasius, of John Hus, of Luther and of Kierkegaard, But to fling a resounding defiance in the face of a church which has no means of persecuting nor desire to do so, is a policy which has no particular virtue attached to it and usually argues ignorance rather than valour.

It is one thing, however, to show that orthodoxy is valuable and desirable. It is quite another to define what orthodoxy is or should be. The preceding pages have shown the peculiar difficulties attending anybody who today desires to state what is orthodox and what not. It must, therefore, be understood that the attempt to do this which follows is done so under all the conditions and reservations mentioned above. This is not the orthodoxy of a persecutor, nor the orthodoxy of a theological precisian, but of those who desire the common life in the body of Christ (*koinōnia, sobornost*) to be expressed in doctrine as well as in worship and action. We shall, therefore, set out five points which we consider to constitute indispensable orthodoxy for Christians.

It may cause surprise that we start with the doctrine of the Trinity, because for many Christians, the doctrine of God as three Persons but one God is a remote and irrelevant subject preserved for a few super-intellectual theologians but quite unnecessary for the ordinary Christian. They never hear it expounded, they scarcely even hear it mentioned. They do not see why everybody should be concerned about it and if they learn, as they would if they read the section devoted to this subject in our earlier book,[2] that this doctrine is a development of what is to be found in the Bible, they would be even less inclined to favour it.

However, we affirm confidently that the doctrine of the Trinity is an indispensable safeguard and expression of Christian belief because it is based on something that is at the very heart of Christianity. We refer the reader on the more detailed aspects of this doctrine to our earlier book: here it is enough to say that the deepest truth which Christianity enshrines is that the one sole true God has poured himself out in love in Jesus Christ for our final and decisive salvation, calling us to return to him in love. It is not enough to say, if we are to be true to the furthest reach of biblical thought, that God has given us an example of love or enacted for us a parable of love or provided us with a religious experience based on love, or inculcated a doctrine or philosophy about love. He has given himself, he has himself in his Son exposed himself to human experience, human limitation, suffering, tension and death, and has done so without ceasing to be God and has thereby established within human history a perennial means of responding to that love, of living in it and expressing it in our lives individually and communally. The doctrine of the Trinity declares that God did not merely, on one occasion, do this, but that in doing so he was expressing his very nature and being. He is a God who is constituted by outgoing and return in love. The doctrine of the Trinity is the proper and necessary corollary to the witness of the Bible about God. It is the specifically Christian doctrine of God, of the difference that Christian belief makes to theistic belief, and it is not just a doctrine. It is an invitation to worship. It is based not just on scholars searching the pages of the Bible but on individuals praying and congregations worshipping. It is by no chance that the document which (for all its undoubted defects) expresses this doctrine most fully and succinctly among the credal statements of the

Christian faith, the Athanasian creed, says 'And the Catholic faith is this: that we *worship* one God in Trinity and Trinity in unity'. The doctrine of the Trinity is a prime ingredient of orthodoxy.

Most Christians would recognize at once that the doctrine of the Incarnation is a necessary part of orthodoxy. They would probably not realize that it presents more difficulties today than many other parts of the traditional Christian faith. There are two reasons for this: the doctrine of the Incarnation was not officially defined (in the year 451 at the Council of Chalcedon) until more than fifty years after the general acceptance of the doctrine of the Trinity within the church, and the terms in which it was defined are so particular and so much influenced by the categories of late Greek philosophy as to make defence of the Chalcedonian formula in all its details a very difficult, if not impossible task.[3] And secondly, this doctrine is necessarily involved with a consideration of the historical career of Jesus, and biblical criticism has made this a peculiarly complicated and sensitive subject.

But because we cannot reproduce *ex animo* the doctrine of the Chalcedonian Formula, we are not obliged to abandon the doctrine of the Incarnation: after all, the Chalcedonian doctrine itself caused an immediate and lasting division in the Christian church of the fifth century, and other versions of the doctrine of the Incarnation have been for long held by large numbers of Christians. As long as Christians continue to worship Jesus Christ as God, there must be a doctrine of the Incarnation. If we see Jesus as the human figure who was laid hold of by God to be the vehicle of his final and decisive revelation of himself, his opening of his heart to mankind, so to speak, we must speak of him in incarnational terms. Our doctrine of the Incarnation need not be, indeed should not be, a doctrine of a deified man so absorbing as to threaten to obscure the figure of God the Father, as, we suspect, it tends to be in some evangelical circles today. Nor need it be a doctrine of a perambulating oracle, more divine than human, omniscient and imperturbable, of God inhabiting a human body as astronauts today inhabit a space-suit, as it was too often in the writings of the early Fathers of the church. Our doctrine must be at once more drastic and subtler than this. It must concede far more to Christ's genuine humanity, and it must be much readier than the Father's to accept the scandal of the cross, and allow for a deliberately accepted suffering and weakness in God. But in whatever terms we express our doctrine of the Incarnation (and the New Testament allows us several different choices and the history of Christian doctrine even more), it must include the affirmation that in Christ we meet God in such a way that he faces us with a final choice of infinite importance for ourselves, that he conveys and communicates to us, if we believe in him, the life (though not the nature) of God himself. It is tempting today, in the light of our greatly increased knowledge of, and interest in, other religions, consciously or unconsciously to water down this doctrine until Christ becomes one (perhaps the highest) among a number of other revealers of God in human history. But the eschatological material in the New Testament, indeed the whole atmosphere of the book itself, forbids us thus to compromise the finality and ultimacy of Jesus Christ. This is not to deny that God has revealed himself in other great religious teachers throughout history. But Jesus Christ represents the communication of God himself for final salvation, final in the sense that it cannot be superseded or reduced by comparison.

When we come to consider the doctrine of the Atonement, the knowledgeable reader here will say, 'But there is no official doctrine of the Atonement!' – and he will be quite right. Perhaps fortunately, no specific doctrine of how precisely Christ has saved us has ever been accepted by the church at large. There have been plenty of instances of sections or denominations or parties in the church expecting everybody to accept one particular account of this subject or another. For a long time, among Presbyterians and Anglicans at least, a substitutionary theory of the atonement was regarded as orthodoxy from which it would be dangerous to waver. Most of the evangelical party within the Church of England and in some other parts of the Anglican Communion today would think of the doctrine that Christ in dying appeased God's wrath or satisfied his justice in our stead when we were unable to do so as the biblical doctrine of the atonement *par excellence*, and might judge the soundness of others' doctrine by this standard. But this particular theory has not been the universally adopted view of the church from the beginning by any means. Some of the materials for it are to be found in Tertullian (fl. 200), but it owes much more to Calvin and Calvinists since the sixteenth century. Many of the Greek-speaking Fathers of the early church had a view of the atonement which almost made the incarnation equivalent to the atonement: once the Word became united to mankind, his saving work was largely accomplished. From the time that Anselm of Canterbury (fl. 1100) wrote his famous book on the atonement, *Cur Deus Homo?*, his particular theory which is called the satisfaction theory was widely influential. And in the nineteenth century the moral or exemplarist theory began to dominate in Protestant theological circles at least.[4] So no one party or section has the right to claim that its view of the atonement is the sole correct or orthodox one.

But this is not to say that it is perfectly permissible for Christians to have no theory of the atonement at all, to say that the expression, 'Christ died for our sins' is an empty and meaningless phrase, or to reduce it to meaning simply that, like President Coolidge's preacher, Christ was against sin. In the fifteenth chapter of I Corinthians, Paul says (v.3), 'for I delivered to you as of first importance what I also received, that Christ died for our sins in accordance with the scriptures'. This was not Paul's own original interpretation of the significance of Christ; he inherited it from the church that had been there before him, and yet he was converted at a very early period of the primitive church's life; indeed, this doctrine that Christ died 'for our sins' must be regarded as one of the very oldest and most original pieces of Christian doctrine. It cannot be pushed aside or reduced to a shadow. In it is contained the important truth that Jesus Christ cannot simply be regarded as a teacher and a paradigm; he must be something more, a mediator, somebody who reconciles us to God, not only by his words and example, but by his very person. Indeed Paul's doctrine of the church as the body of Christ brings us to the same conclusion. This does not mean that Christ is one stage in our move towards God and that there is a further stage beyond, which God the Father represents; it is as he is incarnate that the Son of God is a mediator; he is the form taken by God to approach us and reconcile us to himself so that he becomes man without ceasing to be God, and in the process it is necessary for him to suffer and die, a necessity which he voluntarily imposes on himself. This is the least that the atonement can mean. It is open to a wide range of different interpretations and elaboration according to which strand of thought about it in the New Testament is developed. But it is clearly an indispensable part of the wholeness of Christian doctrine.

As has already been said, Protestants are usually anxious to insist that the church needs the Bible, indeed that the Bible is indispensable to the church. They are not always aware of the equally important complementary truth, that the Bible needs the church, that the church is indispensable to the Bible. The very concept of a New Testament implies a church. Christianity is not only an individualist religion, it is communal. Being united with Christ involves union with all the others, and they worship and live as a community, not simply as an aggregate. This was so evident in the early centuries of Christianity that nobody took much trouble to write about it. But since the growth of a tyrannous and privileged hierarchy in the late Middle Ages in the West and the consequent reaction of the Reformation, many Christians in the Protestant tradition have seen no necessity for regarding the doctrine of the church as an important or necessary aspect of the Christian faith. They think of the church, if they think of it at all, as a loose federation of saved individuals. Or they attach themselves vaguely to a single charismatic individual who runs his own church as rock-stars run their fans, and too often finds the business as lucrative as they. This is a wrong concept of the church, a dangerous distortion of the original idea of the people of God in the Bible and the early church. A low doctrine of the church is not merely feeble and unattractive, it is unorthodox and unscriptural. It should be added that a 'high' doctrine of the church is not necessarily confined to, nor even held by, groups and traditions who look to the unenquiring eye as if they were 'Catholic'. The Church of Scotland, which is Presbyterian in polity, has a high doctrine of the church. So do the Lutherans, many of whom do not have bishops. The Church of Ireland, which is generally classed as 'low' among the provinces of the Anglican communion, has a high doctrine of the church, and conversely some Anglo-Catholics who prefer a very 'Catholic' pattern of doctrine behave in so sectarian a way in practice that one cannot seriously regard them as having a high doctrine of the church. Any Christians who for any reasons cut themselves off from their fellow-Christians in order to form tight little groups, whether they call themselves Gospel Hall Christians or Pentecostals or Continuing Anglican or simply Catholics, are likely to have a defective doctrine of the church and to be lacking in orthodoxy. The immense importance of a sound doctrine of the church has been one of the discoveries of theological scholarship in the twentieth century. With this must go the belief that the church has the authority of Christ and can exercise it within proper limits.

This subject of the sacraments of baptism and of holy communion has been in the past one around which controversy has raged, and it has proved perhaps more divisive than any other. But two considerations should restrain us from dismissing the subject as too explosive and too open to divergent interpretations to form part of orthodoxy. In the first place, these two sacraments have always held a central place in Christian belief and practice and worship. Even the practice of infant baptism, which is open to so much abuse and has given to many wrong impressions of this sacrament, has not removed it from the centre of Christian concern and thought. Even the effect of the Reformation in shifting the centre of attention from the sacrament to the Word, did not wholly obscure the sacrament of holy communion among the Protestants, and in our own day we have seen it restored to a properly central place among many of the sons and daughters of the Reformation. And secondly, during the last ten or fifteen years, a remarkable series of agreements upon these sacraments has been achieved in discussions among representatives of different Christian traditions, some of whom would *a priori* have been thought to be incapable of reaching agreement with their counterparts on these subjects. Should we regard them as rites purely demonstrative of something which has happened independently of them, as simply seals or public declarations of an initiation into Christ in the first case and of a regular renewal of union with him in the second which had taken place already in religious experience? This would mean seeing them as not efficacious, that is to say, as not conveying to the faithful recipient of them that which they symbolize, but merely as symbolizing events with which they are not efficaciously connected. The result of this view would be the gradual disappearance of these two sacraments, for that which is merely peripheral or ornamental in a rite tends ultimately to fade away, like the practice of giving newly initiated Christians milk and honey, which certainly existed in the early church. To regard these rites as necessary to orthodoxy is not necessarily to agree that they must be treated in a superstitious way or allowed to dominate Christian life and belief to the exclusion of other important elements; and a wide scope must be left for different ways of celebrating them. But they must not be omitted.

It may seem bigoted and narrow-minded to insist upon this element as vital to orthodox Christianity. It appears to exclude from this category some who have deservedly won respect for their manner of life and unselfish care for others, such as the Society of Friends and the Salvation Army. But it is not in accordance either with the witness of the New Testament or to the impressive weight of universal Christian tradition to omit and ignore these sacraments, and if we are to be honest, we must say so. We may be conscious that we have something to learn from those communities who have renounced sacraments altogether, but it would be hypocrisy and false ecumenism to pretend that they are standing within the bounds of orthodoxy.

It must be recognized in addition that these five principles of orthodoxy rest upon certain assumptions and carry certain corollaries with them which are not discussed here because this is not primarily a treatise on Christian doctrine. Examples of these are that God exists, that he has created the universe and exercises a kindly providence over it, that he answers prayers, that he rewards the good and punishes the bad, that there is a future life for which this life is a preparation. It would be impossible, or all but impossible, to believe the five principles outlined above without also believing such doctrines as these. What has been attempted here is a statement of the central doctrines of the Christian faith which have traditionally been regarded as constituting orthodoxy, and which even in the confused and uncertain circumstances of today must still be seen to constitute orthodoxy.

This account of orthodoxy is not, it need hardly be said, intended to supersede all previous standards or statements of orthodoxy, but to suffice for a period in which all have come into question. We can and should learn from a study of the history of Christian doctrine, Christian creeds and Christian confessions. The story of the Pelagian Controversy, for instance, can teach us something of the relation of the human will to divine grace; the history of Donatism should convince us that the efficacy of a sacrament is not dependent on the worthiness of the minister. The protest of the Reformers of the sixteenth century should convince us of the gratuitousness of God's love and of the danger of trying to achieve salvation either by good conduct alone or by sacramental or ecclesiastical manipulation. And many other such doctrinal lessons can be learnt from history.

In a more general way, we can also draw conclusions about the right and the wrong sort of Christianity by a survey of the history of the church. By now, we ought to realize that persecution of others for their religious beliefs alone is in all circumstances wrong. We ought to realize that it is unhealthy and in the long run disastrous for Christian churches to be dominated by an all-powerful hierarchy, whether of bishops or kirk sessions or any other, or by purely popular vote irrespective of the education, knowledge and experience of the voters. History should teach us too that religious experience is a good servant but a bad master, that to subordinate all aspects of Christianity, ministry, sacraments, preaching, teaching and worship, to the test of how much thrill or excitement or satisfaction they give to the individual is a recipe for calamity. And we should perceive that all types of Christianity which claim a new revelation given through any individual, Joseph Smith or Mrs Baker Eddy or any other, which modifies or adds to or reduces the revelation given in Jesus Christ is inauthentic and self-condemned.

Here then is a brief and imperfect sketch of what orthodoxy should mean in its barest outlines. This is not intended to be an iron system brutally or fanatically imposed on its devotees, material for gleefully conducted witch-hunts. Orthodoxy when treated like this damages the orthodox as much as their victims. But this account of orthodoxy implies that there are limits, although wide, and a form, though flexible, for the Christian faith, and the church has authority to insist on those limits and in certain circumstances to exclude from its number those who will not or cannot observe them.

We have argued above that certain doctrines of Christianity must be retained or defended at all costs because they are essential to the genius and spirit of that faith. The drive and burden of the New Testament and the character of God to which the Old bears witness necessarily involve the recognition that Jesus Christ is God, though we must add, God revealed in the mode of self-emptying. In order to do justice to this conclusion, to preserve monotheism, and to reflect the doctrine of the Holy Spirit and the eschatological emphasis of the New Testament, a doctrine of God as Trinity is essential. And we must believe that Jesus Christ is the divinely appointed means of reconciliation between God and man; indeed we cannot avoid the conclusion that in the suffering of Jesus Christ

God suffers. And we have upheld the necessity of belief in the church and in the sacraments of baptism and the eucharist.

But these doctrines must be cherished and taught within the conditions imposed by the development of thought, philosophy and science since the founding of Christianity. This is an assumption often challenged by people who are ignorant of the history of Christianity and of the development of the discipline of historical criticism. In fact the church has always been compelled to adjust itself to this necessity. Whether we look at the second-century church achieving the transition from messianic expectation to concentration upon the person of Jesus Christ in the church, or the fourth-century church both using and rejecting late Greek philosophy in order to reach the classical doctrine of the Trinity, or the scholastic theologians of the twelfth and thirteenth centuries assimilating the impact of a revived Aristotelianism, we must come to the same conclusion. The church has always been compelled to maintain a dialogue with contemporary secular thought, and in the course of this dialogue it has always found it necessary to reinterpret and re-assess its traditional doctrine, shuffling the elements and changing the emphases in the fundamentals of its faith, and viewing them with new eyes. This process has been more or less speedy, more or less drastic, more or less conspicuous, according to the rate of influx of new ideas and discoveries and the pace of change in the society in which the church has been living.

Today the requirement to make such adjustment, such reinterpretation, is stronger than it has ever been before, except perhaps in the second century. Not only are we compelled to take account of the enormous advances in scientific discovery made in recent centuries, affecting our understanding of the universe, of the position and nature of this planet, of the origin of mankind and of the purpose and place of man in the world, but the advance of historical criticism has necessitated a new approach to the fundamental doctrines of the Christian faith, to the Old and New Testaments, to the history of Christian dogma and to the traditional creeds. This is a conclusion which cannot be avoided, though there are apparently many educated and ostensibly thinking Christians who believe that it can, and who ought to know better. We can retain fundamentalism neither in our approach to the Bible nor in our understanding of the creeds. This point cannot be laboured here. It is enough to ask a few relevant questions: Do we believe that the whole world is inhabited by small invisible beings, called devils, devoted to working evil on the human race, as was implicitly believed by almost everybody in the ancient and medieval world? Do we believe in a spatial heaven and a spatial hell, as those did who first repeated the words, 'he ascended into heaven' and 'he descended into hell'? How many followers in any parish today are there of Marcellus of Ancyra, whose heresy is rebutted in the words 'whose kingdom shall have no end' inserted in the Nicene Creed of the year 381? One could continue endlessly producing examples to show that 'time makes ancient good uncouth', that words become obsolete and need re-stating, that all the basic documents of the Christian religion are strongly influenced by the periods in which they were written, and that those periods lie far back in the past.

It is therefore the pressing, inescapable duty of the leaders of the Christian church, be they bishops or theologians or any other, to make sense of the Christian faith to their people in the terms of their own day. This is not just the academic exercise of remote and ineffectual dons. It is the life-blood of Christianity, that which shows that it is a living religion and not just a pleasing museum-piece kept in being by people who have a nostalgic longing to retain the past, a kind of Christian Old Curiosity Shop. Historical criticism is not just the plaything of theologians in ivory towers. It is a stern necessity, and the ivory towers are inhabited by those who refuse to recognize its importance. To those who have met this discipline, who have understood and imbibed it, the acceptance of certain conclusions about the contents of the Bible, for instance, is unavoidable, if they are to refuse to do what many clergy seem to be quite happy to do, that is to live with a lie in their soul. To ask people who know what historical criticism is to deny and suppress that knowledge is disgraceful. If they understand how fragile is the evidence for the virgin birth of Christ, if they can assess realistically the evidence for the resurrection, they cannot be expected to agree that the virgin birth is a foundation doctrine of Christianity, nor to take quite literally the fourth of the Thirty-Nine Articles which states that 'Christ did truly arise again from the dead, and take again his body, with flesh, bones and all things appertaining to the perfection of man's nature'. This would be to ask them to deny the deliverances of their intellect and to suppress the promptings of their conscience. Or, to take another example: Careful study of the New Testament makes it very difficult to avoid the conclusion that the knowledge of Jesus Christ was limited and that he did not claim to be divine in the way in which the Gospel of St John represents him as claiming. If public opinion within the church wishes to coerce people who, following the discipline of historical study, have come to these conclusions into disavowing them or refraining from publicizing them in case they disturb the faithful, then we are in precisely the same position as was Galileo when he was required to believe that the sun went round the earth and not vice versa, or as Robertson Smith was when his church expected him to agree that all the stories in Genesis are straightforward, trustworthy historical accounts. The exponents of historical criticism are not an eccentric, esoteric group of intellectuals playing with speculative and far-fetched ideas. They are the realists. Their opponents are living in a dream-world, cocooned from the impact of truth by their own illusions.

If it is the duty of the leaders of the church to make sense of Christianity to the world of the twentieth century, then they should not be timid conservatives. Orthodoxy cannot be defended by sheer conservatism, by attempting to place the gospel in a bullet-proof case, by building an impregnable museum for it. Orthodoxy can only be preserved by creative re-interpretation. The history of Christian doctrine should convince us of this. The great crisis of doctrine in the fourth century was not solved by a resolute refusal to change anything in Christian teaching, by a nostalgic clinging to old formulae in spite of all pressures. One could make out a case for saying that the real conservatism in that controversy lay with the Arians, who had a strict respect for the literal sense of Scripture and could point to several old and traditional ideas which were in their favour. The Nicene Creed of 381 which ended the controversy and rejected the Arian version of Christianity was a creative re-statement of the Christian faith, an employment of new language in order to preserve old truth. The Reformation in the Western church in the sixteenth century seemed to many traditionally-minded people of that age a dangerous, modernist introduction of new ideas and new interpretations which were calculated to disturb the minds of many pious Christians and required a quite new understanding of the nature of Christianity. Today we can see the

Reformation as a largely successful effort to achieve a creative re-assessment of the faith.

From all this we draw the conclusion that a leader of the church – and for Anglicans this means a bishop – is not necessarily called upon to be a conservative, if he is to regard himself (as he should) as a guardian and expounder of the faith. Christian truth is not such as can be preserved either by pious ignorance or timid conservatism. An essential qualification for a bishop is that he should be a theologian, that is one who is at least abreast with the main trends of biblical scholarship and theological debate. If he is not, he deprives himself of the right to speak publicly and representatively about doctrinal matters. He is indeed a custodian of the faith. But he is also a watchman. He must recognize the signs of the times. He must continually relate the Gospel with which he is entrusted to the intellectual climate and the needs of the age in which he lives. He must not regard himself as simply commissioned to refrain from disturbing the minds of the faithful. He must also stimulate and educate them.

5

Development

1. Conditions for Development

We cannot leave the subject of the doctrine of the church without considering briefly the questions of development of doctrine. Ever since John Henry Newman wrote his classic work *Essay on the Development of Christian Doctrine* in 1845 this subject has been more and more prominent in the minds of theologians who know their business. Newman certainly did not give satisfactory answers to all the questions which he raised, but to him belongs the credit for having at least asked the right questions. No theologian since can be said to have produced wholly adequate answers to them.

We have insisted more than once that interpretation of the Bible is a basic necessity of historical Christianity. Those who think that they can simply and directly derive the one and only possible doctrine from the Bible without taking into account the history of creeds, confessions and doctrines are deceiving themselves and only adding to confusion. And we have made the further step of suggesting that traditional doctrines such as those of the Trinity and of the Incarnation represent an actual development or advance in doctrine which, while it is certainly based on the Bible, means in fact an expression of the genius and drive of authentic Christianity derived from the Bible but in one sense enlarging or expanding its witness. The main argument of Newman was based on the fact that the Anglican Church of his day accepted the conclusions of the first four General Councils of the church, those which were concerned with the dogmas of the Trinity and the Incarnation, but remained silent or uncertain about any dogmatic conclusions or accretions of doctrine which had occurred after the date of the last of these four councils, 451. Why exactly, he asked, if you accept the first four councils' decisions, do you not accept the decisions of later councils and the forms of doctrine developed later in the history of the church? In particular, why not accept the medieval doctrines of purgatory, of the nature of the priesthood, and of the invocation of saints? Why should the Holy Spirit have ceased in the year 451 to inspire the church to formulate ever more profound and elaborate doctrines?

Anglican opponents of Newman (who had signalized his defect- ion to the Roman Catholic Church by publishing his *Essay*) almost all failed to see Newman's point, because they insisted that the dogmas of the first four councils were nothing but restatements in a different mode of the obvious truths of scripture. But if we agree with Newman (as we believe we must) that the doctrines of the Trinity and of the Incarnation are not simply restatements but constructive and necessary developments, we cannot be satisfied with this easy reply. Newman's own attempt to answer the question which he had raised was unsatisfactory. It depended on an elabor- ate and unconvincing argument drawn from history, and constantly tended to slip from saying that the Roman Church is the true church because its doctrine is true into saying that its doctrine is true because it is the true church. Some Roman Catholic theo- logians in the first half of the twentieth century were ready to take the bit between their teeth and argue that as the Roman Church is the true church any doctrine which it may declare to be Catholic, scriptural and true must be authentic doctrine because the Roman Church is the only authentic church, and contemplated with com- placency an indefinite extension and development of doctrine in the future guaranteed as true simply on the word of the church. And certainly only such an argument could justify the latest and most remotely elaborated Roman Catholic dogma, that of the Corporeal Assumption into Heaven of the Blessed Virgin Mary, proclaimed in 1950. But ever since the Second Vatican Council such an irrespon- sible view of the development of doctrine has been, rightly, at a discount in the Roman Catholic Church. Few theologians of that tradition, if any, would today support a view of development as uncontrolled as this.

One of the difficulties of this subject is that different bodies within Christianity today recognize different councils as authori- tative. Freechurchmen might recognize the first four, but no more. Anglicans would certainly recognize the first four, and some might, as some have in the past, extend this recognition to the next four also, up to that which took place in 787; the Orthodox regard these as certainly authoritative, but no more. The Roman Catholic Church, on the other hand, recognizes as General Councils no less than twenty-one, of which the Second Vatican is the latest. If only councils can create new doctrine or dogma, then we are in a state of grave confusion. In fact, however, the Roman Church does not agree that only councils can produce newly-recognized dogmas, because two of its latest examples, those of the Immaculate Conception of the Blessed Virgin Mary and that of her Assumption (in 1854 and 1950 respectively) were proclaimed by the Pope without any preceding council, though he claimed on each occasion to have consulted the church beforehand. Anglicans may well agree with the Roman Catholics that it is unnecessarily restrictive to the life of the church that only General Councils can develop doctrine. The history of the councils of the ancient church is not one of unsullied integrity and imperturbable impartiality. Probably only a body as authoritatively run as the Roman Church could successfully bring off a General Council in modern conditions; even with all its discipline the Roman Church has not found it easy to digest the conclusions of Vatican II.

But if we allow that development of doctrine can take place apart from the activity of councils, this does not commit us to agreeing that an acceptable alternative is the method of a single authoritative figure like a bishop of Rome defining apparently new dogmas on his own initiative and expecting us to accept his word that before he defined them as *de fide* he had consulted the whole church. This, in fact, is one of the worst ways of attempting to achieve development in doctrine, as the two dogmas defined by the Pope alone in recent centuries strongly suggest. Development of doctrine need not be confined to dogmas inserted in creeds. It may well be that the period when formal creeds served a useful purpose has passed. One could range through Christian history picking out examples of doctrine which has owing to various circumstances been enunciated and has been learned by the church thereafter. In the fifth century in the West it was learnt that the imperfection of the minister does not hinder the effect of the sacrament; and Augustine's struggle with Donatism taught the church something about the operation of grace on the human will. The scholastics of the later Middle Ages taught us, among other things, that grace does not supersede nor destroy nature but completes or perfects it. And the Reformation of the sixteenth century might, in fact must, be regarded as a prime example of the development of doctrine. There is no reason why development should not take the form of a return to earlier and less corrupt doctrinal authorities and sources, and every reason why on occasion it should. The impact of historical criticism will certainly result in some development of doctrine, probably in the field of christology.

It would be easy to solve the problem of development of doctrine superficially and unrealistically by saying that no development can take place till the whole church can pronounce on the subject. In the past this has not been the case, and the likelihood of any body genuinely representing the whole church being assembled in the foreseeable future is remote. The wisest course seems to be that of laying down conditions in which authentic development can and should take place and leaving future generations to apply these criteria whenever the opportunity or the necessity should occur:

1. Any development must be one which involves the whole nature of the Christian faith, and is likely to be achieved as a result of a crisis in doctrine, perhaps a controversy, perhaps one of those moments when historic decisions are necessary. The formation of the doctrine of the Trinity is one such example, and the crisis which we call the Reformation is another. Dogma or doctrine should not be developed irresponsibly, for the sake of adding to a dogmatic structure. One cannot help concluding that the charge of irresponsibility can be made against the Marian dogmas of 1854 and of 1950. There was no crisis of belief, no controversy, to justify them in either case; the rest of Christendom apart from the Roman Catholic Church dissented from this dogma-making and protested against its gratuitousness. To say that these dogmas were defined because Christianity was at stake is manifestly absurd.

2. Statements designed to develop or publicly formulate dogma must cover subjects which are within the competence of those who make the statements. In the fourteenth century Pope John XXII made a formal pronouncement about the extent of the poverty of Jesus Christ, a subject then of hot controversy. In fact there is not enough evidence in the New Testament to determine exactly how

poor Jesus was, though he certainly was poor. Popes and councils can err in failing to recognize their limitations.

3. Developments of doctrine must be well and firmly based on scripture, not merely on some verses or verse somewhere in scripture. Newman never seems to have appreciated this point. It is not enough, for instance, to teach that we are all finally destined to share God's *nature*, on the basis of one verse in II Peter 1.4, whereas the rest of the New Testament speaks only of our sharing God's life. The curious idea still dear to the hearts of many Protestants that Christians are meant to observe the first day of the week in the same way as Jews regard themselves as bound to spend the last day of the week, so that Sunday can be called the Sabbath, must be discarded on the grounds of entire lack of support in scripture. How the Marian dogmas, and the dogma of the infallibility of the church (and Pope), formulated by the Roman Catholic Church in 1870, fare when presented with this test, we leave the reader to determine himself.

4. Development of doctrine must not contradict nor be inconsistent with the worship and spirituality of the great majority of Christians through the ages. The idea, floated by some contemporary theologians, that we might quietly abandon the doctrine of the divinity of Christ in the face of historical criticism, contradicts the very mind and heart of the church's worship and spiritual experience. From a very early period indeed Jesus Christ the Son of God has been worshipped by Christians; theological thinking about his divinity went parallel with this cult.

5. Development of doctrine must be capable of sustaining a dialogue with the intellectual climate and demands of the age in which it is formed; it must not arise out of mere antiquarianism nor romanticism nor enthusiasm uninformed by right reason. If, for instance, fundamentalists were so to prevail in the Christian church at large as to commit the church to statements about the Bible or about Christian doctrine which were directly contrary to the conclusions of sober scholarship (a not completely impossible event), these could not be described as authentic developments. Authentic doctrine must face and wrestle with the problems presented to it by its age, as the scholastic philosophers of the twelfth and thirteenth centuries wrestled with the problems created by the resurgence of Aristotelianism. Development must not be an escape into illusion.

6. It must be recognized that what matters in the development of doctrine is not just the words themselves, the formula, but the intention behind them. Thus, there is no single ecumenically agreed formula for expressing the doctrine of the Trinity, not even the Nicene Creed. Different theologians through the ages have expressed it rather differently, but it can be recognized as the same doctrine. Again, words in any language change and grow obsolete. The word *ousia* (substance or being) which the great theologians of the fourth century used to express their account of the Christian doctrine of God, borrowed from Greek philosophy, is not one which most theologians would today use in speaking of God. And we can recognize that both the framers of the Chalcedonian Definition about the Incarnation of 451 and also some of those who disagreed with them and refused the formula had the same intentions and were trying to say the same thing in different words.

7. Finally, the slogan of developers of doctrine should be 'Wait and see!' It takes some time before history makes it evident whether doctrine officially pronounced will be accepted by the mind of the whole church, and conversely doctrines which when first formulated attracted no great attention may become in process of time central and important. Two medieval councils, in the twelfth and fifteenth centuries, apparently achieved a formula of reunion between the separated Eastern and Western churches. Both were ultimately rejected by the great body of Eastern Christians. On the other hand the Council of Constantinople of 381 produced a creed which at the time attracted very little attention; but it finally became the Nicene Creed as we know it today, the great ecumenical creed of the whole church. This last principle ensures that it is the consent and mind of the faithful at large which finally decides doctrine. The Eastern Orthodox Church has always held this sound belief, and it is one which the West might well adopt. The most authoritatively pronounced dogmas must stand the test of time, and perhaps some of those whose original enunciation was attended by the greatest solemnity will come worst out of this test.

It only remains to add that it should not be surprising that a great universal religion like Christianity should in the course of many centuries prove to have consequences and corollaries and significances which were not evident in its early years. As it has met the chances and changes of history Christianity must inevitably have in some sense itself changed. It is not that Christ has changed, but our understanding of him has. Newman saw rightly that it is proper to expect an enrichment and enhancement of Christian doctrine in the course of history. His, perhaps pardonable, mistake was to imagine that this process was confined to the doctrinal tradition of the Roman Catholic Church.

A pertinent question to ask in connection with this subject of the development of doctrine is, on what model should we conceive of the development? We have already rejected the idea that Christian doctrine should be allowed to develop indefinitely at the whim of popular devotion or at the *ipse dixit* of a wayward Pope. Newman in his famous work favoured, though not exclusively, the biological model, that is the model of an acorn growing into an oak or of a boy growing into a man. This model has grave drawbacks in it. It suggests a steady continually increasing increment of doctrine following an uninterrupted course, and this makes no allowance for the discontinuities, accidents and returns to a more primitive pattern which are characteristic of all intellectual movements in history (cf. the history of ancient Platonism). It also suggests that the apostles and first Christians who witnessed the very source of revelation were in fact in a less favoured, more rudimentary situation than later generations who were enriched by the harvest of later developments. Various other models have been suggested in order to reach a true and acceptable idea of how doctrine, if it does develop, should develop. Perhaps most theologians will try to combine more than one model to reach a fuller understanding of the subject. But it seems to us that the best (though not exclusive) model is that of the development of some humane discipline, like the history of painting or of drama or of legal studies, or even of literary criticism. In each of these there has certainly been a movement, a history, partly brought about by accident, partly by fashion, partly by each succeeding age bringing to bear on the subject a new and usually valuable understanding. But the history has been controlled in each case by the existence of the matter of the discipline itself, by the pictures or the plays or the body of law or the literature. None has advanced with steady, uninterrupted consistency; all have learnt from the past, both from its mistakes and its achievements.

In like manner both the Bible and Christian tradition have been interpreted differently during different ages by different people with different presuppositions and preoccupations through the centuries. Age after age has made its own characteristic mistakes and found its own way of misunderstanding the text.

Athanasius in the fourth century, for instance, saw with resolute clarity what was at stake in the main controversy of his time, and fought successfully to establish his insight as orthodoxy. But he also presented an impossibly unrealistic picture of the incarnate Son in which the Word of God wore a human body as an astronaut wears a space-suit. And both these doctrines affected the theology of later generations. Nor was the result of his work entirely one of accumulation of doctrine. The triumph of the Nicene Creed in the same century represented an unmistakable development of Christian doctrine, but at the same time it meant the extinction of a traditional and ancient *Logos*-theology whereby the pre-existent Christ was used as an ingenious philosophical device. The solution of the Arian controversy, in fact, resulted in both addition to and pruning of doctrine. Similarly the Reformation in the sixteenth century achieved both a return to earlier tradition and the appearance of new kinds of theology in Lutheranism and Calvinism. The advent of historical criticism has produced a seismic change in our understanding of the Bible whose tremors have not yet subsided, destroying many well-worn ideas and doctrines, but also making an opening for new truths about the Christian faith.

Each succeeding age, then, while displaying its peculiar blind spots in looking at Christianity has also gained its own insights into Christianity and contributed its own share in reaching a fuller understanding of it, so that there has been a recognizable deposit of valid and true interpretation. And we can apply a practical test to the Christian faith, because we can express it in prayer and worship and in our tradition of Christian behaviour. And finally, at the end of the day we cannot turn back the clock and question Jesus Christ and his first disciples. In one sense we cannot improve on the text of the Bible or do better than Jesus and his apostles. We are constricted by the limitations of history. But we can recognize the necessity of development and ensure as far as possible that the development is true and not false.

The process of forming Christian doctrine is controlled by two facts. First, Christianity is not just a book, nor just an idea or philosophy, not just an institution, though all these things contribute in some way to its nature. It is a living force in history and one which has made a deep mark upon history. To believers it is a divine power and mind working in history, but even unbelievers must recognize that it is a force making its mark on history. This was at least one of the things which Newman meant when in his *Essay* he so constantly spoke of the 'idea' of Christianity. And historical forces produce development, change and often an increasing self-understanding and inwardness. The development of the British Constitution might be taken as an example of this. But Christianity is also a religion which is inextricably centred on a single figure in history, that of Jesus Christ. The only satisfactory guarantee that the Christian faith shall not desert the figure of Christ, drifting off into Gnostic speculations or mounting into some wild space-flight or irrelevant elaboration, is the body of documents witnessing to the historical origins of Christianity which the church early in its career registered or singled out or canonized as those which most effectively give this witness, and which are called the Bible. Christian doctrine therefore is the intellectual understanding of the Christian religion and of its interaction with historical events, and the Bible is the check or norm continually to be applied to this understanding to make sure that it is faithful to the original lineaments and significance of the figure of Jesus Christ. How in present circumstances scripture can be applied as a norm will be considered presently.

If the case is presented in this way, the question may well be asked, how can any continuity be preserved in Christian doctrine, and indeed this is a hard question. Those who have had a considerable acquaintance with the history even of only early Christian doctrine, up to, say 451, may be pardoned if they sometimes ask themselves what serious connection is there between the way the ancients, for instance, handled the Bible and the way in which the history of European thought compels us to handle it now. But if we recognize that the intentions and purposes of the men and women of antiquity in forming doctrine were the same as ours (and we believe that it can be shown that they were), then we should not despair of seeing a thread of continuity in Christian doctrine through all the obfuscations, misunderstandings and follies of

Christian exposition. It is helpful to regard the relationship of scripture and tradition as one of dialogue. Christian doctrine has always, even in the darkest moments of its history, attempted to return to the Bible as its source and norm. Even at periods when misguided people were attempting to construct from scripture systems and patterns which it is not capable of yielding, even during periods of the most infatuated bibliolatry, some regard was paid to the necessity of making sense rather than sanctified nonsense and to the history of the Christian tradition itself. Sometimes tradition has appeared to overwhelm the Bible in speculative or systematic darkness. But the Bible has a capacity of asserting itself unexpectedly, as it did at the Reformation and as in the opinion of some it did at the Second Vatican Council. Sometimes the Bible has seemed to disappear or disintegrate under the weight of critical investigation, as some people think may be happening in the present day. But Christian faith, worship and spirituality, to which no less attention is being paid today than in the past, continues to find in the Bible nourishment and life, and, we may confidently predict, will continue to do so indefinitely. Christian doctrine is always subject to this double pull or pressure. This is a tension which is part of its essence.

Mariology might be regarded here as a test case. In 1854 and 1950 the Roman Catholic Church promulgated or registered two dogmas concerning the Blessed Virgin Mary which were wholly uncongenial and deeply shocking to the minds of Protestants of all complexions, how shocking perhaps Roman Catholics even today do not fully realize. The first of them had only the frailest of frail support in scripture, the second none whatever (indeed it was apparently concerned with an event which took place many years after the resurrection). They were very insufficiently supported by the writings of the Fathers of the early church. The first of them used the extraordinary argument that Mary had been rendered immune from sin from her conception in view of the foreseen merits of the yet unborn Jesus. This grotesque argument about foreseen merits had been used by Arian heretics in the fourth century in their doctrine of Christ (not of Mary), as Newman had pointed out in 1845, The doctrine of Mary's Assumption first appears, as far as can be ascertained, at a late stage in the history of early doctrine among suspiciously Gnostic circles in Egypt. Every test which the Protestants could apply to see whether these doctrines were sound doctrine damned them. But since the nineteenth century several things have happened to ameliorate this apparently unhappy situation. The result of the theological movements which produced the Second Vatican Council caused Roman Catholic theologians to return with renewed interest to scripture and to the doctrine of the early church and one result of this was a markedly reduced emphasis upon these Mariological dogmas. In his book, *The Foundations of the Christian Faith*[1] (no insubstantial volume), Karl Rahner devoted only about four pages to Mary. Again, deeply though the cult of Mary is involved with the life and devotion of the Roman Catholic Church and far though that involvement goes back in history, the concept of a 'hierarchy of doctrines' whereby some can be regarded as more central and others as more peripheral, a concept accepted by Vatican II, offers hope of better understanding. Protestant thinkers too, have begun to realize that while they need not subscribe to the recent dogmas it is a little odd to say nothing whatever about Mary, who, after all was the human mother of the Saviour, except to deny Roman Catholic doctrines. Further acquaintance with the Eastern Orthodox Church also has brought home both to Protestants and Catholics the realization that Orthodox theologians have for long been accustomed to considering the theological significance of Mary, because her cult has been for long as deeply interwoven with the life and spirituality of the Orthodox Church as it has been with those of the Roman Church, but that their doctrines about her, while honouring her not less highly than in the West, are much less speculative and rationalist and have not been incorporated into a series of official dogmas comparable to the dogmas of the Nicene Creed, as, if we are to take Roman Catholic claims at their face value, they have been in the Church of Rome. We can envisage a movement of thought whereby each of these three different doctrinal traditions, Protestant, Roman and Orthodox approach each other more closely and come to a better understanding upon the subject of the Blessed Virgin Mary in an authentic dialogue of scripture and tradition.

This test case points to the solution of one very thorny question: how is orthodoxy to be achieved? We cannot and should not attempt to enforce orthodoxy by force of arms or coercion by government. The circumstances of today make it wholly unlikely that it can be achieved by General Councils which because of the size of the Christian church would be unwieldy and unmanageable. But the success of the ecumenical movement, which has not yet been in existence for as long as a century, and the ease of modern cummunications which are beginning to make different Christian churches and traditions better acquainted with each other, and the kind of Scholars' International which exists among Christian theologians today, suggest that a broad agreement upon orthodoxy could be achieved and perhaps will be achieved gradually, quietly, as Christian scholars and saints and believers come to know each other's minds better. As barriers of prejudice and misunderstanding dissolve, so not only Christian comity and Christian co-operation but also Christian orthodoxy is likely to emerge. As God has given us a church which it is our business to discover and realize, so he has given us Christian truth which it is our duty to identify together. The particular machinery for expressing this consensus has yet to appear, but we have good reason to hope that the Holy Spirit is leading us towards a period when it will emerge.

2. Scripture as Norm

It is urgent that we should try to make clear in what sense scripture should be a norm for the church in both doctrine and practice. From what has been said so far it might be concluded that we had rejected scripture as a norm altogether, since we have assumed that we cannot regard scripture in the same light as it was regarded by all Christians till about two hundred years ago. In order to make this point clear, it will help if we first show how far we are prepared to go in modifying traditional assumptions about scripture. We will begin by setting down four such assumptions and explaining why they cannot be accepted today. Then we must explain in what sense scripture can be our norm.

1. *Everything commanded or commended in scripture is mandatory for the church.* Almost nobody takes this precept with complete literalness. In the first place, it cannot apply to the Old Testament. In the Old Testament all sorts of things are enjoined on Israel, sacrifices and ritual acts for example, that no Christian would dream of regarding as obligatory on the church. But even within the New

Testament there are very authoritative mandates which do not make sense today. Consider for example the letter sent by the 'Council of Jerusalem' to the Gentile churches as recounted in Acts 15.24–29. Even if complete agreement were to be reached as to what exactly is meant by 'you are to abstain from blood, from anything that has been strangled, and from fornication', no body of Christians today pays any attention to the first two requirements of this recommendation. It has become culturally outmoded. Or again, in I Cor. 11.1–12 Paul vigorously condemns the practice of women appearing bare-headed at divine worship. Today in the West at least no regard is given to this clear command. Even the ultra-conservative Greek Orthodox Church does not observe it. Hence we must use some discrimination about what we regard as mandatory in scripture.

2. *At least our Lord is infallible: what he believed we must believe without further question.* Until relatively recently this argument would have carried weight with all Christians. But in the light of New Testament criticism, it can hardly be defended. We may take two examples which have often been cited. In Mark 12.35–37 (and parallels in Matthew and Luke) Jesus cites Ps. 110.1 as the work of David. And in Luke 11.29–32; Matt. 12.39–41; 16.4 Jesus is represented as referring to the story of Jonah with the obvious implication that Jonah was an historical character to whom the events described in the Book of Jonah really happened. These references have been used in order to establish positions about the authorship of that Psalms and the historicity of the Book of Jonah respectively: 'if Jesus, whose authority for Christians is infallible, held that David wrote Psalm 110 and that the story related of Jonah in the Old Testament really took place, then Christians are bound to accept these conclusions'. But the experts in Old Testament criticism would for the most part maintain the Psalm 110 comes from a later period than the time of David. And all of them would agree that the Book of Jonah is not history but a story with a moral. Does this mean that one cannot be at one and the same time a believing Christian and an Old Testament critic? No. It means we must accept the fact that Jesus, because he was really and genuinely a man, was conditioned by the culture in which he was born and grew up, as all men are. Nobody among the Jews, who were his own people, doubted that David wrote the Psalms or that the Book of

Jonah gives an authentic historical account of the adventures of Jonah. Jesus did not have privileged knowledge given him from heaven about mundane matters. If he had, the genuineness of his humanity would be suspect. Consequently we may differ from him in matters of biblical criticism, while still accepting his supreme authority in the things that matter most.

3. *The New Testament offers us a blueprint for the structure of the church and of the ministry.* This has been believed for centuries by all Catholics and by some Protestants. Catholics have believed that our Lord not only founded the church but also gave it a duly authorized ministry; and Roman Catholics have added that he arranged for that ministry to be ordered and ruled by Peter and his successors as bishops of Rome for ever. Among Protestants, only Calvinists have claimed that a blueprint for church and ministry is available in the New Testament. John Calvin was convinced that he had discovered the form of ministry which our Lord had really intended for his church – not, it need hardly be said, identical with the form of ministry in use in the medieval church in the West – and he proceeded to model the Reformed Church according to the plan he had 'discovered'. Lutherans, Anglicans, and other reformed Christians make no such claims, except that some old-fashioned Anglicans still fondly believe that our Lord intended the episcopal form of ministry to be the norm for his church. But well-informed members of the Reformed Churches today are not inclined to maintain that Calvin had discovered the form of ministry intended by Jesus, since they agree with the great majority of New Testament scholars who hold that Jesus did not plan any particular form of ministry for his church. But we examine these matters in greater detail below when we consider the ordained ministry.

4. *Scripture is at least internally consistent.* This is a view adopted by many thinking Christians after the first impact of biblical criticism had been to some extent absorbed. 'Scripture', they would say, 'can no longer be regarded as infallible or inerrant. But it does give us a consistent picture of God's revelation of himself in Jesus Christ. In particular it shows us a Jesus who from the very first had a superhuman element in his nature and who was conscious in some sense of being divine.' Attractive though this modification of the traditional view is, it will hardly prove adequate to meet the situation. In the first place, it cannot be stretched to include the

Old Testament. In the Old Testament we find a developing understanding of the nature of God; the earliest concepts of God in the
Old Testament are quite incompatible with the highest concept of
God even within the Old Testament itself; and certainly they are
incompatible with the concept of God in the New Testament. Most
of those who hold this fourth view would admit this much. But it is
on the question of christology that the issue of internal consistency
becomes most acute. In fact the various presentations of Jesus
which we meet in the New Testament are not entirely consistent
with each other. The Jesus of Mark is hardly consistent with the
Jesus of John. Christology in the New Testament does not represent either a harmonious whole or a steadily developing process in
which originally implicit elements are only made explicit in later
writings. The New Testament presents us with a number of different pictures of Jesus. Nor is it true that the earlier pictures give
us a relatively 'low' christology and the later ones a 'higher' christology. Paul, who wrote well before the Gospel of Mark was composed, has a 'higher' christology than has Mark; and I Peter, which
most experts would date early in the second century, has a 'lower'
christology than that which we find in the Fourth Gospel, which
can be dated around the year 100. Drawing our doctrine from the
New Testament is therefore a more complicated business than any
of the above rather simplistic views would suggest.

So far we have been almost entirely negative. We have only shown
how not to use scripture as a norm. It is time that we turned to the
positive side. In what sense may we regard scripture as normative
for the church? We set out four main principles, followed by two
important conclusions:

(*a*) Though scripture is not guaranteed to be internally consistent, it does present an undeviating pattern of God's activity. This
is what is called 'salvation history'. It shows God as a saviour, a
living God who is actively concerned for man's well-being. More
than that, it shows us a God who manifests self-giving love as the
constituent element in his character, a love which is in some real
sense willing to undergo suffering on behalf of mankind, a love
which never compromises with moral evil but takes the consequences of human wrong-doing on itself. This revelation has very
definite consequences for what we believe: it implies, for instance,

that a doctrine of hell which requires that all who have never known Jesus Christ, whether through their own fault or not, shall suffer eternal damnation, must be utterly rejected. But equally it requires that God does not compromise with evil in order to attain his ends. For example, he does not approve of torturing or threatening with a violent death those who have mistaken beliefs, in order to compel them to accept true beliefs. This does not mean that there is no such thing as hell; only that the threat of hell is no proper inducement to persuade people to accept the good news of God. This revelation of God's character the church may not reject; in so far as it does so it ceases to be Christian.

(b) We can go farther than this: scripture shows us the nature and being of God. This is a more difficult principle to defend, because the doctrine of the Trinity, which is what we are concerned with here, is not explicitly taught, nor even believed, in the New Testament. But the witness of the New Testament as a whole to the nature of God as revealed in the entire career of Jesus Christ, including his ressurrection, poses inexorably the question: what is Jesus' relation to God? If full justice is to be done to the witness of the New Testament here, it is impossible to stop short of saying that the revelation in Jesus Christ demands a modification in the strict monotheism of Judaism. This in its turn leads on to a consideration of the place of the Holy Spirit in the godhead. Hence the post-apostolic church was right to work out a doctrine of God as three-in-one. Nothing less would satisfy the witness to God-in-Christ which we meet in the New Testament. The doctrine of the Trinity is not a New Testament doctrine in the same sense that, for example, the doctrine of the Son's pre-existence is. But the materials for the doctrine of the Trinity are to be found in the New Testament, and the concept of God implied in the New Testament can only be satisfactorily expressed by means of some form of a doctrine of God as Trinity.

This in turn has far-reaching implications for the belief of the church. It means in the first place that Christianity is not just a deviant or modified form of Judaism. Though our relation to Judaism is closer than it is to any other religion, we are not Jews. It means also that we cannot make room for Islam within Christianity. Islam's monolithic monotheism is incompatible with Christian belief, though we should not on that account refuse to listen to what the Quran has to say about the unity of God, or deny that Muhammad had a prophetic message for his day. But there is another consequence which perhaps comes nearer home: we must reject Unitarianism. Unitarianism in England is largely the product of the Enlightenment, though it can trace its lineage back to the age of the Reformation in the form of Socininism. It denies both the doctrine of the Trinity and the divinity of Christ. Several distinguished modern Anglican theologians have recently professed beliefs which are indistinguishable in essence from Unitarianism, most notably perhaps the late Professor Geoffrey Lampe. This does not mean that the Church of England, still less the Anglican Communion, is Unitarian; it does apparently indicate that to hold a non-Trinitarian doctrine of God is not incompatible with being in good standing as a priest in the Church of England. In a period such as the present when there is taking place a widespread re-assessment of traditional ways of expressing the doctrine of the person of Christ, it is no doubt inevitable that some sort of a Unitarian doctrine will be among the options put forward. We should not therefore demand the instant expulsion from the church of those who profess such views. But in our opinion the Trinitarian doctrine of God is essential if we are to defend the witness of the New Testament. It is the coping stone of the doctrine of Christ's person.

(c) Scripture shows us the centrality and the sole mediatorship of Jesus Christ. This rules out any attempt either to by-pass, or to supplement, the place of Jesus Christ in God's economy of redemption. It seems probable that the Epistle to the Colossians was written in order to oppose the first of these errors. Some people in Colossae were apparently teaching that Christ was only one of a line of mediators between God and man, not even perhaps the highest at that. The author of the epistle replies by emphasizing the sole and supreme place of Christ in God's scheme of salvation. On the other hand some doctrines advanced in the Roman Catholic Church during the period betwen the two Vatican Councils (1870-1963) certainly seemed to be attempting to supplement the mediatorial work of Christ. If the Blessed Virgin Mary is declared to be the mediator of all grace, no matter how much effort may be made to find a superior place for the Son between God and us, it would seem inevitable that the sole mediatorship of Christ should be infringed. One can say the same thing perhaps about some accounts that are given of the role played by the intercessions of the saints. It has often been proposed by respectable theologians in both the Roman Catholic and the Orthodox Churches that we might well hesitate to approach our Lord directly in prayer, in view of our sinfulness and his divine majesty; but if we approach first the Blessed Virgin or the saints, who have privileged access to his presence, we can surely hope for a better reception. All such ideas are ultimately based on the belief that God, or God-in-Christ, has still to be reconciled to us, and that those who knew the Saviour best while he was on earth, or who by their saintliness have earned a place close to him in heaven, are likely to be more merciful or more cognisant of our condition than he. But the essence of the gospel as witnessed in scripture is that God in Jesus Christ has declared his reconciliation to us by means of the cross. We do not need to approach him by other means. If we try to do so, we are doubting his mercy.

(*d*) In ecclesiology scripture shows us the priesthood of Christ and the derived priesthood of the church. This is really a corollary of the last principle, and it is worked out more fully in our section on the ministry. But we mention it here in order to show that scripture can and must be the norm for us in our ecclesiology as well as in the rest of our belief. Just because it is no longer possible for those who are intellectually honest, and who are acquainted with the technique of biblical study today, to hold that Jesus Christ prescribed the form and structure of the ministry for the church, it does not follow that scripture has no light to throw upon the subject. We hope to show that it is quite the contrary.

We may now mention the two important conclusions which follow from these four principles which we have just outlined. The first is this: *scripture interpreted by the tradition of the church is sufficient.* We do not need, and should not seek, any other basis for our faith. This may seem sufficiently obvious; but at various times during the history of the church attempts have been made to supplement scripture as the basis of the church's witness. During the second and third centuries certain Gnostic sects claimed that their doctrine was based on a secret teaching which Jesus gave to one or other of his disciples. It had been carefully preserved and handed down until it reached the contemporary leaders of the sect.

Indeed recently discovered documents such as the *Gospel of Truth* exhibit this characteristic. We need hardly say that there is no historical evidence whatever for the truth of such claims. In more modern times defenders of the later developments of Roman Catholic doctrine have sometimes spoken as if 'the tradition of the church' meant an unwritten oral tradition that had been preserved in the church from the earliest times. When challenged to produce evidence of this tradition during the first few centuries, they have of course been unable to do so. The statements of Vatican II about the sources of revelation must have discouraged any such tendency today. It is on the grounds of this conclusion also that Christians reject such deviations as the Latter Day Saints and the Christian Scientists. The first group claims that the historical scriptures have been supplemented by a relatively recently revealed scripture called 'The Book of Mormon'; and the latter group seems to place the writings of Mary Baker Eddy on a level with the scriptures.

The second conclusion is this: *the church's structure should reflect something of the relation of Christ's relation to his disciples*. In fact we know quite a lot about this: though his authority was supreme he did not desire to lord it among his followers. His leadership was one of service and self-giving. It is easy to say that these should be the characteristics both of the Christian and of the ordained ministers of the church. But we must go further than this and say that these qualities should be visible in the structures of the church and of its ministry. In this respect, it must be admitted, church history tells us that practice has frequently fallen far below theory. If this second conclusion is correct, the church's structure should not be an autocratic one. But for by far the greater part of the period during which the Western Church has existed it has had, in theory at least, a stongly autocratic structure; and half the Western Church still exhibits such a structure today. Again, one would imagine that if this theory were valid there would be no room for a privileged class in the church. But at all times and under nearly all church orders the clergy have claimed a privileged place for themselves. Only the other day we witnessed a communion service in the Orthodox Church in Russia; when it came to the time for communion the administration of the elements to each bishop lasted three minutes each time, to each priest two minutes, and to those few members of the laity who ventured to communicate, ten seconds.

Examples of clerical privilege could of course be multiplied among the main-line reformed churches as well. Similarly, if we take as our example the relation of Christ to his disciples, we would conclude that order, obedience and mutual submission would be leading features of the church's life and ministry. But too often Protestant churches have put a premium on carelessness in worship, over-emphasized the right of the individual Christian to do as he liked without consulting others, and exalted the position of the preacher to the great spiritual peril of those who held that position. In this respect we have all, Catholic and Protestant alike, sinned and fallen short of the glory of God. The reshaping of the structures of the church so as to make them more truly reflect the relation of Jesus to his disciples is an urgent task for the church today.

We may therefore reasonably claim that, despite our altered view of scripture today, we can and do use it as a norm for the most critical and essential area of our belief and practice.

A critical use of the Bible to supply a norm for doctrine such as has been exemplified in the preceding pages seems to demand a new way of looking at the authority of scripture. The traditional way of setting forth the authority of scripture is to speak in terms of its inerrancy and inspiration. It must have been made quite clear enough in the argument of this book so far that it is impossible any longer to believe in the infallibility of the Bible. But to dispense with a belief in its inspiration seems to many an unnecessarily drastic measure. It is, however, impossible to formulate a doctrine of the Bible's inspiration which does not apply to some other Christian literature as well or does not amount to enunciating some statement which refutes itself by its very banality, such as that the Bible is a very impressive book. That the Bible is inspired because it is inspiring is a half-truth which applies to much other literature as well, and to attempt to prove from the Bible itself that it is inspired is to commit the logical fallacy of assuming in your proof that which you want to prove. [2]

The proper category in which to place the Bible if we wish to be clear about its function as a norm is that of witness. It constitutes as a whole a unique body of witness to the activity of God towards man in his chosen people and in his chosen redeemer, Jesus Christ. What we have a right to ask of the Bible when we employ it as a norm is not inerrancy but *sufficiency*, i.e. that it should be sufficient to witness to that by which we can be saved. This classification of the Bible does not require that it shall be inerrant, only that its witness shall be sufficiently reliable to guide us into the way of salvation. Nor does it require that the Bible, either in the Old Testament or in the New Testament, shall be entirely consistent with itself nor present a wholly coherent theology. As far as the New Testament is concerned, indeed, it is helpful to think of its various contents as, so to speak, a series of lenses through which we view the same object, or a series of pictures of the same person painted by different artists. We are given a number of different, sometimes diverse, interpretations of the career and significance of Jesus, some of them fragmentary, some distorted by such pre-judices as the mistaken belief that the Jews as a whole were being punished for putting Christ to death. They are of different origins and ages, deriving from different backgrounds and written under different motives. But all are early and irreplaceable, and the whole constitutes a unique record. To apply the words 'inerrant' and 'inspired' to this collection is irrelevant, unnecessary and mislead-ing. These epithets represent compliments paid to the Bible by early Christian theologians. They were well-meant compliments, but in the history of Christian thought they have produced little but confusion and misunderstanding.

The Bible, in short, provides the raw material for Christian doctrine, and it provides the raw material in the form which has just been outlined. It does not provide ready-made, pre-fabricated doctrine, already prepared for the text-book and the pulpit. The Bible is too human a document, too much concerned with real people and real human issues and situations and decisions to be that sort of book. It is the business of the church to find its doctrine in the Bible, to make doctrine out of the raw material provided by the Bible, and the church has always, in all ages, endeavoured to do so, with greater or lesser success. Perhaps the reader will now see why we have insisted on the one hand that the Bible must be interpreted, that the concept of a 'Bible without notes' or 'the Bible and the Bible alone' is a meaningless illusion, and on the other that for the church to attempt to dispense with, by-pass or suppress the Bible would be a betrayal of the purpose for which the church exists. Perhaps too it has become obvious why, though we cannot do other than use the Bible, our use of it must be conditioned by historical criticism, or in other words by the comparatively recent discovery of the true nature and origins of the Bible.

3. Catholicity

When we recite either the Apostles' or the Nicene Creed we affirm our belief in the holy *Catholic* Church. 'Catholic' is a Greek word which originally meant simply 'universal'. It is first used of the church by Ignatius of Antioch about the year 113, where it seems to distinguish the assembly of worship of the great church from an informal gathering or a sect. It was freely used during the ensuing centuries to distinguish the traditional church first from Gnostic sects and then from schismatical bodies that might be relatively orthodox in belief. Thus by the year 1000 it bore the meaning of 'universal, the original body as founded by our Lord, the assemblage of Christians holding the orthodox faith'.

After the schism between the Eastern and Western Churches in 1054 the term 'Catholic' was more often applied to the Western Church, the Eastern Church preferring to use the term 'Orthodox'. The Reformation brought a new development: on the whole the reformed bodies tended to drop the word 'Catholic' as applied to themselves, preferring to use the term 'Protestant', a very poor substitute for 'Catholic' since it has a purely negative connotation. But until very recently the branch of the Anglican Communion in the USA officially described itself as 'the Protestant Episcopal Church of America'. To this day many Protestant Christians would innocently say 'We are not Catholics', a statement which in earlier days would have been the equivalent of saying 'We are heretics'.

However, there have always been some Anglicans who protested against the monopolizing of the word 'catholic' by the Roman Catholic Church. Ever since the Oxford Movement a hundred and fifty years ago well-informed Anglican laity as well as clergy have claimed that their church has as much right to the epithet 'catholic' as has the Roman Catholic Church. Unfortunately the word has too often been used in a merely party sense. We hear of 'the catholic wing', 'catholic worship', even (worst of all) 'catholic truth'. Thus until the advent of the ecumenical movement the adjective was popularly used of the Eastern Orthodox Church, the Roman

Catholic Church, and of those members of the Anglican Communion who inclined to be 'Anglo-Catholic'. It was also claimed by some breakaway bodies from the Roman Catholic Church, e.g. the Old Catholics in Europe.

Such popular usage has however become somewhat outmoded today. In the first place, the progress of biblical and historical criticism has put a question mark against some of the 'catholic' claims of the ancient churches. For example, when a 'catholic' of any complexion claims 'my church is the original body which goes back to the apostles', he can no longer justify such a claim on strictly historical grounds, since the specific sign of apostolic authority which emboldens him to make this claim, to wit episcopal succession back to the apostles, cannot be maintained. The only body that goes uninterruptedly back to the apostles is the whole body of Christians.

Next, the opposition between the appeal to scripture and the appeal to catholic tradition does not make much sense nowadays. The old Protestant line of argument was that scripture alone was sufficient foundation for belief and practice; the tradition of the church through the ages can be ignored. As long as tradition was regarded, as it tended too often to be, by Catholics, as an independent source of doctrine which needed no foundation in scripture, this Protestant position was sound enough. But now it has become plain that scripture has never existed without a tradition of interpretation, and that scripture is not self-explanatory. This should have been one of the lessons of the Reformation experience: when the slogan *sola scriptura* began to be used by reformed Christians, one small section among them took this with deadly literalness, and soon found that neither the doctrine of the Trinity nor the co-equal divinity of the son can be conclusively *proved* from scripture. Hence to take *sola scriptura* to its logical conclusion is to end in a form of Unitarianism, which was very far indeed from the intentions of the great fathers of the Reformation, Luther and Calvin.

On the other hand, in quite recent times the Roman Catholic Church has been showing an awareness of the need for continual reform which it had violently repudiated when the traumatic experience of the Reformation came upon it in the sixteenth century. From about fifty years ago many scholars and theologians in the church began to feel that they had gone too far (or at least quite far

enough) in the direction of relying on tradition rather than on the
Bible. Certain dogmas, notably perhaps the dogma of the assumption of the Blessed Virgin Mary, formally made an obligatory part of
the creed for all Roman Catholics in 1950, are wholly devoid of any
foundation whatever in scripture, and very poorly supported during
the first few centuries of the church's history. It was felt that a
return to scripture was over-due. This is in fact what has happened: in liturgy, in preaching, in devotional practice there has
been a great new appreciation of the Bible. In some ways it is as if
the Roman Catholic Church was accepting some of the deepest
insights of the sixteenth-century reformers.

At the same time as 'Catholics' are becoming more reformed,
'Protestants' are becoming more catholic. The spread of the liturgical movement to nearly all sections of the Western Church has
meant that all the main-line Christian bodies now have a eucharistic liturgy which, if they use it, is fully catholic in all essentials.
Protestants are beginning to make use of catholic techniques of
prayer and contemplation. There are even a few monastic or quasi-
monastic communities to be found among Protestants. The old
Protestant prejudice against ornamentation in church buildings or
the use of liturgical vestments is considerably diminished. In the
church of the third world, where Western denominational traditions and prejudices have never been as strong as in their countries
of origin, the mingling of Catholic and Protestant is often more
marked and goes further than it does in the West. Only in areas
such as Northern Ireland, where denominational and political divisions unhappily coincide, does the old Catholic-Protestant barrier
remain very largely unbreached.

The word 'catholic' can still be legitimately used to characterize
a number of practices and institutions which go back to the early
centuries of the church's existence. These are such things as
episcopacy, liturgy, monastic orders, and the tradition of mystical
prayer. But, as we have seen, such things can be shared by all and
are not confined to the 'catholic' part of the church, if by that we
mean the Roman Catholic and Orthodox part. All Christians
should want to claim the adjective 'catholic'. We Anglicans ought to
encourage our reformed brethren not to throw away the name or to
allow it to be monopolized by others. Roman Catholics nowadays
are proud to call themselves 'evangelical'. Protestants ought to want
to be Catholics.

We can even discern the emergence of what might be called a reformed catholic tradition. This is a tradition which, based on scripture, appeals back not only to the period of the first few centuries of the church's history, an appeal which is traditional in Anglicanism, but also to the genuinely catholic aspirations of the great reformers. Martin Luther at any rate did not plan to found a new church or an evangelical sect. He wanted to reform the medieval church, which, it is universally admitted today, was in desperate need of reform. If we look at Luther's eucharistic doctrine, or even at his liturgical tradition, we can perceive a genuine effort to return to the belief and practice of the undivided church. The same can be said to a modified extent of Calvin. Some of the most important features of Calvin's theology are as much 'Catholic' as 'Protestant', as for example his doctrine of our Lord's presence in the eucharist and his conception of ministerial authority. The truth is that neither Luther nor Calvin, for all their protestations, desired to return to the church as it was in apostolic times. (In fact the state of historical research in their day was not such as to enable them to discover what the apostolic church had been like in any detail.) What they wanted was a return to the church of the early centuries. This is of course even more characteristic of Anglicanism; the establishment of a Church of England that repudiated the authority of the Bishop of Rome was a deliberate attempt to reform the church without transforming it or deforming it. As we have already remarked, nobody in the sixteenth century had sufficient historical knowledge to be able to reproduce a model of the apostolic church. The great reformers, and the leading theologians of the Church of England, would have been content with a return to the faith and practice of the early church.

This is on the whole the basis on which the only successful act of union between 'Catholic' and 'Protestant' elements in the church has been founded. The Church of South India was formed in 1947, followed by the Church of North India in 1970. Both churches are composed of Anglicans, and various Free Church traditions, not including Lutherans, but, in the case of CNI, including some Baptists. Certainly the experience of the early years of the Church of South India has shown that when questions of faith or practice on which scripture gave no guidance came up for decision, as inevitably happened from time to time, the standard according to which they were decided was the faith and practice of the early church. Likewise in the discussions between the reformed churches and the Roman Catholic Church which have taken place in various parts of the world since Vatican II, it seems that the faith and practice of the undivided church has proved to be an excellent starting point, one which has often led to surprisingly fruitful results: 'Let us turn away from the controversial terms in which our disagreements were expressed in the sixteenth century, and see whether we cannot find a deeper union by looking at the way in which these matters were expressed before the great divisions of the church.' This is the method by which a remarkable degree of accord has been achieved. If ever the great 'Catholic versus Protestant' division is to be healed, this is surely the tradition on the basis of which unity will be won.

So that word 'catholic', instead of being a divisive term, can be a healing one. We can all agree to see ourselves as members of the One, Holy Catholic Church.

4. Religious Experience and Doctrine

In 1834 Friedrich Schleiermacher died, acknowledged in his day and ever since as being one of the seminal theologians of the nineteenth century. His great achievement was that he made a courageous and largely successful attempt to restate traditional Christianity in terms which were not vulnerable to the intellectual criticism to which Christianity as traditionally expounded was exposed in his day. The Christian church has always had three sources of authority, the Bible, Christian tradition (or the church's memory), and religious experience. In Schleiermacher's day the Bible was being apparently undermined by the beginnings of biblical criticism. As a Lutheran, Schleiermacher did not set much store by the authority of the church, and in any case the church's official apologia in his day was manifestly unequal to coping with the attacks of its critics. This left religious experience, and on this foundation Schleiermacher built up a system of theology which seemed to restore almost everything that traditional theology had defended. Hence right up to the first quarter of the twentieth century, when Karl Barth launched a violent reaction against nearly everything that Schleiermacher stood for, religious experience has played a big part in Protestant attempts to defend the substance of traditional Christian belief.

Today matters have altered in two respects: the psychologists (notably Freud) have questioned the validity of religious experience; and the Barthian movement has run out of steam. This has meant that on the one hand Christian theologians, while in no way obliged to accept Freud's outdated positivistic approach to reality, have to tread very carefully if they appeal to religious experience in order to vindicate their belief. On the other hand they are faced in the West with a philosophical climate that is strongly empirical; hence they like where possible to provide an empirical test for the truth of what they claim. They have therefore found that they cannot afford to dispense with the appeal to religious experience, as Karl Barth at times gave the impression that he would like to do.

The attempt to base Christian theology on religious experience is not the only claim on our attention that Schleiermacher has. He had also certain very profound insights about christology which cannot be ignored. But we are concerned with his main thesis because it gives a very short and often popular answer to our question: what is the relation of religious experience to doctrine? Doctrine, replied Schleiermacher, is the systemization and expression in intelligible form of religious experience.

We must say at once that we think this is a misleading way of formulating the relationship. This is because the basic Christian gospel, the foundation on which all doctrine must rest, is not a statement about, or an offer of, religious experience. It is a statement about what God has done: God in Christ has manifested himself in saving power for the benefit of all who approach him in faith. There is nothing here, except the reference to faith (to which we revert later on), that necessarily implies religious experience. The gospel is therefore first and foremost a claim concerning God, not concerning man, though man is of course necessarily involved. The temptation to alter this, so that the centre of the Christian message is expressed in terms of religious experience, is always present to the church, never more so than it is today. This corruption of the gospel takes two forms: a Protestant and a Catholic. The Protestant form is that to which evangelicals are most prone (we use 'evangelicals' in its Anglo-Saxon not its continental Lutheran sense). The evangelical will often present Christianity in the form of a challenge: 'come and have the conversion experience which is necessary if you are to become a real Christian'. Often preachers will seek to induce this experience by the use of emotional evangelistic campaigns, where rousing hymns and mass emotion are powerful incitements to accept and share the conversion experience. In extreme cases Evangelicals will not accept anyone as a genuine Christian unless they have had the conversion experience of the variety which they favour. This approach is quite untrue to the New Testament. Paul in his letters does not appeal for emotional conversions (whatever be the nature of his own conversion). He appeals for faith. In Gal. 1.11–17, where he refers to his own conversion experience, he writes as follows: 'But when he who had set me apart before I was born, and had called me through his grace, was pleased to reveal his Son to me (literally "in me"), in order that I might preach him among the Gentiles, I did not confer with flesh and blood ... etc.' Paul distinguishes clearly between the gospel (the content of his preaching), and the moment when he apprehended it. The two are not identical.

The Catholic version of this particular corruption of the gospel is much more varied. It consists in permitting authentic Christianity to be heavily diluted with folk religion. Folk religion has plenty of room for religious experience of the most diverse sort, from the temple prostitutes of Old Testament times to the excitement caused by the annual liquefaction of the blood of St Januarius in Naples in our own day. What is common to all forms of folk religion is that it is essentially the attempt of natural man to safeguard himself against the influence of superhuman powers. When Christianity accepts too strong an infusion of folk religion the central affirmation of the gospel is inevitably pushed into the background, and something else, often a thrilling experience, or a sentimental story, takes its place.

Doctrine is the attempt to safeguard the central affirmation of Christianity from the various corruptions to which it is exposed by the *Zeitgeist*. This means that the expression of doctrine will vary from age to age, but always what is being defended or expounded is a claim, a statement, not an experience. We cannot of course exclude religious experience from Christianity. The rise and fall of the 'Death of God' theology of the sixties is a clear demonstration of this. A statement about what God has done is quite futile if there is no reaction on the part of man. But if the reaction is substituted for the statement disaster follows. The function of doctrine, however, is not merely to serve as an intellectual formulation of religious experience. In this respect Schleiermacher was wrong.

However, it can be asked whether religious experience can be used to check doctrine or vice versa? There is a sense in which this question should be answered with a Yes. If the expression of a doctrine includes the assertion that certain events have taken place in a heavenly sphere to which we have no access and of which we have no knowledge it becomes suspect because it appears to be making speculations for the truth or falsehood of which there can be no test whatever. For instance, certain theories of the atonement have claimed that through the life, death and resurrection of Jesus Christ a transaction took place between God and the devil whereby the devil agreed to release the whole of mankind from the bondage of the devil which they had incurred through the fall in return for the humanity of Christ, which God allowed the devil to take possession of and destroy. Or, to follow Anselm's more sophisticated theory of transaction, Christ by his death established a claim on God which he asked the Father to commute in favour of mankind, or even, to mention a doctrine which is still popular with many Christians of all traditions, it is said that the risen Christ now in heaven induces the Father, who otherwise would be hostile to us, to look on us mercifully. All these theories have this in common that some transaction took place in heaven, or is taking place in heaven, to which we are not a party and to which there can be nothing corresponding in our experience. In this sense it can be said that religious experience should provide a check on doctrine.

But sometimes religious experience is used as a test of the reality of one's Christianity, or even of one's orthodoxy. To take an extreme example, some Pentecostal Christians maintain that one is not a real Christian unless one has spoken with tongues or received 'the baptism of the Spirit', a form of conversion experience. When an evangelical asks you 'Are you a real Christian?', he will not normally be content with the reply: 'I believe in God made known in Christ'. He will want to know what experience you have had of God in Christ. Now this in itself is not an illegitimate question; it is a perfectly proper thing for Christians to talk about the work of God the Spirit in their lives. What is illegitimate is that religious

experience should be made a test of committed church membership or of orthodoxy. Even that fine Christian poet and theologian
Charles Wesley is not entirely innocent in this respect. How often
in his poems does he refer to feeling as the test of faith!

> Jehovah in thy person show,
> Jehovah crucified;
> And then the pardoning God I know
> And feel the blood applied.

If feeling is made the test of commitment, or the justification for
one particular doctrine of the atonement (in this case 'application of
the blood'), something has gone wrong.

We are in deep waters here, for it might seem that at least one
basic doctrine of traditional Christianity, the doctrine of the Trinity,
can have no relation to religious experience. That is indeed why
Schleiermacher had very little use for it in his theological system.
We must indeed admit that we should not claim to be able to
experience the blessed Trinity. True, the claim has been made by
some mystics, but should probably be treated with reserve. However, this is no reason for rejecting the doctrine of the Trinity
because, as we have seen, the sole function of doctrine is not to
formulate religious experience but to safeguard the gospel. In any
case the doctrine of the Trinity is not, like the heavenly transactions
to which we have just referred, entirely divorced from experience.
We can know that God is Father, Son, and Spirit; we can only
know him in the Spirit. Spirit is the form in which we know him as
God, Father, Son, and Spirit. The doctrine of the Trinity is an
attempt to make intelligible the Christian understanding of God,
which itself, most notably perhaps in the realm of the Holy Spirit, is
capable of being related to religious experience. Indeed the doctrine of the Trinity, far from being a disproof of what we have been
saying about the relation of religious experience to doctrine, is an
excellent example of the right relationship: doctrine is based on the
gospel, not on religious experience, but at many points doctrine can
be checked by experience.

But the doctrine of the Trinity can be related to religious experience in other ways also. It seems likely, for instance, that one of the
main reasons why by the end of the first century the church was
worshipping Christ as God was that common Christian experience

demanded it. Though the practice faced the theologians with a major problem, the pressure of Christian experience could not be resisted. We find in some of the later and less theologically sophisticated writings of the New Testament a naïve application of the word *theos* (God) to Jesus. See for example Titus 2.13; II Peter 1.1. The resolution of this problem in intellectual terms had to be undertaken by the author of the Fourth Gospel, with his introduction of the concept of the *Logos* or Word of God, whereby a distinction within the Godhead could be made. In a very similar way the church in the course of the second, third, and fourth centuries allowed the Holy Spirit to be accepted as a co-equal partner in the Trinity. One of the main reasons for this (though not the only one) was that the presence of the Holy Spirit in the experience of the church was a datum that could not be ignored. Were we to concentrate on the evidence of the New Testament alone, it is very doubtful whether we would reach the conclusion that the Holy Spirit must be regarded as co-equal with the Father and the Son. In the New Testament the doctrine of the Holy Spirit is still in process of formation and there are obscurities and ambiguities in the expression of how the Holy Spirit is related to Christ and to the whole economy of God. It needed some generations of the experience of the Holy Spirit in the church before he could be seen as fully integrated into the Christian doctrine of God as three in one.

We must now ask the reverse question: can doctrine be used to check religious experience? Yes certainly, in some circumstances. Paul makes this clear in II Cor. 12.1–10, where he gives us a dramatic account of his religious experiences, how he was snatched up to heaven and heard words incapable of utterance. In this context he speaks of the 'revelations' which he has received; but he deliberately refrains from drawing any doctrinal conclusions from them. These revelations did nothing to modify his belief in the gospel of God in Christ. This is very significant indeed. It seems that there are not going to be any revelations which could in any way modify or cancel out the one great revelation of God in Christ. Throughout the history of the church of course there have been people who claimed special revelations, some of which if true would have drastically modified the traditional Christian understanding of the faith. About the year 1200 the abbot Joachim of

Fiore in Calabria claimed to have received a revelation to the effect that the third age of the world, the age of the Holy Spirit, would begin in about fifty years' time, at which point the 'Spiritual Church' would appear. Only the other day we met a lady who told us that she had been privileged to learn that she would not die before the *parousia* came, thereby claiming actually to be better informed than was the incarnate Lord (see Mark 13.32). It is reported that on one occasion when John Wesley was granted an interview with the great bishop Joseph Butler, the bishop remarked: 'Sir, the pretending to extraordinary revelations and gifts of the Holy Ghost is a horrid thing, a very horrid thing.'

In other words, religious experience alone must not be used as a proof of doctrine. Catholics are sometimes tempted to do exactly this. When in 1858 the Blessed Virgin Mary appeared to Bernadette Soubirous at Lourdes she is reported as saying to the child: 'I am the immaculate conception.' Quite apart from the question of the authenticity of this apparition, it must not be used as a proof of the doctrine of the Immaculate Conception. Sometimes during the period between the First and the Second Vatican Council Roman Catholic apologetic concerning the resurrection of our Lord has taken the form of saying: 'The church knows it took place; the church was present at the event.' This is in effect a claim to a special revelation concerning a point of doctrine. Expressed in this form it is spurious. The temptation to use this sort of argument is even stronger when we are dealing with an event less well evidenced than the resurrection of our Lord, the assumption of the Blessed Virgin, for example. The total lack of either credible historical evidence or scriptural foundation for this event has tempted some apologists to claim that the church has known it was true ever since it took place. But the argument is hollow. The ultimate criteria for such an alleged event are historical evidence and the church's rule of faith based on scripture. Religious evidence alone must not be used as a proof of doctrine.

The question of whether there is a Christian norm of spirituality is essentially the same as the last question as to whether doctrine can act as a check on religious experience, but is made more pointed by being restricted to the realm of prayer. Before attempting a reply we should make two observations which are relevant to our enquiry:

(*a*) There seems to be an experience of God common to mystics in many religious traditions, one which is not confined to Christian mysticism. This has become clearer in recent years during which inter-faith dialogue has become a prominent feature of the religious scene. Christian mystics find that they speak the same language as mystics in very different religious traditions, whether Hindus, Buddhists, Jews, or Muslims (Sufis).

(*b*) The New Testament does not seem to be very much interested in contemplative prayer. It is indeed true that passages may be found in the New Testament which can easily be interpreted in terms of contemplative prayer, especially perhaps in the Fourth Gospel. But when New Testament writers actually mention prayer it is nearly always intercessory or thanksgiving prayer. Nowhere in the New Testament are Christians specifically urged to be quiet with God in the sense which is intended by most practitioners of contemplative prayer.

We should not attempt to deny the validity of this common mystical experience. It is in itself a very strong indication of the existence of God, one which Freudians and others who try to discredit religious experience deny at the cost of falling into the category of Philistines and barbarians. The difference between Christian mystics and others lies not in the experience itself but in the interpretation of the experience. This is precisely where doctrine or the rule of faith come in. As for the apparent lack of interest in contemplative prayer which we meet in the New Testament, we must recall once more the central affirmation of the gospel: God in Christ has acted for the salvation of mankind, calling for the response of faith. Faith is undoubtedly to be classed as religious experience, but it is a very basic form of religious experience. It is essentially an act of the will, an act of obedience. Indeed 'the obedience of faith' (Rom. 1.5; 16.26) is the only form of religious experience which is essential for all Christians. Anything more than this must not be required, though the obedience of faith will normally lead on to other forms of religious experience. Some very fine Christians may never have actually experienced anything more than this: no emotional conversion, no 'heart strangely warmed', no vision of Christ, nor angels, nor Mary, simply the hearing of a call and the obedience to that call. Anything more than this is of the grace of God. But God's grace is manifold

(Eph. 3.10) and to those who seek it shall be given. If there are Christians who have never known anything but the obedience of faith, it may be because some of them have not sought with that importunity which our Lord commends in his parables.

Doctrine therefore can, and must in certain circumstances, be used as a check on religious experience. If a Christian mystic announces that the pursuit of the mystic way has led him to the conclusion that, like the Hindu *advaitin*, he is actually and substantially part of God, then we must say that he has ceased to be a Christian mystic, for such a conclusion is not compatible with the gospel. If a Christian attempts to explore what St John the Divine calls 'the deep things of Satan' (Rev. 2.24) by means of prayer, he must be if possible dissuaded and certainly repudiated, whatever realities he may claim to have encountered. Any Christian mystic who claims that by virtue of his religious experience he has attained a superiority over other Christians, or has become a member of a Christian élite, or has gained a special knowledge unavailable to others, has gone wrong and must be put right. Within limits such as these the realm of religious experience is open to all Christians.

6

The Ordained Ministry

In this chapter we shall be working out in fuller detail the theology of the ordained ministry which we outlined in *Reasonable Belief*.[1]

1. The Ordained Ministry in the New Testament

The notion of ministry as such is very prominent in the New Testament. Our Lord came 'not to be ministered to but to minister' (Mark 10.45), and we find Paul describing himself and his fellow workers as 'servants (*hupēretēs*) of Christ and stewards of the mysteries of God' (I Cor. 4.1). But until late in the New Testament period we do not encounter what we would today recognize as an ordained ministry.

It used to be held by many Anglicans, and still is officially held by Roman Catholics and Orthodox, that our Lord commissioned the apostles (the eleven at least) to be the rulers of his church and that they handed on their authority to successors, who in turn handed it on to others, until the period when we can distinguish the first bishops. From those bishops, it was believed, our Lord's authority has been handed on to the bishops in today's church. This provided an apparently impeccable pedigree for the episcopal ministry and cast very grave doubt on the legitimacy of those ministers who do not have episcopal ordination in the historical succession. This theory of the legitimacy of episcopacy was called the doctrine of the apostolic succession.

The progress of critical study of the New Testament has, however, undermined both these claims. In the first place, very few scholars would maintain that Jesus intended the twelve to be the rulers and officers of his church. As we have seen in Chapter 1, there has always been a church, but it is very difficult to find any passage in the New Testament where Jesus actually gives authority to the twelve as such to be the rulers of the church. We do not know how long Jesus expected the community of disciples whom he had gathered round him to continue after his death, because we do not know how long he expected the present age to last. But it seems very unlikely that he clearly envisaged a long and turbulent history for his church, or that he took any steps to make provision for its government. There are indeed various tests that have been quoted in defence of the view that the twelve were appointed as rulers of the church, Matt. 16.13–20 for instance, and Matt. 18.15–20. The first is the most important of the 'Petrine' texts and we shall deal with it separately later on. The second is closely connected with it. If any piece of teaching attributed to Jesus in the New Testament bears the marks of being the product of the early church rather than of its Lord, Matt. 18.15–20 is surely one such. Then there is John 20.21–23, where the risen Lord commissions his disciples and gives them authority to forgive sins. But in this passage John does not describe the group commissioned as the twelve. Indeed he shows marked reserve about the twelve in his Gospel and seems not at all interested in the ordained ministry, The commission would seem to be given to the infant church rather than to its officers. In Matt. 28.16–20 it is the eleven disciples who are sent out by the risen Lord to make disciples, to baptize and to teach. In Luke 24.33–53 the group whom the risen Lord addresses are described as 'the eleven and those who were with them', though in Acts 1.2 the same group is referred to as 'the apostles'. And of course when the gift of the Spirit is granted at Pentecost it is not confined to the twelve.

There are a number of passages in Matthew and Luke where the disciples seem to be spoken of as servants bearing authority in the Lord's household. One such is Matt. 24.45–51 with its parallel in Luke 12.41–48. This is therefore a passage from Q, that uncertain source of material common to Matthew and Luke. Similar to this is Matt. 19.28 (parallel Luke 22.30), where the promise is made to faithful disciples that they will sit on thrones judging the twelve tribes of Israel. All these passages are orientated towards the *parousia* and it would be rash to draw from them any clear evidence about the ordained ministry.

The other claim, the assertion that the apostles passed on their authority to the first bishops, is equally dubious in the light of our modern understanding of the New Testament evidence. In fact, in the New Testament we never find the apostles passing on their authority to anyone else. When we seem to have instances of this they invariably prove to be illusory. This holds good even if we understand 'apostle' in the wider sense that includes Paul and perhaps others such as Barnabas and James the brother of the Lord. For example, Acts 14.23 represents Paul and Barnabas as appointing presbyters in every city in which they had recently founded churches. But in the authentic Pauline epistles we never find the term 'presbyter' used in connection with the churches founded by Paul: it seems likely that the author of Acts is reading into an earlier period the conditions that prevailed in his day. Similarly in I Tim. 4.14 and II Tim. 1.6 there are references to Timothy having been ordained by the hands of Paul and/or the presbyters. But the great majority of New Testament scholars would put the Pastoral Epistles late in the New Testament period, so we do not have in them an authentic record of church practice in Paul's day.

We have referred already to the 'Petrine' texts. These are the texts on which the see of Rome has traditionally based its claim that our Lord granted to Peter rule over the church, a rule which was to be handed on to Peter's successors in the bishoprick of Rome. We need not examine the historical basis for the association of Peter with the see of Rome, but we must look at the texts. They are Matt. 16.18–19; Luke 22.31–32; John 21.15–17. The apparent uniqueness of the promise to Peter in Matt. 16.18–19 is very much qualified by the fact that almost the same promise is made to all the disciples in Matt. 18.18–20. As for the other two passages, no one would think of interpreting them in terms of a supremacy granted to Peter if they were considered by themselves. Only if we look at them through the spectacles of a later age, when any see that could claim a connection with an apostle gained considerable prestige and power, do they appear to have anything to do with an appointment of Peter as prince of the apostles. It might of course, be argued that Matt. 16.18–19 is evidence at least for the belief that Peter had special authority in the church, and this is quite true. But if we ask whether this passage is good historical evidence that Jesus intended Peter to have such authority, we must return a doubtful

answer. There is no hint of this in the other Gospels and we do not
find Peter exercising a unique authority either in the Pauline epistles or in Acts.

This is not to deny that both the twelve and Paul had authority in
the early church. Paul certainly treats the church in Jerusalem, of
which the twelve were the nucleus, with respect; and he himself
claims the authority of a founding apostle in his own churches. It is
notable, however, that when he wants one of his churches, that of
Corinth, to discipline one of its members who had sinned grossly,
he expects the church as a whole to act and shows no sign of
wanting to place the duty in the hands of any church officials (see I
Cor. 5.1–5). We also find members of Paul's churches who have
taken upon themselves pastoral oversight: Paul urges the local
church to be obedient to such people; see I Thess. 5.12–13; I Cor.
16.15f.; and cf. Col. 4.17. We find in addition an obscure reference
to *episkopoi* and *diakonoi* in the greeting to the church in Phil. 1.1.
But these are all local ministries. There is nothing to connect them
with wider church authority. We have no reason to believe that Paul
ordained any of these local figures.

It is therefore a reasonable conclusion that during the first
generation of the church no one was concerned about passing on
ministerial authority, still less that anyone imagined that Christ
had instituted or ordained a ministry bearing authority in the
church. The lists of persons serving the church which we find in
I Cor. 12.28; Eph. 4.11 are, with the exception of apostles (a non-
transferable status), lists of functions not of offices. To this we may
add Rom. 12.6–8. The salient feature of all these lists is their
miscellaneous quality. None of them can possibly be regarded as
consisting simply of a list of offices in the church. Thus the passage
in I Cor. 12, though it begins with what appear to be offices
(apostles, prophets, teachers), ends up with 'powers', gifts of healing, ability to speak with tongues and to interpret them. In any case
it does not seem likely that there ever was an office of prophet.
Similarly in Rom. 12 we begin with prophecy; then comes a vague
term, 'ministry', then teaching, then exhortation, generosity
in giving, undertaking leadership, service of the unfortunate.
Ephesians 4.11 shows us something much nearer the conception of
office, but then it is very unlikely to be Pauline. It probably belongs
to the period when specific offices were just beginning to emerge.

Even here, however, prophets come very high up on the list; it does not look as if 'evangelists' and 'pastors', next on the list, were ever meant to be names for offices. The conclusion must surely be that during the first generation of the church the distinction between 'ordained' and 'lay' simply did not exist. It only begins to be formulated towards the end of the first century. A study of I and II Corinthians, however, leaves one with the distinct impression that the church had a ministry to carry out (*diakonia*), that this was Christ's ministry, and that Paul and his fellow workers were conscious of a duty to hand on this ministry to each church which they founded. This ministry must be described in the very widest terms; it was not a ministry of the sacraments only. In essence it had the obligation of nothing less than living out the life of Christ in the world. If we read such passages as I Cor. 4.8–13; II Cor. 4.7–15; 6.1–10, we must surely conclude that someone is carrying out a very strenuous, existential, Christ-centred ministry which seems to consist primarily in reproducing the life, atoning death, and resurrection of Christ in the life of the local church. The ministers here can be no others but Paul and his fellow workers, Sosthenes, Apollos, Titus, Timothy, etc. But, unlike the ordained ministry of a later period, they do not regard themselves as clerics ministering to laity. On the contrary, the whole purpose of their ministry is to enable the Corinthian church as a whole to become themselves responsible for this activity, this reproduction of the life of Christ. Thus we find in Paul's writings the conception of ministry and of ministers. But it does not seem to be an ordained ministry and there is no distinction between ministers and those ministered to except in what they are actually doing.

However, Paul does give us a hint which by analogy may throw light on the doctrine of the priesthood of the ordained ministry. In his Corinthian letters he is concerned at various points to describe the life which he and his fellow missionaries (whom he calls 'apostles') lead. He does not do this merely in order to elicit sympathy or admiration, but to encourage his converts to live just such a life. Consider such passages as I Cor. 4.6–13; II Cor. 4.7–15; 6.1–10. There are other similar shorter passages also. What Paul says is that the strenuous, dangerous life, led by the missionaries is a reproduction or representation of the life of Christ, so that the sufferings, death, and resurrection of Christ are in some sense reproduced in their lives, as is also his atoning power. It is not that the 'apostles' add something on to the value of Christ's atonement. It is rather that this atonement, once for all brought about through his cross and resurrection, is brought into action in the life of the church by its being reproduced in the lives of his servants.

In this sense each apostle (in Paul's sense, not meaning just the twelve) could be described as *alter Christus*, a title sometimes used in the Catholic tradition for the role of the priest. But if we accept this description we must notice two very important qualifications:

1. Paul is not actually writing about what we would understand as an ordained ministry. The difference between 'the apostles' in his sense and the Corinthians is not the difference between the clergy and the laity. It is the difference between the inaugurator of a process and those who follow in his footsteps. Paul would no doubt apply the same language to anyone who founded the church anywhere. Compare Rom. 16.7, where Andronikos and Junias, a pair of completely unknown disciples, are described as 'prominent among the apostles'. It *may* be because they were the founders (or among the founders) of the church in Rome. A still more shocking conjecture is that one of them may have been a woman, if the well-attested reading *Ioulian* is correct.

2. If we may apply Paul's language by analogy to the ordained ministry we must remember that these apostles are not substitutes for the laity. On the contrary, Paul uses this language precisely because he wishes to encourage the Corinthians to take up this ministry themselves. Thus the concept of *alter Christus* is just as much applicable to the laity, if we are to continue to use the anachronistic language of a later period. If we may apply Paul's language to the ordained ministry, we must confess that we have the conception of an enabling ministry, or (to use a phrase which we have used elsewhere) a pioneer ministry, not a ministry which performs functions of which the rest of the church is intrinsically incapable.

Since there is no ordained ministry in the Pauline churches, there are no names for offices (with the exception of the obscure reference in Phil. 1.1). But names for offices begin to emerge in the post-Pauline period. In Acts we find the office of presbyter in the

Jerusalem church, probably derived from the elders who were responsible for the running of the Jewish synagogue. The general name for any sort of minister is *diakonos*; but some time in the second half of the first century this name came to denote a special office distinct from that of presbyter. Luke in Acts seems to use *presbuteros* and *episkopos* (the word from which our 'bishop' is derived) as synonyms. See Acts 20.17,28 where the same group of people is first called *presbuteroi* and then *episkopoi*. Some scholars maintain that *episkopos* is simply a translation into Greek of the name of an office of overseer in the Qumran Community, *mᵉbaqqer*. But this is rather speculative. It is very remarkable that none of the words which the church came eventually to use for the various grades in the ordained ministry has a cultic or sacerdotal significance. In secular Greek a *diakonos* meant any sort of servant. A *presbuteros* simply meant an older man. An *episkopos* was any sort of overseer, from an inspector of markets to an auditor of temple finances.

Nobody in the New Testament makes any attempt to link Christian ministry or ministers with the Jewish Levitical temple priesthood of the Old Testament. That cult, early Christians believed, had been superseded by the sacrifice of Christ. Consequently only Christ in the New Testament is called *hiereus*, a priest of the Christian church. The writing in which this idea is worked out most fully is of course the Epistle to the Hebrews. There are, however, a few passages in which Christians as a whole are described as a corporate priesthood; e.g. I Peter 2.1–10; Rev. 1.6; 5.10; 20.6. This priesthood is often described today as 'the priesthood of all believers'; but this is not a phrase found in the New Testament and it would be more accurate to speak of the priesthood of the whole church. Thus, as far as the New Testament is concerned, Christ's priesthood is inherited by, or more accurately exercised through, the priesthood of the whole church. The New Testament does not envisage an ordained ministry as mediating between the priesthood of Christ and that of the church. If any continuity of authority from Christ to the first bishops is to be sought, it must be sought in the church as a whole and not in an ordained ministry.

'A curious fact about the New Testament', writes Avery Dulles, 'is the absence of any precise indication as to whether there were officers specially designated for cultic functions'.[2] A regular structure of ordained ministry does, however, appear within the period of the writing of the New Testament. It is certainly to be found in I Peter, where a group of presbyters seems to be in charge of each local church (I Peter 5.1–4). Their task is to shepherd the flock (cf. Acts 20.28). The chief shepherd is not Peter but Christ. There is no mention of *episkopoi*, but the verb *episkopein* 'to oversee' is used of the presbyters. Dating I Peter is difficult, but most scholars would perhaps put it in the second decade of the second century.

The Pastoral Epistles (I and II Timothy and Titus) give us a much fuller picture of the ordained ministry. We read of presbyters and deacons. The qualifications for these offices are carefully detailed, but not their duties. The word *episkopos* is also used of the presbyters, but there are one or two places where *episkopos* is used in the singular as if it referred to a separate office, e.g. Titus 1.7. The most probable explanation for this is that the author of the Pastorals knew that there was no monepiscopacy in Paul's day and that it was only just appearing in some of the churches to which he was writing in his day. He therefore deliberately used language that could apply to a church in either situation. In the time when the Pastorals were written there certainly was a ceremony of ordination; see I Tim. 4.14; II Tim. 1.6. It was carried out by the group of presbyters in the local church laying hands on the candidate. He may well have been previously marked out by the voice of prophets in the congregation (I Tim. 1.18). In the Pastorals Timothy and Titus are represented as exercising an authority that transcends the bounds of the local church. This was probably not a feature of the author's own day, as there seems at that time to have been no authority that extended beyond the bounds of the local church. Some scholars have attempted to show that figures such as Timothy and Titus form a link in authority between the apostles and the first bishops. But once we have recognized that the Pastorals are not Pauline, but belong to a period very early in the second century, this argument loses much of its force. The author is trying to reproduce the situation in Paul's day, when Paul's assistants did indeed tour his churches carrying Paul's authority with them.

One notable feature of the ordained ministry in the Pastorals is that many of the functions which Paul expected the whole congregation to exercise are now exercised by the ordained ministry only, e.g. discipline; see I Tim. 5.17–24 (verse 22 probably refers to readmission to communion of those who had been under discipline rather than to ordination). The main functions of the ordained ministry seem to be church discipline, teaching and defending the faith, and leading worship. See I Tim. 2.1–6; II Tim. 3.16–17; 4.2–5; Titus 1.9. There is no suggestion of apostolic sucession in the later sense, though the author is very anxious to preserve what he believes to be the authentically apostolic teaching of Paul. He is not concerned to trace the origin of the teaching any further back than that.

As we read the Pastorals we cannot help being impressed by the very unsacerdotal quality of the ordained ministry. There is no explicit mention of the sacramental activities of the ministers. One might almost describe it as a domestic ministry. Great stress is laid on the domestic virtues required in bishops, presbyters, and deacons. The ideal of clerical celibacy has not yet dawned on the horizon. Leadership, an exemplary domestic life, ability to teach, these are the desirable qualities. When we have made every allowance for the middle-class, almost bourgeois background of the author himself, we must still confess that we are very far indeed from the sacerdotal, authoritarian hierophant which is what the Christian minister has become three centuries later.

Before passing on to trace the development of the form and the ethos of the ordained ministry which took place in subsequent ages, it will be useful to sum up some of the conclusions that may legitimately be drawn from this brief sketch of the ordained ministry in the New Testament. We may tabulate them thus:

(a) No denomination today is justified in claiming that it possesses in its ministry a direct link of delegated authority going back to our Lord or to the apostles. Such claims are still made and will continue to be made for some time by the Orthodox Church, the Roman Catholic Church when speaking authoritatively (though some of its best scholars and theologians tell a very different tale), and by some Anglicans, though without ecclesiastical authority. But these claims are empty, supported by the bare word of ecclesiastical authority or by an arbitrary determination to believe where there is not sufficient evidence. Those who make them have no privileged information about the history of the early church – quite the contrary.

(*b*) It follows that no denomination today is justified in claiming that its form of ministry possesses a divine approval which is denied to other forms. This is not to say that all forms of ministry are equally good. And some can certainly claim a much longer history than others, notably episcopacy of course. But episcopacy, despite its impressively long history, cannot be said to be approved in the New Testament as the correct, or only, form of the church's ordained ministry. Later in this work we discuss the claims that can legitimately be made for episcopacy. They are by no means negligible.

(*c*) In the New Testament the ordained ministry is not defined in terms of its relation to the sacraments but to the wider pastoral task of the church. As we shall see, this has great significance for the theology of the ordained ministry.

(*d*) Ordination is the conferring by the church of authority on certain persons in order that they may carry out certain functions on behalf of the church. In effect, as it gradually became apparent that the *parousia* was not to take place in the immediate future, the church found that it had to have a duly authorized ministry if it was to carry out its task in the world. This was not an unhappy degeneration nor a temporary makeshift, but a development guided by the Holy Spirit quite as much as was a little later the emergence of liturgies and the compilation of the creeds.

(*e*) From the very first the church has claimed to exercise authority. The appointment of an ordained ministry is one of its main ways of exercising that authority, but it is not the only one. The death of the martyrs, for example, is another.

2. Ministry to AD 200 and Beyond

By the year 200 the threefold ministry of bishop, presbyter and deacon was securely established almost everywhere throughout the church. These ministries were, as has already been pointed out, in their origin very much *ad hoc*. Even as late as 200 they might have been thought by an ordinary Christian to represent merely a superintendent, an older man and a helper, which is what their names indicate. They were not consciously formed on Old Testament models. No widely recognized theological significance had yet been attached to them. By far the most significant was the bishop, who was regarded as the custodian of doctrine, the main dispenser of discipline and the normal celebrant of the eucharist.

From about the year 200, however, begins the practice of calling the bishop, and much less frequently the presbyter, a 'high-priest' (Greek *archiereus*, Latin *sacerdos*). The main reason for this must have been that, now that an official ministry was securely established, the church's activity in all its roles must be represented in the activity of its chief minister and this high-priestly role was one of them. As the ministers begin to do what the whole people of God were originally called to do, i.e. witness, preach, worship, heal, administer discipline, so the chief minister now fulfils the priestly role of the people of God. Anyway, for whatever reason, the year 200 marks the emergence of the practice of calling the bishop a high-priest. It must be emphasized that this was not 'the institution of a priesthood'. There is no evidence capable of enduring five minutes' examination that Christ or his apostles or anybody else in the ancient church 'instituted a priesthood'. This long-standing fiction should now be abandoned. What happened was that an existing ministry began to be *called* a priesthood about the year 200.

This priesthood at first was not specifically connected with the eucharist. The prayer for the ordination of a bishop in Hippolytus' *Apostolic Tradition* (about 220) makes no mention of his celebrating the eucharist but rather emphasizes his capacity to forgive sins, i.e. administer the church's discipline, as well as his more clearly pastoral role. But in course of time, first in the West with Cyprian, bishop of Carthage, and later in the East, the priestly activity of the bishop is associated with his capacity to consecrate the bread and the wine in the eucharist. In fact Cyprian goes much further than any of his contemporaries in envisaging the bishop (and to a lesser extent the presbyter) as a Christian counterpart of the Old Testament high-priest. Like the high-priest, his person is sacrosanct; like him he is a cultic official, offering sacrifice, in this case, not the sacrifice of praise and thanksgiving, which was the universally agreed Christian sacrifice before that period, but the sacrifice of Christ himself in the consecrated elements. Cyprian's doctrine of priesthood was quickly adopted in the West. Similar ideas developed and found widespread acceptance in the East a little later. The old, primitive doctrine of the priesthood of all baptized people and of the Christian sacrifice as that of praise and thanksgiving continued for long side-by-side with these new concepts of priesthood and sacrifice. It must be understood that at this period and from the moment when any Christian official begins to be called a priest, it is the bishop who is the priest *par excellence*. The presbyter is only a priest by delegation from him.

Another development in the Christian ministry which begins to appear in the third century is the gradual reduction in importance of the deacon. He could not be thought to have any weighty cultic significance, and although deacons on innumerable occasions prove to be important people in the third to fifth centuries it is not because they are specifically deacons but because they are clergy, as distinct from laity. During the centuries that follow in both East and West the deacon sinks further into insignificance. He ends by becoming what he is today, an interesting historical relic employed as an apprentice priest. For any episcopally governed church in the twentieth century to claim that the threefold ministry, *as threefold*, is inviolable, is ludicrous. Indeed, it is an impudent claim. Orthodox, Roman Catholics and Anglicans have made nothing of the diaconate. We cannot possibly claim that it is an essential ministry, unless we fall back on the exploded theory that the diaconate was instituted by Christ or his apostles.

In both East and West the Middle Ages saw the Christian ministry develop into a sacerdotal caste: in the East all bishops were chosen from among celibate monks; in the West all clergy above the rank of deacon were supposed to be compulsorily celibate. The cultic capacity of the bishop and the presbyter was emphasized strongly. In the West the presbyter gradually came to be regarded as the priest *par excellence* because the bishop was developing in such diverse and unecclesiastical directions. During the Middle Ages in the West the bishop was used for a variety of functions quite unconnected with his office or with the original intention of his order. He became a civil administrator, a judge, a great land-owner, a feudal baron, a secular ruler, even a general equipping and leading troops into battle. When the historian Anna Comnena witnessed the arrival of the First Crusade at Constantinople at the end of the eleventh century, she was shocked to observe that Western bishops put on armour and fought in battle. However, the ordinary presbyter in the parish (when parishes developed) could be observed every Sunday celebrating Mass. Consequently, everybody forgot that it was the bishop who was primarily the priest and gave to the presbyter/priest the credit of being the significant priestly figure rather than to the distant and preoccupied bishop. Medieval and post-Tridentine theology obligingly regularized this state of affairs by teaching that the presbyter was the true priest and that the bishop was no more than a priest with special added powers conferred on him. This theology suffered from a double delusion, that our Lord had directly instituted bishops or priests in the persons of the apostles, and that in this priestly institution the presbyter was the significant figure and not the bishop.

It must be made clear that during the whole of the Middle Ages the priest was defined and evaluated by his cultic function, his capacity to consecrate the bread and the wine in the eucharist. The more general priestly function which was apparently in the minds of those who first began calling bishops high-priests was forgotten or subordinated to the other aspect.

At the Reformation in the sixteenth century most Reformed traditions abolished priests and bishops altogether. It is not surprising that they did so. It was impossible to recognize in the powerful secular figure which the word 'bishop' then denoted, in a Cardinal Wolsey or a Cardinal Beaton, in the Archbishops of Mainz and Cologne of Luther's day, the pastorally-minded Father-in-God which was the original conception of a bishop. The Reformers particularly disliked the late medieval cultic interpretation of the priest because it contributed largely to the contemporary eucharistic theology and practice which they attacked above all other targets. Priesthood then, absorbed as it was into its cultic aspect, had little chance of surviving the tidal wave of Reformation. In a few places, however, such as Sweden and England, the offices of both bishop and priest were retained, but were given a different interpretation, in short, reformed rather than abolished. In the Church of England (as in Anglican churches within the British isles in communion with the Church of England) the Ordination Service was so altered as to make it quite clear that the church continued to intend to ordain both bishops and priests, but their functions and significance were differently defined. They were not defined by (though not deprived of) their cultic capacity nor activity. They were given power to forgive sins and celebrate sacraments, but their significance was stated in terms which were much more deliberately pastoral. The bishop was to guard doctrine, to feed his flock, to govern the church wisely, firmly and mildly. The priest was to be a watchman, a steward, a pastor, preacher and teacher. Owing to the connection of the Church of England with the state it was long before the Anglican bishop could free himself from the embrace of the government, which wanted to exploit him for secular ends. But gradually he has been able to become more like what the ordinal indicated that he should be. The change made in the role of the priest by this Reformation manifested itself earlier. In the long run both re-interpretations of the offices have been an immense improvement. They have effected a Reformation of the traditional ministry of the church which was both scriptural and Catholic.

3. Validity

In the year 1896 Pope Leo XIII published a bull *Apostolicae Curae* in which he gave an official pronouncement on the validity of Anglican orders. This meant a decision as to whether at the time of the Reformation in England the Church of England had retained the same intention, and the minimum necessary element of the same form, as the pre-Reformation church had had when ordaining men to the priesthood. Leo XIII's conclusion was that Anglican orders are 'absolutely null and utterly void'. By this he undoubtedly meant that those who were ordained by Anglican bishops had no orders at all and were no different from laymen.

The reasons he gave for this decision were various, but there was one that ranked highest in importance and that must have had most influence in bringing him to this decision: at the Reformation, he said, the changes that were made in the ordinal of the Church of England indicate clearly that this church had abandoned the intention to ordain a sacrificing priesthood. In order that a man should be validly ordained to the priesthood, he held, it was necessary not only that he should be ordained by a bishop standing in the apostolic succession, and that the rite should be accomplished by means of the prayer and the laying on of hands (both of which conditions he admitted that the Church of England fulfilled), but it was also necessary that there should be present in the minds of those who ordain the intention to ordain a sacrificing priest. The only way that this intention can be clearly known is by studying the words of the ordinal used. In the ordinal used by the Church of England after the Reformation there is no hint of any such intention. Therefore the Church of England cannot confer valid orders.

There is a sense in which Leo XIII was quite right: the reformed Church of England had no intention of ordaining sacrificing priests. But then neither had the early church. The earliest Roman ordinals contain no suggestion of ordaining sacrificing priests. The archbishops of the Church of England in their *Responsio* to Leo XIII's bull had no difficulty in showing that the notion of a sacrificing priesthood had no support in scripture nor in the earliest Fathers, and that the expression of such an intention only entered Western ordinals hundreds of years after the time of the apostles. If Anglican orders are invalid because of this defect, then so are those of the entire Western church from the earliest days and for centuries thereafter. This would of course invalidate the orders of all subsequently ordained.

It might seem that there was no hope of reconciliation between the Roman Catholic Church and the Anglican Communion on this subject. Certainly if theological formulae can commit a church forever, Leo XIII did his best to ensure that his view of priesthood should last for eternity in his church. But beliefs change under the pressure of historical research and other forces, and formulae cannot be guaranteed to keep beliefs petrified eternally. A number of leading Roman Catholic theologians are beginning to reassess their doctrine of priesthood in the light of a less dogmatic approach to the evidence, and their work is bound ultimately to bring about a change in the way in which the Roman Catholic Church understands its doctrine of the priesthood. Thus Raymond Brown in his book *Priest and Bishop, Biblical Reflections*[3] freely admits that a clear succession of authority from our Lord through the apostles to the first bishops cannot be proved. Robert J. Daly SJ in *The Origins of the Christian Doctrine of Sacrifice*[4] makes it clear that the earliest concept of the eucharistic sacrifice in the church was that we offer ourselves, or our prayers and praises, not that we offer (or the priest offers) Christ. E. Schillebeeckx in his rather controversial book *Ministry*[5] has at least shown how very far from primitive models and how extreme in emphasis has been the concept of the priesthood held in the Roman Catholic Church since the Council of Trent. Such views as those advanced by these theologians would not of course be accepted by the official theologians of the Roman Catholic Church in the Vatican, who would no doubt stoutly defend Leonine views on the question of orders. But it is the truest, deepest, and best theologians, not necessarily the most conventional, who ultimately prevail. There is every reason to hope that a fruitful discussion on the subject of orders and priesthood can be held in the future between Roman Catholics and Anglicans.

We must next ask: what do Anglicans say about non-episcopal orders? The Anglican Communion has never officially pronounced upon the validity of non-episcopal orders in the way the Church of Rome has upon Anglican orders, and never will. But ever since the Anglican Communion came into existence in the nineteenth century successive Lambeth Conferences have made episcopal orders a *sine qua non* of intercommunion; and throughout the Anglican Communion if a man in non-episcopal orders wishes to be accepted as an Anglican priest he must accept ordination by a bishop. Hence it is quite clear that Anglicans do not recognize non-episcopal orders.

This does not answer the question, do we Anglicans regard non-episcopal orders as invalid in the same way as Rome regards our orders as invalid? To this there is no clear official answer, because attitudes on this question vary widely within the Anglican Communion. Perhaps the best way we can examine the question is to take four adjectives, expressing descending degrees of disapproval, and try to see the consequences of adopting each of them in turn:

'*Non-episcopal orders are invalid.*' This is certainly held by some Anglicans. It would imply that we regard such orders exactly as Rome regards ours: the Free Church minister as far as authority is concerned is no different from a layman. Though this was a very popular view among Anglo-Catholics in the last century, it is not widely held now. Various Anglican assemblies have recognized the spiritual efficacy, even the reality of non-episcopal ministries. It is agreed that Christ is in some sense present at their eucharists. Such ministries are used by God and are means of grace. If we are willing to go thus far – and most Anglicans are – we can hardly accept that word 'invalid'.

'*Non-episcopal ministries are illegitimate.*' This was the view of the

great bishop Charles Gore. He held that Christ intended an episcopal ministry for his church, and had seen to it that such a ministry
was duly provided and authorized. Any other sort of ministry
therefore could not be regarded as intended, or indeed approved,
by God. Because of God's unconvenanted mercies non-episcopal
ministries were not entirely deprived of God's grace. But we have
no right to presume on this. We have already noted the historical
difficulties attached to this theory. Besides it has to contend with a
great deal of practical evidence against it. It is relatively easy, for
instance, to pronounce that Methodist orders in England are illegitimate, because everywhere there is an established church to
supply their place. But go to South India, where the Methodists
have established a numerous and flourishing church wherein the
sacraments are devoutly celebrated and a ministry possessing clear
authority has existed from the first, and you will find it much more
difficult to be so certain about the illegitimacy of non-episcopal
orders. If God really disapproves of a non-episcopal church such as
this, he has a curious way of showing it.

'Non-episcopal orders are defective.' This is probably the opinion
about non-episcopal orders that would receive the greatest measure
of assent from thoughtful Anglo-Catholics today. They would not
want to deny the efficacy of such orders; nor would they describe
the non-episcopal minister as a layman and nothing else. But they
would affirm that there is something lacking in such orders. They
themselves would in (almost) no circumstances avail themselves of
the services of a non-episcopally ordained ministry just because of
this defect. In one sense we can accept this epithet. Non-episcopal
orders are defective because as long as the church exists in a state
of internal schism all orders are defective. But beyond this it is not
easy to see in what the defect in non-episcopal orders consists. If
you say they are defective in authority, are you really meaning
anything more than what we have just said? We all lack the authority which a fully united church would confer. Otherwise the use
of the word 'defective' would seem to be nothing very much more
than a nostalgic attempt to hold on to the belief that there exists a
'Catholic' church consisting of all those who possess an episcopal
ministry, a church to which 'non-Catholics' do not really belong, or
of which they are at least defective and second-class members.
Such a doctrine of the church we have already repudiated.

'Non-episcopal orders are irregular.' Writing as Anglicans we would
be prepared to accept this statement. Judged by the standard of the
practice of the vast majority of the rest of the church and by the
tradition that has prevailed ever since early in the second century,
non-episcopal orders are a relatively recent innovation, an emergency move made necessary by the extreme corruption of the
church in the West at the end of the fifteenth century. It is indeed
true that Calvin believed that in his system of elders he had redis-
covered the pattern of church orders which our Lord had originaly
intended for his church, but most well-informed Presbyterians
would not now defend their form of church order on these
grounds. Non-episcopal orders are irregular, but they work. They
have been owned by God. Non-episcopal ministers celebrate as
valid a eucharist as does any Catholic priest. Such ministers
do possess churchly authority. We should recognize most Free
Church ministers as our fellow-presbyters. But because their orders are irregular it is much to be desired that they should be
brought within the aegis of the episcopal ministry as soon as prac-
ticable. It must be confessed that a great many Free Church
ministers in this country would profess themselves perfectly ready
for such a move if a scheme could be devised that does not seem to
deny the reality of their existing orders. What has so far frustrated
every such scheme devised in this country is a residual conviction
among some Anglicans that non-episcopal orders are invalid or
illegitimate. Any attempt on the part of Anglicans officially to admit
their reality as a means of integrating them into an episcopal system
has so far been resisted on the grounds that it would seem to be
betraying a principle which is vital to Anglicanism. In our opinion
that principle is historically indefensible.

We must therefore submit the whole concept of validity of orders to
a closer scrutiny. What do we mean when we say that someone's
orders are invalid? Leo XIII, as we have seen, meant that the
ceremony at which such orders had been conferred was an empty
charade, and the person who received the laying on of hands at
such a ceremony had no more authority or commission from God
after it than he had before it. He would have added no doubt that
when such an individual fondly believed he was celebrating the
eucharist, he was in fact failing to do so, in the sense that he could

not change the bread and wine into the body and blood of our Lord by uttering the words of consecration as a validly ordained priest can do.

Very few people, even Roman Catholics, would define invalidity in such extreme terms today. We live in an ecumenical age, and Roman Catholics are anxious to take the best possible view of such orders as they do not officially recognize. Perhaps the following statement from the *Decree on Ecumenism* of the Second Vatican Council would express what a great many Roman Catholics believe: 'ecclesial communities which are separated from us lack the fulness of unity with us which should flow from baptism and ... we believe that they have not retained the authentic and full reality of the eucharistic mystery, especially because of the absence of the sacrament of orders'. The defect here is expressed in terms of the eucharistic mystery. Now one might take this in the very moderate sense that ecclesial communities separated from the Roman Catholic Church do not have an adequate eucharistic liturgy, so that the worshippers are hindered from apprehending the full range of the meaning of the eucharist. And we must admit that this often happens. We recollect attending a eucharist in India conducted by a Baptist minister in the course of which it became clear the celebrant had very little idea why Jesus had given us this rite (since there was no liturgy but we were dependent on his free prayer he was able to say this several times). We were celebrating the service, it seemed, simply because Jesus had told us to do so.

But this interpretation can hardly be correct. In the first place, before the liturgical movement began in the early years of this century it could reasonably be claimed that no tradition in Western Christendom had a liturgy that adequately expressed the full meaning of the eucharist. This would apply to the Tridentine mass as to the Anglican *Book of Common Prayer* or to the free services of the non-episcopal churches. Secondly, during the last thirty years all the main traditions in the church have provided themselves with new eucharistic liturgies. However much they differ from one another in detail, they all bear a family resemblance, and the great majority of them would be regarded as quite adequate by any competent Roman Catholic theologian.

So we ask again, still limiting ourselves to the area chosen by the *Decree on Ecumenism*, what is wrong with the orders which Rome does not recognize, as far as the eucharist is concerned? We have already set aside as unacceptable the answer, 'Nothing happens at an invalid eucharist; our Lord is not present'. What then does happen? One could reply 'We do not know; we can have no assurance that our Lord is present as we have in the case of a validly celebrated rite'. This sort of reply would be made by a good many Catholics. It is an unsatisfactory one because it gives us a picture of a God who has promised to be present if certain rules are observed, but who is not obliged to be present if they are not. He may actually be present out of a sense of decency, but we cannot be sure. Frankly, this is not the sort of God whom we recognize in Jesus Christ. God revealed in Christ is a God of infinite self-giving, who in Jesus Christ came down to our level while we were yet sinners. He is simply not compatible with a God who refuses (or might refuse) to be present when a group of Christians in good faith celebrates the eucharist, however mistaken their views on the subject of the church. We do not want to be left with the image of a God who says in effect 'I would very much like to be present at the rite which these well-meaning Anglicans or Methodists or Baptists celebrate, but unfortunately I have tied my hands. I can only operate where there are valid orders'.

We are reduced therefore to the last resort of those who deny the validity of the eucharist of any one or more groups of Christians: 'Christ is present at a eucharist celebrated by an invalidly ordained minister', they say, 'but not as fully as he is at our altars'. This introduces the idea of there being various grades of eucharistic presence of grace. It is as if non-Roman Catholics enjoy an inferior brand of eucharistic grace; Roman Catholics have the real thing. Once again, we must protest that God is not that sort of person. There are no degrees of eucharistic presence or eucharistic grace. We can never hope to be able to devise a eucharistometer which will register the degree of eucharistic grace available at any given celebration.

Before we come to any conclusion about the concept of validity as applied to orders and the eucharist, we ought to make one point clear. We have approached the question from the point of view of the Roman Catholic Church in its relation to other ecclesial communities. But what we have said would apply just as much to the attitude which some Anglicans take towards the eucharist celebrated by the non-episcopally ordained minister. Indeed one of the more ridiculous aspects of church history in England during the last century was the way in which Anglo-Catholics applied to non-episcopal orders exactly the same derogatory epithets which they had heard Roman Catholics applying to their own. The last century in this country was one in which a great many Christians felt constrained to vindicate their own position at the expense of that of their fellow-Christians.

What is our conclusion about the question of 'invalid' orders? We suggest that it is best to dispense with the concept of validity altogether in this area of theology. It is a concept brought in from the law-courts and is inappropriate in a context such as the eucharist where grace implies a personal relationship. Let us admit straight away that Christ is always present, as he has promised, whenever his people celebrate the eucharist in good faith. An invalid eucharist would be one celebrated not in good faith, i.e. as a deliberate mockery.

Why then do the great majority of churches require that an ordained minister must preside at the eucharist? It is because the eucharist is the church's worship not a private devotion. The presidency of the authorized minister ensures that the eucharist is the church's act, not merely that of a single Christian or group of Christians. If this rule were to be widely disregarded there would be serious danger that the eucharist would develop into a private devotion, like the Catholic saying the rosary or the Protestant having a quiet time. The church's practice of baptism affords an excellent analogy: in theory anyone may baptize and most churches recognize lay baptism. But if the church were to encourage, or even permit, lay people to baptize indiscriminately according to their own judgment, chaos would ensue. There would be no certainty as to who was being admitted to the church and how they were to be looked after. The two great Gospel sacraments are the church's act from first to last. It is therefore necessary from the point of view of order, though not of efficacy, that an ordained minister should preside at both. Incidentally we can cite William Temple in favour of this view.[6] We do not agree with Temple's view as to the relation of the ministry to the church as a whole, as we shall be making clear presently. But here, we believe, he was right.

Finally we should say here that our views about the validity of orders do not imply that we think any and every form of ordained ministry to be equally satisfactory or that anyone who sets himself up to be an ordained minister has equal authority with all other ministers. But our explanation for this must await our fuller exposition of our doctrine of the ministry below.

4. Theology of the Ordained Ministry

A satisfactory doctrine of the ordained ministry must meet a number of requirements. It must justify the existence of an ordained ministry, something we cannot take for granted. It must show how the ministry is related to scripture, and if possible link the ministry with the gospel, whether directly or by some other means. It must explain what is the function of the ministry and how it carries that function out. It must also explore the limits of the ordained ministry and show what it cannot or should not do. It must outline a doctrine of priesthood or ministerial responsibility – and here it is particularly important to keep in line with scripture, because as we have already noted the New Testament never uses the word priest (*hiereus*) for any minister of the church. And finally such a doctrine must say something about the structure of the ministry, the three orders of bishop, priest (or presbyter) and deacon.

We have already expounded the theme of the ordained ministry in the New Testament, and have maintained that it is impossible to show with any degree of probability that there is a line of ministerial authority descending unbroken from our Lord through the apostles to the first bishops in the early second century. Nor is it easy to defend the view that the apostles deliberately handed on their authority to successors. The ordained ministry as we understand the term today first appears towards the end of the first century; but we must wait another hundred years before we can say that the ministerial system consisting of the three orders of bishop, presbyter, and deacon was universally established. Hence the very existence of an ordained ministry must be defended on the grounds that it is the creation of the church of the first century, not of Jesus or of the apostles.

This does not mean that the ordained ministry was a mere afterthought, or a temporary expedient, or a regrettable necessity occasioned by the failure of the second-generation church to live up to the high standards of the first generation. It was in fact, an inevitable development once Christians realized that the *parousia* was not going to take place immediately or even in the foreseeable future. It was the necessary accompaniment of the church's realization that it had to exist in history, because history was not going to end very soon. From the first the church (and this usually meant the local church because the universal church had as yet no organs of expression) had claimed authority, the authority of Christ. But soon situations began to arise where there was an urgent need for the church to exercise its authority, most notably in cases of discipline, but also in other circumstances, such as the need to have someone who was competent to preside at the eucharist and utter the prayer of thanksgiving. Christ's authority, entrusted to the church, had to be brought to bear. The only way was to commission agents who should be seen to bear the authority of the church. Only gradually did the nomenclature for these agents become standardized; it took some time before the presiding bishop was everywhere distinguishable from the group of presbyter-bishops. But eventually everything fell into place. By AD 200 we find in every local church a bishop assisted by a group of presbyters and served by a body of deacons. The ordained ministry therefore has as much claim upon our attention as has the New Testament (much of which is only a little older than the ministry), the earliest liturgies, and the earliest creeds. These last two are in fact, later in appearance than the ministry.

Thus the ordained ministry is the product of the church. Let us rather say it is the product of the Holy Spirit acting in the church. We must not claim, as the Catholic tradition still does, that the ministry descends by transmission with a clerical order from Christ independently of the church. This claim is made crudely and unreflectively by official statements from the Roman Catholic and Eastern Orthodox Churches. It is also occasionally made by some Anglicans. Consider for example this extract from a presidential address to the Convocation of Canterbury made by the great Archbishop William Temple in May 1943:

> When we go back to the first records of the Church we find neither a Ministry which called people into association with it, nor an undifferentiated fellowship which delegated powers to a Ministry; but we find a complete Church, with the Apostolate

accepted as its form of administration and authority. When the Lord's earthly ministry was ended, there was found in the world as its fruit and its means of continuance this Body, in which the distinction between Ministry and Laity is already established. The Apostles were in no sense ministers of the Laity; they were ministers of Christ to the Laity, and to the world waiting to be won. They took steps for the perpetuation of the ministry, and it has descended to ourselves. So when I consecrate a godly and well learned man to the office and work of a bishop in the Church, I do not act as a representative of the Church, if by that is meant the whole number of contemporary Christians; but I do act as the ministerial instrument of Christ in His Body the Church. The authority by which I act is His, transmitted to me through His apostles and those to whom they committed it; I hold it neither from the Church nor apart from the Church, but from Christ in the Church.

This statement is impressive and carries great authority still, because William Temple was a great Christian leader and a fine philosopher. But he was no expert in the New Testament. The accuracy of the statement as an account of the origin of the ordained ministry must be challenged at several points. Temple assumes that the distinction between apostles (whom he apparently identifies with the twelve) and other Christians is the same as the clergy-laity distinction with which we are all familiar. This is very doubtful. Even more questionable is his claim that the apostles 'took steps for the perpetuation of the ministry'. This is precisely where the evidence completely fails. The consequence of this misinterpretation of the New Testament evidence is that Temple presents us with a picture of the origin and continuance of the ordained ministry which makes it out to be a clerical order within the church independent of the church and not apparently responsible to the rest of the church. Avery Dulles has well described this as 'a ruling class that perpetuates itself by cooption'.[7] This is of course what the ordained ministry developed into in the course of the first few centuries, but as an account of the origin of the ordained ministry it is completely misleading. Temple claims that he does not hold his authority from the church, but he adds that he does not hold it apart from the church. He does not make it clear how he can be described as holding it within the church at all. On his premises, if he were to ordain his chauffeur as a bishop in his back drawing room in the teeth of the opposition of the rest of the church, the chauffeur would have to be accepted by the rest of the church as a validly ordained bishop.

So the ordained ministry is the authorized agent of the church. We must be honest and say that by 'church' we mean the contemporary church. Some theologians hold a theory of the existence of an apostolic college to which every newly ordained bishop is joined at his consecration, a college which consists of all who have ever been validly consecrated bishops, whether living or dead. This, they maintain, is the body to which every contemporary bishop should regard himself as responsible, and not the contemporary church. One is driven to ask whether the authority of the bishop is even destroyed if he finds himself in hell! Such transcendental speculations have no foundation whatever in scripture and carry with them the danger of divinizing the power of the ministry. Christ does not confer on his ministers arbitrary and irresponsible power. The ministry exists for the sake of the church and not *vice versa*.

At the same time the ordained ministry is not the slave, or the football, of the church. Authority is conferred through the church by means of its ordained ministers; and it can only be taken away by those who gave it in the name of Christ in the church. There are occasions when the ordained minister has to speak out against the church (often perhaps the local church) in the name of Christ. But he is never justified in ignoring his responsibility to the church. He must not refuse to listen to the rest of the church, or even to be judged by them if necessary. The ultimate judgment lies with God, and it has happened that those whom the church officially condemned are vindicated by the verdict of history. We think of such figures as Jon Hus and Joan of Arc. It is not easy to pinpoint exactly the balance that should be achieved between the authority of the ordained ministry and the authority of the church as a whole which the minister is supposed to be exercising. One thing is clear: no minister should claim unlimited, absolute, or irresponsible authority.

This is exactly what happened in the church in the West in the Middle Ages. The ordained ministry succeeded in monopolizing all power and authority in the church, leaving the laity in theory at least entirely at the mercy of the ministers. It need hardly be added that the ministers misused and corrupted this power which they claimed. The question must therefore arise: what limit should be placed on the authority of the ordained ministry?

The basic principle is this: the ordained ministry must at some point be answerable to the whole contemporary church. As we have already emphasized, it is not satisfactory to make it responsible to a church most of whose membership is in the hereafter and therefore conveniently cannot be consulted. There must be machinery for making the ministry responsible to the contemporary church. Until recent centuries this has never been attempted in any regulated way, though during the Middle Ages kings did in fact interfere with church administration again and again. This was unavoidable since the church was so inextricably mixed up with society. At the Reformation and in the next two hundred years this interference continued in both Catholic and Protestant countries in Europe. But of course the people of God, the *plebs sancta Dei* as such, had nothing to say in the administration of the church. Once in the early centuries the primitive custom of consulting the laity was abandoned, the only way the people of God had of making their views felt was by rioting, a method which they used extensively. This is still the situation in the Roman Catholic and Eastern Orthodox Churches. If over a long period the members of the ordained ministry monopolize power and abuse it, disruption results. An internal schism takes place, and the ordained ministry in the new body has to seek its authority from some source other than that of the old ministry. This is what happened at the Reformation. Various methods were sought for authorizing the new ministry. Luther boldly appealed to the priesthood conferred in baptism, and declared that in the special circumstances of his day the local Christian congregation was competent to confer authority in ordination. Calvin had a theory of his own: he believed that by study of the New Testament he had discovered our Lord's real intentions about providing his church with a ministry, and he proceeded to furnish the body of Reformed Christians who followed his teaching with a ministry conforming to his own ideas. Most modern Presbyterians would not now claim that Calvin was right in his interpretation of our Lord's intention. The way the matter was managed in the Church of England was unique, or very nearly so (the Church of Sweden furnished a partial analogy). The

crown ordered the Church of England to repudiate the jurisdiction
of the Bishop of Rome. Ordinations by bishops went on uninterruptedly. Thus it is inaccurate to say that the Church of England
received a new ministry at the Reformation.

We are therefore faced with the question: when is it justifiable to
break with the existing ministry and to begin anew? That it is
sometimes justifiable we have assumed; and we have also assumed
that God does not necessarily refuse to honour such a new ministry, so that it bears Christ's authority and functions as steward of
the mysteries of God. We repudiate the view that there is only one
'catholic' ministry which alone possesses Christ's authority and
which alone guarantees the validity of the sacraments which it
administers. The reasons for this we have already made sufficiently
clear. But the position we have taken requires that we give some
indication of when we believe such a break and new beginning is
justified.

We cannot draw up a set of rules which any would-be reformer
can apply. Such an attempt would be absurd. But we can make two
points which should help to illuminate the question:

1. There are circumstances in which making a clean break with
existing church authority is justified. The Reformation was certainly an example of this. For at least a century the Western church
had been attempting to reform itself. The so-called Lateran
Council of 1512, summoned by Pope Julius II with the deliberate
intention of obviating any serious reform, had made it plain to all
thinking people that the church was incapable of reforming itself by
constitutional means. Only a disruption could precipitate reform.
The disruption came by the agency of Luther, and the shock
administered by the series of schisms which he occasioned finally
moved the continuing Catholic Church to reform itself. The Reformation in fact sparked off the Counter-Reformation. Para-
doxically the papacy probably owes its continuing existence to
Martin Luther. Had the disruption not taken place, the papacy
would probably have gone the way of the caliphate in Islam.

2. If a break has to be made and a new authority for the ministry
found, Luther's way is the best. There is a priesthood conferred in
baptism, the priesthood of the whole church which represents and
exercises Christ's priesthood. It was in virtue of this priesthood that

the primitive church originally produced the ordained ministry. In times of emergency, such as the state of affairs in the Western church at the opening of the sixteenth century, appeal may be legitimately made to this basic priesthood. Another such occasion in the history of the Church of England was probably the late eighteenth century when the Methodist Church was set up. In the last analysis the continuity of the church is constituted by the whole people of God, and not by the ordained ministry. In time of emergency it must be the authority of the priestly body that repairs the broken chain of authority.

We have next to consider the nature of the authority that is conferred in ordination. It has already been observed that, though the minister is never called a priest (*hiereus*) in the New Testament, before many centuries had passed we find the presbyter or bishop described as *hiereus* in the East and *sacerdos* (priest) in the West. The Church of England, followed by almost the entire Anglican Communion, retained the word 'priest' for the second order of the ministry in its ordinal, though in Laud's Scottish Prayer Book of 1637 the word 'presbyter' was used instead. Moreover the Church of England and the majority of the members of the Anglican Communion have accepted as validly ordained those who have been ordained as 'presbyters' in the Church of South India and the Church of North India. We must therefore as Anglicans decide what we mean by priesthood in this context.

Perhaps we can do this best by showing first where we differ from the official Roman Catholic doctrine on this point. The Roman Catholic Church teaches that the essence of priesthood lies in the ability to offer the eucharistic sacrifice. This ability is irreversibly conferred in the act of ordination consisting of the laying on of hands by the bishop with prayer. Once the newly made priest is ordained he has the power to change the substance of the bread and the wine into the body and blood of Christ when during the eucharist he utters the words of consecration 'This is my body ... This is my blood, etc.'. Roman Catholic doctrine also teaches that ordination imparts an indelible character to the ordinand, so that he is henceforth made able to consecrate the eucharist, and nothing can take this power away from him. He may of course, for disciplinary reasons, be suspended from saying mass, but whenever he does celebrate mass, whether under suspension or not, he cannot fail as long as his intention is genuine and he is not merely play-acting, to bring about a valid eucharist.

We have already noted that it was on the basis of this doctrine that Leo XIII in 1896 declared Anglican orders to be null and void. Leo was certainly right in his conclusion that from the reformation onwards the bishops of the Church of England had no intention of ordaining sacrificing priests in the sense in which Leo defined it. But the question is whether the early church had any such intention either. The earliest ordinals show no trace of any such idea, as the English archbishops pointed out in their reply. But the arch-bishops' official reply to *Apostolicae Curae* was followed shortly afterwards by a book written by R.C. Moberly which is probably the most weighty exposition of the Anglican doctrine of priesthood that has ever been published.[8] He criticized the Roman Catholic doc-trine on two main grounds. First he said that it unduly restricted the scope of priesthood; by defining it in essentially eucharistic terms we put in the centre what should be only a part, though an important part, of the priest's functions. The doctrine of the priest-hood should be based on Mark 10.45: 'The Son of Man is come not to be ministered to but to minister, and to give his life a ransom for many.' The task of the priest is to further the entire pastoral work of the church, his concern is for the good of all the faithful as well as for their worship. As we have seen, this is very much the function of the ministry when it first appears on the stage of history. In the Pastoral Epistles the ordained ministry is startlingly non-cultic, and completely unsacerdotal. Thus the Roman Catholics, following what was really a medieval distortion, have made what should only be a part of priesthood into the whole.

Following on from this Moberly makes his second criticism of the Roman Catholic doctrine. They are describing, he says, what is essentially a *vicarious* priesthood, whereas true Christian priesthood is *ministerial*. By 'vicarious' he means that the priest in official Roman Catholic doctrine is a surrogate for the laity: he has his own sacrifice to offer distinct from that of the people as a whole. At one point in the mass he prays: 'May my sacrifice and yours be accep-table.' There should not be any distinction between the two sacri-fices, says Moberly. The Christian priest is the minister of the people's offering in the eucharist. He does not offer something over and above theirs. He exists in order to enable the offering of their sacrifice. If we were writing a treatise on the eucharist we would go on to insist that the sacrifice which is offered in the eucharist is not an offering of Christ by either priest or people, but an offering of themselves by the people in Christ to the Father, by the agency of the ordained minister. But we need say no more than this. The Roman Catholic teaching about the reception in ordination of an actual capacity to change the elements in the eucharist is something which many modern theologians, including some Roman Catholics, would like to modify or at least express differently. Eucharistic theologians of all traditions are anxious to get away from the idea of a sacred formula effecting a miraculous change, and to regard the whole action of the eucharistic rite as that which consecrates.

What about the *character indelebilis*, the irrevocable power conferred in ordination? Anglicans certainly would not want to express it like that, since they regard ordination as conferring authority rather than any mysterious power. But we, like Roman Catholics and indeed many of the Free Churches, regard ordination as unrepeatable, like baptism. If a priest, having for any reason been suspended from exercising his priesthood, is permitted to act as a priest once more, he is not re-ordained.

We have been defining our doctrine of the priesthood by contrast with the official Roman Catholic doctrine. Perhaps we should now compare it with doctrines of ordained ministry found in other reformed traditions. There is not likely to be very much difference between Anglicans and Presbyterians or Methodists on the subject of priesthood. Indeed Moberly in his book heartily commends the work of Dr Milligan, a Scottish divine who had written on the doctrine of the ministry a few years previously. But the farther we proceed in the direction of the heirs of the radical reformed tradition, Congregationalists, Baptists, Mennonites, for example, the more we find the line between the ordained and non-ordained becoming blurred, and the less attention we find paid to the authority of the wider church in the rite or ordination.

We must therefore state that in the Anglican view the ordained priest possesses an authority which the unordained layman or laywoman does not have. At certain important points in the church's life the priest can act with the church's authority, notably in matters of discipline and in presiding at the eucharist. This authority which the priest possesses comes from Christ in the church. It should never be so separated from the church as to be made the unchallengeable possession of a clerical caste. The priest only possesses his priesthood because the church possesses a priesthood, the derived priesthood of Christ. Christ our great high priest exercises his priesthood through the church, and the church in virtue of this corporate priesthood authorizes certain people to act on its behalf. It does this by ordaining them at the hands of duly authorized ministers, but these ministers are themselves respons-ible to the church as a whole. They should not act, as they have acted during many centuries of the church's existence, as if they were only answerable to God and not to the church. This is the link between ordained priesthood and gospel to which we referred above. It is therefore clearly an indirect link. The New Testament as a whole does not have a clear doctrine of ordained priesthood; we can only infer it from Christ's priesthood and from the priest-hood of the church, both of which are clearly set out in the New Testament. But the priesthood of the ordained ministry, under-stood in the sense in which we have explained it, is a legitimate inference from the priesthood of the church. After all the ordained ministry does appear in the later pages of the New Testament, and this would seem to be the obvious theological justification for it. We may well add that this priesthood had no connection whatever with the Levitical priesthood of the old dispensation, which the New Testament writers unanimously regard as having been abrogated by Christ.

We have perhaps appeared rather controversial in our discussion of priesthood, but the last word on the subject should be more ecumenical. Roman Catholic attitudes towards the priesthood and ministry generally are not inflexible. Doubts about the validity of the traditional 'apostolic succession' argument, and a realization that the early church did not express the function of the presbyter in sacrificial terms, are already producing some new and original thinking on the topic by Roman Catholic scholars. Anglicans are no longer divided, as they were fifty years ago, into two camps, one of which held a traditional doctrine of apostolic succession derived from the uncritical approach to the New Testament of the Tract-arians, and the other of which had virtually no doctrine of the ministry at all. Lutherans, Reformed, and Methodists, especially when they find themselves (as they often do in the third world) the only church in any given area, are realizing the need for the exercising of an effective authority in the church, and are often finding that this authority has a place in their own traditional structures and formularies. The doctrine of the priesthood is not necessarily one about which there will be irreconcilable disagreement among Christians for ever.

We have still one flank of our position to define and defend. One could imagine a critic from the Catholic tradition saying something like this: 'Your willingness to recognize in effect everybody's orders leaves you with no protection against the unjustified schism or the sect founded upon ignorance and bigotry. Our doctrine of recognising only "catholic" orders at least has the merit of enabling everyone to know exactly where we stand.' In other words, are there any limits to our willingness to accept the efficacy and reality of non-episcopal orders? We would base our reply on the important principle set out by Oliver Chase Quick in the earlier years of the century: in a situation of internal schism such as prevails in the universal church today the orders of all of us are to some extent lacking in full authority. It is not the case (*exempli gratia*) that half the church possesses fully valid and authorized orders, whereas the other half possesses orders which are of doubtful validity. As long as we continue in disunity the orders of all of us lack something of full authority. Consequently, if we encounter anywhere a small sect or conventicle, however it originated, its orders will have very little authority. If, in other circumstances, the authority of the ordained ministry is obscured, weakened or dispensed with altogether, the part of the church where this occurs will have the greater difficulty in demonstrating and exercising its authority. But, as we have already pointed out, from the very first the church has claimed to exercise the authority of Christ. From this it does not follow that every such claim made on every occasion necessarily bears Christ's authority. As with our own decisions as individual Christians, so the church's decisions, made and executed by the agency of the church's ordained ministers (though not necessarily by them acting alone without the laity being represented), are made in faith. We may as individuals make the wrong decision, even if we make it in faith. If so, subsequent events in which we may discern the hand of

God will make this plain to us. So with the church. Christ does not give the church a blank cheque, he does not grant it free permission to use his authority with the certainty that he will approve whatever the church decides in his name. But the church must act in faith, must exercise authority, must strive to display the genuine authority of Christ. We return to the topic of the church's authority later on, but must now test our theory by an actual example.

We have said that wherever we encounter a small sect or conventicle, however originated, it will wield very little authority. Let us take what looks like an example of this taken actually from the area of the Anglican Communion, so that there may not be any individious sniping at non-Anglican bodies. There exists in Portugal a very small body of Christians, not more than two thousand in all, called the Lusitanian Church. This originated in the last century from an evangelical movement among some Portuguese Roman Catholics. But the leaders of this schism were not content to exist on their own as a small non-episcopal sect. They appreciated the heritage of Catholicism and wanted if they could to have an episcopally ordained ministry. They therefore approached the Archbishop of Canterbury and asked him to ordain their candidates for priesthood and eventually consecrate a bishop for them. This the archbishop was unwilling to do, but eventually they found that the Anglican Archbishop of Dublin was willing to give them what they required. The consequence is that today this tiny body is in full communion with the Anglican Communion and has a bishop of its own. We would therefore conclude that the Lusitanian Church does not fall into the category of 'small sect or conventicle' just because it has shown a genuine desire to be in communion with as much of the rest of the church as possible, even though it had decided to go out of communion with the Roman Catholic Church for doctrinal reasons.

Thus we should now be able to answer the difficulty which seemed to have arisen at the end of our section on validity. The rebellious layman who sets up his own conventicle and ordains ministers has little or no authority. When such ministers celebrate the eucharist they are in effect turning the eucharist into a private devotion. Christ will never refuse to be present to those who act in sincerity. But an important element in the significance of the eucharist will have been obscured. The sectarian group will have cut themselves off from the benefits of the fuller fellowship. The church's authority will have been diminished. For the sake of the discipline of the greater church the authority of such ministers should not be recognized.

Traditionally the ordained ministry has been divided into three orders, bishops, priests (or presbyters), and deacons. We need not concern ourselves with the medieval tendency to run together the orders of priest and bishop, nor yet with the minor orders, fossilized relics of varied functions in the early church such as subdeacon and lector. These distinctions cannot be traced back earlier than the early part of the second century. Before that the distinction between bishop and presbyter disappears. But this in itself means that the threefold orders of the ministry have a very long history indeed. All through the Middle Ages, though there were schisms in abundance and no lack of sects opposed to the authority of the great church, no one thought of initiating a new ministry. That this did happen at the Reformation is an index of how far the episcopal order had been secularized and corrupted. We who today are accustomed to bishops of impeccable lives, great pastoral zeal and moderate incomes, must not judge those who rejected episcopacy as if they had rejected episcopacy as it is today. For them the bishop usually meant a great feudal lord with magisterial powers, often one who exercised over his flock the right of life and death. The bishop had become a top civil servant who was thought of far more as a juridical than as a pastoral figure. Very often he would be immensely rich, totally worldly, and not infrequently very loose in his morals. He was about as unlike the spiritual father that the second or third century bishop appeared to be as one could well imagine. Nevertheless presbyteral government as we meet it in most of the reformed churches was an emergency measure. We have already rejected Calvin's claim that he had discovered our Lord's true intention regarding the ministry. So the traditional threefold ministry has a very strong claim on the attention of all Christians. An actual commendation of episcopacy in its operation over against other forms of ministry we leave until later.

All Catholics in the West, however, are on shaky ground when they claim as a merit to have preserved intact the threefold form of the ministry from the early days of the church, because in fact they have allowed the diaconate to lose all its distinctive significance. In the Roman Catholic as in the Anglican Church the diaconate is now nothing more than a preparatory stage for the priesthood. This development had already taken place long before the Reformation and at the Reformation the Church of England did nothing to put it right.

In the early church the deacon had distinctive functions: he was especially the assistant and minister of the bishop. He had financial and administrative duties in connection with the church's charitable work. He also had certain liturgical functions. In Rome the group of deacons was a very important body, and for some hundreds of years during the Dark Ages the Pope was always chosen from among the deacons and not from among the presbyters. Some of the reformed churches succeeded in reviving the office of deacon as a distinctive function. In some forms of Presbyterianism he is quite different from the elder. The Congregationalists and the Baptists have set an example to the rest of the church in recovering the office of deacon. He is an officer of the church, usually not stipendiary, on whom rests the responsibility of seeing that the local community is organized and equipped to carry out its ministry.

The fading out of the diaconate as a separate function left a gap that needed to be filled in the organization of the local church in Catholicism. In the Roman Catholic Church this was to a large extent met by the religious orders, both men and women. But monastic orders were abolished in the Church of England at the time of the Reformation and have only gradually been re-established on a relatively small scale since the last century. Consequently there developed in Anglicanism the lay office of reader. Beginning in 1886, this office has increased and developed remarkably throughout the Anglican Communion, especially during the last thirty years. Women are now admitted as readers and it is quite normal for a reader to administer the cup at communion. Obviously this office meets a need. Though it was originally given the name of a minor order it functions in fact in a way much more like the original office of deacon. It would therefore be an admirable move if all readers, men and women alike, were to be ordained deacon. Anglicans would then have freed themselves from the accusation of hypocrisy or at least make-believe which they incur as long as they continue to extol the virtues of the threefold ministry but fail in practice to do anything with the third order except to use it as a preparatory stage for the second.

There is another point where the Church of England, as distinguished from the rest of the Anglican Communion, is less than convincing in its defence of the threefold ministry. Like all Anglicans, we insist on the virtues of the episcopal system and demand that all who would unite with us should adopt it. But in practice our bishops are unable to exercise anything but a very imperfect episcopal oversight because the dioceses to which we appoint them are so vast. The average population of a diocese in the Church of England is 1.1 million. Of course the vast majority of this population takes no active interest in the church and would not recognize a bishop if they saw one. But the diocesan and his clergy still have an obligation to meet their spiritual needs, and millions of English men and women who never go to church on Sundays still expect to be baptized, married, and buried by the ministers of the established church. The diocesan in the meantime finds himself in charge of a large administrative system the running of which must absorb most of his time. He can only hope to meet a tiny fraction even of the faithful, and in most cases cannot expect to know the majority even of his clergy except in the most superficial manner.

Ever since Saxon times the English diocesan has probably never been very well acquainted with most of his laity. But the situation was worsened by the industrial revolution, as a result of which there was a population explosion during the late eighteenth and early nineteenth centuries. The Church of England woke up to this during the first half of the nineteenth century, when the church was still closely connected with the state and British prime ministers still acknowledged some responsibility for looking after the Church of England. Vast dioceses such as York and Lincoln were subdivided. But to create a new diocese requires an act of Parliament, which is expensive both in money and in parliamentary time. As the nineteenth century wore on prime ministers, especially Liberal ones who depended on the votes of Nonconformists, became more and more unwilling to concede the time needed for such acts of Parliament. Matters came to a head in 1870, when Archbishop Tait asked Gladstone if he could introduce a bill to create new dioceses. Gladstone refused. Tait then took advantage of an act originally passed in 1534 whereby the crown could appoint suffragan or assistant bishops without resort to Parliament. Since then though some new dioceses have been created (e.g. Wakefield and Guildford), the process of appointing suffragan bishops has proceeded apace. Today there are more suffragans than there are diocesans in the Church of England. The average regular church-goer in the Church of England is far more likely to encounter a suffragan bishop than his diocesan. A suffragan bishop is better than no bishop at all, but he is an unsatisfactory substitute: he does not have the responsibility of a diocesan and is therefore less well qualified to represent the great church. The growth of suffragans in the Church of England indicates a process of bureaucratization. The process should be stopped and reversed. At whatever cost to social prestige or hallowed historical associations, vast sees should be subdivided and the diocesan enabled once more to experience a personal relationship with all his clergy and with many more of his laity. Instead of forty odd dioceses and fifty odd suffragans we should have two hundred diocesans. Until the church of England takes some such action we are not likely to make many converts to the beauty of episcopacy.

The Roman Catholic Church also employs auxiliary bishops on an alarming scale. But here we can find another corruption of episcopacy as well. When some priest is appointed to an important office in the Curia (the bureaucracy of the Roman Catholic Church in the Vatican) he is often consecrated bishop purely in order to enhance his status. He is appointed to some nominal see and has no pastoral or episcopal duties. Thus episcopacy is used as an honour not as an office. This goes further in the direction of rendering meaningless the spiritual office of a bishop. As long as the Roman Catholic Church continues to exist in a condition of acute and historically unprecedented centralization it will no doubt continue to need a central bureaucracy. But that is no reason why it should in the process degrade and corrupt the bishop's office. Let us hope that the day will soon come when Monsignor Smith can move from his diocesan post to becoming an official in the Vatican without in the process being made bishop of Rumti-Foo.

We have had to make careful distinctions about the various ordained ministries as they exist in the Christian church today. But the way forward lies not in a process of condemning or rejecting our respective ministries, but in the endeavour to inaugurate a method of convergence and integration of all ministries into one ministry which can be recognized by the great majority of Christians. There can be no reasonable doubt that such a ministry, whenever it comes, will be episcopal.

7

Particular Problems

1. The Ordination of Women to the Priesthood

We have already seen that anything recongizable as an ordained ministry in the traditional sense of the term only appears at the end of the New Testament period. Certainly when it does appear there is no evidence that any women were admitted to it, and it does not seem to have occurred to anyone that they should. An argument against the ordination of women to the priesthood is sometimes drawn from the fact that Jesus did not include any women among the twelve. But, since we have already agreed that the twelve were not intended to be ordained clergy in the traditional sense, not very much can be made of this argument. For any direct evidence on the question of ordination of women, therefore, must turn to the writings of Paul and his successors.

(a) *I Corinthians 11.2,8,12.* In this passage Paul is arguing in favour of women wearing their hair long and of their covering their heads when engaged in public worship. But in the course of his argument he tells us something of what he believes about the proper relation of women to men. In verse 3 he says that the man is the head of the woman, as Christ is the head of man. By this he means that man has a natural authority over women. In verses 8-9 he explains this by adding that the man was not created for the sake of the woman, but the woman for the sake of the man, and this is shown by the fact that the woman was created from the man and not the man from the woman. He is referring, of course, to the second creation account of Genesis 2.21–23. He elaborates this in verse 12 by saying that, though the woman was made from the man, man comes by means of the woman. He is referring presumably to the natural process of gestation and birth.

From this we may certainly conclude that Paul would not have approved of women bearing formal authority in the church, not at least if it meant women having authority over men. But we should observe that Paul is not here considering the question of authority in the church but of authority at the natural level. His argument would be just as strong against a woman headmistress in a mixed school, a woman prime minister, or a woman judge. If therefore we are to quote I Cor. 11 against the ordination of women, we must be prepared to reject a great deal else that is considered perfectly legitimate by the vast majority of Christians.

Again, Paul's argument is based on a literal interpretation of Gen 2. Paul accepted the view of Gen. 2 common to most Jews of his day: he thought it was a straightforward account of the actual historical origin of mankind. Today, if we are not to be intellectually dishonest, we cannot possibly accept this. Though there is much to be learned of value from the story in Gen.2, it is not a literal scientifically accurate account of the origin of man. For that we must turn to the biologists.

On the other side , we can see from this passage that Paul seems to have no objection to women praying aloud or prophesying in church; see verse 5. Whatever 'prophesying' meant, it must imply some sort of comprehensible utterance which was regarded as likely to benefit the church. Also verse 12, to which we have already referred, is only written in order to reinforce the argument of verse 11, which is that men and women are mutually interdependent. We may add that Paul himself used the ministry of women extensively. We have the example of Chloe (I Cor. 1.11), and in I Cor.16.19 Prisca is mentioned with her husband Aquila. Even more remarkable is the place which women hold in the greetings in Rom. 16. Prisca and Aquila are mentioned again as Paul's fellow workers (16.3), Phoebe earns special praise as 'the helper of many, including myself' (16.2); and, as we have already noted, it is even possible that a woman is described as 'well-known among the apostles'.

In short, this passage from I Corinthians 11 either proves far too much about the place of women in the church, or is to be regarded as having the same amount of authority as Paul's views on women wearing hats in church.

(*b*) *I Corinthians 14.34–35*. Here it is said in plain terms that women must be silent when the local community gathers for worship. They are to be subordinate (we must understand 'to their husbands'). The reference to the law is no doubt to Gen. 3.16, where Eve after the fall is told: 'yet your desire shall be for your husband, and he shall rule over you'. If they fail to understand anything that is said, they can ask their husbands afterwards, for 'it is disgraceful for a woman to speak in church'.

This is a puzzling passage, since it seems to contradict I Cor. 11.5, where Paul certainly contemplates the possibility of a woman uttering prayer or prophecy in church, and does not disapprove. It is not surprising therefore that many scholars hold these two verses to be a later interpolation. This is not arbitrary speculation, for there is textual evidence to support this suggestion. In some early manuscripts verses 34–35 do not come after verse 33, but after verse 40. The main witnesses to this form of the text are the mysterious Codex Bezae, G (a ninth cent Greek uncial manuscript now in Dresden), some manuscripts of the Old Latin, and a very few Fathers. On the other side are an early papyrus fragment, the third hand in Codex Sinaiticus, Codex Alexandrinus, Codex Vaticanus, and many other Greek uncials and other authorities. It must be said that the great bulk of the manuscript tradition is against the transposition. But one must ask, how did the transposition come about? Transposition can certainly in some cases be a sign of an interpolation. A good example is Rom. 16.25–27, which comes in some manuscripts at the end of Rom. 14 and in some at the end of ch. 15. A great many scholars would regard Rom. 16.25–27, as not from Paul's pen. The conjunction of the apparent inconsistency with I Cor. 11.5 together with the evidence for displacement makes out quite a strong case for the theory of interpolation. Some have even suggested that the interpolation was made by the author of the Pastoral Epistles.

However, let us suppose for the sake of argument that Paul did write I Cor. 14.34–35, and that the inconsistency with 11.5 can somehow be explained. The passage can hardly be used with very much force by Anglicans at any rate, as an argument against the ordination of women, since throughout the Anglican Communion we have ignored its injunction from at least the last ten years. We have allowed women to become Readers; we are often using them to administer the consecrated elements in the eucharist, which in itself requires that they speak in church. After approving the admission of women to Readership, to use this passage as an argument against their admission to the priesthood would be to incur the charge of hypocrisy.

(c) *I Timothy 2.11–15*. This passage seems to follow on from the last. Women must be silent and obedient. The writer does not permit women to teach, nor to domineer over a man. The precept is backed up by evidence from the story of the fall. Woman, it is implied, is more gullible than man. She was beguiled by the serpent, as Adam was not. However, she may be saved by childbearing. There are other interpretations of verse 15, but this is far the most likely.

It is not likely that Paul wrote these words, since in Galatians and Romans he quite certainly holds that no one can be saved by anything that they do or suffer. We also gain the impression from Rom. 7 at least that the basic sin which caused the fall was pride, rather than sensuality of gullibility, as is implied here. We note, of course, that the argument depends on a literal interpretation of Gen. 3, with the possibility of a little legendary embroidery (the view that Eve was actually seduced by the serpent). We have already pointed out the difficulties which this involves.

But the most important feature about this passage from the point of view of its relevance to the question of the ordination of women is that it is almost certainly not from the pen of St Paul. The great majority of scholars are now agreed that the Pastoral Epistles are not by Paul, but by some admirer of his who wrote perhaps forty years after his death. This would explain the incompatibility between the theology of man implied here and that of the genuine Paul. So this passage does not have Paul's authority behind it. When viewed on its own it must be regarded as one of the less important passages in the New Testament. In any case we in the Anglican tradition (and this applies to the Roman Catholic Church also) have already ignored the teaching of this passage, for we do permit women to teach. Indeed we encourage them to do so. It is therefore too late for Anglicans to cite this passage as a witness against the desirability of ordaining women to the priesthood.

There seem to be five arguments, apart from the arguments from scripture, which are used by the opponents of the ordination of women to the priesthood to-day. We can ignore the crude and superstitious refusal to accept the consecrated elements from the hand of a woman which one sometimes encounters. These arguments are as follows:

1. 'The church up to this point in its history has never ordained women to the priesthood. Such a move has the entire witness of tradition against it. So violent a break with tradition in the matter of orders should only be made with the consent of the whole church. The ministry is not ours to do what we like with; it is a gift descending to us from the time of the apostles. One branch of the church, such as is the Anglican Communion, is not justified in taking unilateral action in this matter.'

2. 'For two thousand years the church has done without women priests. Why this pressure for ordaining them now?'

3. 'Christ incarnate was a man. The priest represents Christ; therefore the priest must be a male.'

4. 'God is Father; the priest represents God, therefore the priest must be capable of being a father, not a mother.'

5. 'The very notion of a priestess is pagan not Christian.'

Let us now consider these arguments in order:

1. The mere fact that something has never been done is not an insuperable argument against it. The same argument could be used against having women as Readers, or allowing them to administer the elements at the eucharist. Tradition is just as much opposed to these innovations yet we have accepted them without difficulty. The argument about awaiting the consent of the whole church is a way of postponing the ordination of women until the Greek Kalends. There never will be a time within the foreseeable future when what the proponents of this argument understand as the church will be sufficiently united to agree on anything. Indeed this argument depends on a doctrine of the church which we have already rejected, i.e. that it consists of those bodies of Christians who have preserved intact the episcopal ministry from medieval times. Nor can we honestly regard the ministry as a gift which has descended from the apostles. It has very much the same authority as have the canon of the New Testament, the earliest creeds, and the earliest liturgies. None of these today do we receive with complete literal adherence. The 'catholic' ministry cannot claim to

have God's approval in the way that other forms of ministry have not. It is not therefore an unalterable system which we are forbidden to modify. It is sometimes added by those who use this argument that if the Anglican communion as a whole were to ordain women to the priesthood this would constitute an insuperable obstacle to reunion with the Roman Catholic Church. This is a most doubtful statement. There is plenty of pressure within that church for the ordination of women. Some of their best theologians have said that they can see no objection to it.

2. Why this pressure today to ordain women? Because today in the West, and increasingly in other parts of the world, social circumstances have made it possible. A good analogy is the attitude of the church towards slavery. For centuries the church accepted slavery as part of society. And, when the medieval form of slavery, serfdom, began to wane in Europe, the church complacently accepted a new and much more drastic form of slavery, the kidnapping and deportation of Africans in order to make them work in the American plantations. Only in the eighteenth century did Christian opinion begin to turn against slavery as incompatible with Christianity. Today in the West we are experiencing a very far-reaching social change whereby women can now have a career of their own without foregoing marriage. Simply because this has not been possible before, we are not justified in denying *a priori* that the Holy Spirit can call women to the vocation of priesthood.

We will take (3) and (4) together. Both arguments that the priest represents God or Christ directly. This is not so. Christian ministerial priesthood comes through the church. It is the church that in the first place inherited the priesthood of Christ. But the church is made up of women as well as men, so women are as eligible to be priests as are men. In any case, why should maleness be singled out as an attribute of Christ which must not be omitted from Christ's representative? It would be as logical to say 'Christ was a Jew, therefore all priests must be Jews'. We must also maintain that when we call God Father we are using an image. Like all language which we apply to God, it can only be used in an analogical, quasi-symbolical sense. God is as much Mother as he is Father. It would be absurd to say that God is male, not female. Both these arguments, (3) and (4), carry the extreme implication that, even if the church wanted to ordain a woman a priest, it could not do so.

'Women are biologically incapable of receiving priesthood. If they were to go through a ceremony of ordination, their priesthood would not work. Nothing would happen if they celebrated the eucharist: the necessary change in the elements would not occur.' One has only to state the implications of these arguments to realize how absurd they are. They degrade priesthood to the level of a quasi-mechanical operation.

The final argument (5), describes women priests as 'priestesses' and claims that this is a pagan concept. In the sense used in this argument the notion of priest is equally pagan. The New Testament priest is not a hierophant appointed to offer sacrifices. Christian priesthood is *sui generis*, and depends on what Christ has done and is doing *in the church*. We only use 'priest' of the Christian minister in a derived sense which depends on the priesthood of the church. Moreover, in those parts of the Anglican Communion where women have been ordained to the priesthood there is no suggestion that their priestly ministry is ineffective, offensive, or unorthodox. Quite the reverse. They have proved themselves effective and acceptable ministers of work and sacrament. Naturally, there is a specifically feminine way of exercising priesthood, just as there is a specifically feminine way of preaching the word or of carrying out pastoral ministry. But it is none the worse for that. We have still to explore fully the way in which God wills women to exercise the priesthood. But we cannot do this until we decide to ordain them priests.

Consequently the church universal, and the Anglican Communion in particular, is entirely justified in ordaining women to the priesthood, where social circumstances make such a move acceptable.

2. The Papacy

There is one school of thought in Protestantism that would simply dismiss the question of the papacy with Voltaire's cry when he was writing about the persecution of French Protestants under Louis XV: 'Écrasez l'infâme!', 'Remove the shameful thing!'. In other words, they will have nothing to do with the papacy. This is not an attitude which thoughtful and well-informed Anglicans ought to adopt. In the sixteenth century the Church of England for very good reasons repudiated the authority of the Pope. We believe it was a right move at the time and we confess that the Church of England benefited from this break in communion. But neither the Church of England nor the papacy has remained unchanged since then. We are not therefore justified in dismissing the very notion of a papacy out of hand. As Anglicans we must give careful consideration to the question of the position and authority of the Bishop of Rome.

The evidence from the New Testament which has been traditionally cited in defence of the divine right of the Bishop of Rome to have jurisdiction over all other Christians is, in the light of the critical study of the Bible, not at all impressive. Peter certainly had a position of leadership in the early church, but it is by no means clear that this position stemmed from the direct authority of Jesus himself. The key passage is Matt. 16.16–20. It is not at all certain that Jesus did actually utter the words recorded here. If he did utter them, or something like them, it does not follow that this constituted an act of appointing Peter alone as head of the church. Most of the promises made in this passage are also made to all the disciples in Matt. 18.18–20. What evidence we have for Peter's leadership in the rest of the New Testament does not suggest that anyone regarded him as leader by divine appointment. If Peter wrote I Peter (which is not very probable), he shows no awareness in the epistle of his unique position.

In any case there is no evidence at all in the New Testament or anywhere else that Jesus intended the leadership of the church to be perpetually connected with the See of Rome. Peter did not found the Roman church. It was already securely founded when Paul wrote his letter to the Christians in Rome. Peter probably did die as a martyr in Rome; but his arrival in the city must have come after Paul's writing his epistle. The later belief that Peter (or Peter and Paul) consecrated the first bishop for the church in Rome is not borne out by the earliest evidence. Indeed it is very doubtful whether the conservative Roman church had any figure which we could identify with a bishop presiding on his own before about the middle of the second century.

Modern Roman Catholic scholars, who are fully aware of these difficulties, tend to talk about 'a Petrine ministry' which the papacy could exercise in the church. The suggestion is that the position of Peter in the early church can afford an analogy for the position which the See of Rome might occupy in a future re-united church. The idea is not to be dismissed without consideration as long as two conditions are observed:

(a) There must be no suggestion that the See of Rome has any divine or scriptural right to jurisdiction over the rest of the church.

(b) A 'Petrine ministry' must be regarded as a possible option for the church in the West at any rate, but not as mandatory for all, or indeed any, Christians.

We must next state categorically that it is monstrous that one diocese should claim absolute, despotic, or dominant power over the whole of the rest of the church. This claim has been made by a number of Popes, most notably by Boniface VIII in 1302, and has never been repudiated. But the mere notion of one see having superior status and authority is not necessarily to be rejected. We in the Church of England have inherited a system in which the See of Canterbury has superior status over all the other dioceses in England. Increasingly the Archbishop of Canterbury is being accorded a position of authority (though not of jurisdiction) in the entire Anglican Communion. When we study the history of the church in Western Europe we see that from very early times the Bishop of Rome has been regarded as Patriarch of the West, a position which the Eastern Orthodox Church is still willing to give him. For at least nine hundred years of its history the Church of England acknowledged some sort of papal jurisdiction. The definite and demanding character of that jurisdiction grew steadily throughout that period until by the beginning of the sixteenth century it had become intolerable. We should not deny that on some occasions the papacy has stood on the side of the spiritual freedom of the church against the pretensions of medieval monarchs. In the reign of Henry VIII what the Church of England repudiated was the *tyranny* of the Bishop of Rome. If the Bishop of Rome were to cease to be a tyrant and behave like a spiritual father, who asks only for a status of honour not of jurisdiction, an opportunity to serve and not to command, a position free from both adulation and compulsion, there is no reason why Anglicans should not give him careful attention. Ever since the Reformation there have been Anglicans who have professed themselves quite willing to enter into communion with a papacy suitably reformed.

What we have in mind is the acknowledgment on the part of the Church of England at least of the Pope as Patriarch of the West, on the analogy of the way in which the Archbishop of Canterbury is a sort of Patriarch without jurisdiction of the Anglican Communion. This would not give the Pope the right to interfere in our episcopal elections; we would be completely free to order our own affairs. The Pope's position would be a primacy of honour.

However, we may well ask whether we want a *universal* primacy. Is there any reason why American, Japanese, African or Indian Christians should acknowledge the primacy of the Bishop of Rome? The truth is that the notion of a universal jurisdiction for the Pope grew up in medieval Europe when the size of the world was unknown and a universal primacy meant a European primacy. Even that was never conceded by the church in Eastern Europe. Only with the spread of Christianity to America and after that to the third world did the concept emerge of a primacy which should be acknowledged by all Christians everywhere in the world. Thus stated, the idea seems unjustified. Why should Christians in New Guinea acknowledge the primacy of the Bishop of Rome? Such a primacy is a leading feature of the church in Western Europe and should be regarded as a purely Western phenomenon. We have no more justification for exporting papal primacy to the third world than we have for building Gothic churches there.

We cannot reject as inconceivable for Anglicans some sort of a primacy for the See of Rome, in the West at least. This does not mean of course that we could possibly accept the Pope as he is now or as he has been for many centuries. Indeed it may truly be said that the present position of the Pope is more intolerable for Anglicans from the theological point of view than it was at the Reformation. Since the Reformation the Pope has not only been declared infallible under certain conditions, but he has, without consulting a council of the church, even of his own church, defined a number of dogmas as necessarily to be accepted by all orthodox Christians (Immaculate Conception 1854, Assumption of the Blessed Virgin Mary 1950). It is not only grossly immoral Popes, such as John XII (ob.964) or Alexander VI (ob.1503), but also more recent Popes of impeccable private morality who have proved a scandal to the church as a whole. Future historians may very well conclude that Pius IX by his identification of the church with reactionary politics, and Pius X by his inflexible opposition to any accommodation between Christian belief and modern knowledge (coupled with his ferocious anti-modernist campaign), did more long-term harm to the church as a whole than ever did any of the Renaissance Popes with their mistresses and their dynastic ambitions. But Pius X at least, far from being repudiated, has been actually canonized. It is conceivable that in the future a reformed papacy could be a blessing to the church as a whole. At times in the past it has been a scandal and even today is a doubtful asset.

However, there is no reason why we should not attempt to conjecture what advantages might accrue to the church from a reformed papacy. Let us then suppose that the Bishop of Rome has been accepted by all Anglicans as Patriarch of the Western Church, without jurisdiction but enjoying a primacy of honour. What benefits might we expect to receive from this? We can see three.

1. Acknowledgment of the See of Rome as the supreme see in the Western Church should help to rid the Church of England of its insularity. This besetting temptation to a church which has been out of communion with the rest of Christendom for more than four hundred years. Though the concept of national autonomous churches is one which is congenial to Anglicans, this carries with it the temptation to confuse Christianity with national interests, even the temptation to become nothing more than the religious voice of the nation. A link with a centre outside England, one open to influences from all over the world, might counteract this tendency. The papacy could also act as an international clearing-house for the church as a whole, where new ideas from all over the world could be shared (instead of being a place where new ideas are suppressed). It might be the place where we could have a fully Christian university, instead of having several Roman Catholic ones as is the case at present. A link with Rome might strengthen some national churches under pressure from nationalist governments. In a word, the papacy could be a rallying point for the entire church.

2. The See of Rome might provide a supreme court of appeal for all Christians. It acts in this capacity at the moment for all Roman

Catholics. But Anglicans would want to see the appeal procedure greatly modified compared with what it is now. Proceedings would have to be more open. Proper opportunities for the defendants to make their case without prejudice should be provided. Judges should be drawn from all over the church, not from the Curia. The great objection to the present procedure as far as concerns cases of heresy and theological judgment is this: it is not by any means certain that the judges are always competent to assess the rights and wrongs of the question (this was certainly the situation when Edward Schillebeeckx was examined); it is not clear that the accused is allowed to defend himself fully and without prejudice; and the judges do not always give reasons for their verdict. But if these grave deficiencies could be removed the papacy could certainly act as an appeal court for all Christians.

3. The Pope could act as a representative figure for all Christians. Here we are on difficult ground, for in fact the present Pope, John Paul II, does in some measure act in this capacity already. A Pope of charismatic quality, who is an expert in the art of public appearance, has arisen in an epoch when modern technology has made it possible as never before for one man to speak and appear before millions of people. Modern methods of travel enable him to visit every part of the globe relatively easily. Whether in fact this is the job of the Bishop of Rome may well be questioned, and is questioned by some Roman Catholics today. The cultivation of the arts of popular communication does not necessarily improve the judgment, or ultimately enhance the reputation, of one who is certainly the representative of the largest body of Christians in the world. Notwithstanding we must admit that if there is to be one single figure representing all Christians, there are at the moment no rivals to the Bishop of Rome in the field. Perhaps we should conclude that, since modern methods of communication make it inevitable that some representative must be found, we should consider how best the Pope can be induced to be a satisfactory representative of all Christians, not only of Roman Catholic Christians.

The notion of a national church, independent of all external control, is one which is congenial to Anglicanism. This is because Anglicanism as such came into existence when in 1534 Henry VIII induced Parliament to declare that the Bishop of Rome has no authority in the realm of England. This move was based on the assumption that a national church has a right to order its own affairs without the interference of any outside ecclesiastical jurisdiction. In the subsequent development of Anglicanism the tendency had been to organize new provinces on national lines: we have the Episcopal Church of the United States of America, the Anglican Church of Canada, the Anglican Church of Australia, etc. This principle is not always adhered to. In West and East Africa provinces span several national churches, but each national church still preserves its own identity. Where Anglicanism is newly planted the aim is always to set up an indepenent national church.

In the past this practice certainly led to Erastianism as far as the British Isles is concerned. This is a state of affairs in which the church is regarded as a department of state. From the Reformation until the nineteenth century with few exceptions the Church of England was the servant and tool of the crown. The fact that during the Commonwealth period episcopacy and monarchy were both abolished tended to cement this bond all the more strongly when the Restoration came. During the latter half of the seventeenth century and during the eighteenth century episcopal appointments were predominantly political. Bishops were expected to vote with the government in the House of Lords and promote government policy in their sees.

This connection began to be loosened in the nineteenth century, though the established church was still regarded as a bastion of the established order. But this disestablishment of the Church of Ireland in 1869 was a significant indication that the state had not much further use for the church. Today real relics of establishment remain, but the old sneer that the Church of England is the Tory party at prayer is no longer justified. Whatever the merits and demerits of the establishment of the Church of England, its leaders are no longer under any obligation to support the government. Parish clergy are no longer regarded as mouthpieces of government policy.

There are, of course, dangers inherent in the scheme of the national church, as we have indicated above. One is the danger of isolation, a weakness from which the Church of England certainly suffered between 1560 and 1960. Even in the contemporary Church of England indications of insularity are not far to seek:

it is almost inconceivable, for instance, that the Archbishop of Canterbury should not be a graduate of either Oxford or Cambridge. Nor is it at all likely that he should ever be appointed from among the ranks of bishops in the rest of the Anglican Communion. Another danger is that a national church could become merely the sounding-board for nationalist sentiment, consecrating the nation's ambitions and blessing the nation's arms however they are used. The Church of England has not always successfully resisted this temptation, witness its behaviour during the First World War. But national churches are under no moral obligation nor historical necessity to behave like this. A national church is well placed to act as the nation's conscience, as to some extent happened during and after the Falklands conflict in 1982. A national church may also be in a good position to maintain links with Christians in enemy countries during the war, and to renew them immediately after hostilities are ended. The history of the Second World War gives some evidence that this actually took place.

It is possible for a national church to act responsibly towards the nation even when it only represents a small minority of population. In India for example the Christian community as a whole, though by far the smallest of the three main religions of India, has on occasion been able to act in some areas as something of a mediator between Hindu and Muslim, and in a small degree to set an example in service to the victims of discord and violence. It may even be that on some occasions a national church can voice the genuine and laudable sentiment of the nation. This happened at the time of the Glorious Revolution at the end of the seventeenth century. It is happening today in Poland – which shows incidentally that the concept of a national church is not incompatible with a very considerable degree of external ecclesiastical influence.

We will make two final comments on the question of the papacy:

1. If the Church of England ever were top integrate itself into a system whereby the See of Rome was acknowledged as the patriarchate of the West, it ought to review its own organization. At the moment the Church of England is divided into only two provinces, about forty dioceses, and about seventy suffragan bishops. We should have more provinces: a province for London is under consideration; there was once for a brief period in Anglo-Saxon times

a province of Mercia. This could well be revived. Our dioceses are far too big and need to be split up into at least twice as many as we have now, better still four times as many. We need to do away with those bureaucratic anomalies, suffragan bishops. Only thus will we equip ourselves to be integrated into a truly European church.

2. The papacy must be decentralized, decurialized, purged of its age-old atmosphere of absolutism. The unpleasant aura of infallibility at present hanging over the Pope makes it impossible to admit doctrinal errors in the past. Such a scheme seems utopian, but is ardently desired by many thoughtful Roman Catholics. To sum up: Anglicans do not need to reject the notion of a papal primacy, but the papacy must first be reformed to an extent to which, it must be admitted, few Roman Catholics are prepared to recognize.

3. Schemes of Reunion

This is a subject about which it is quite impossible to be 'objective'. There is no viewpoint within the church from which one can make impartial judgments about the merits of this or that reunion scheme, because every Christian exists in one denomination or another. A viewpoint of someone who is outside the church altogether would be equally biassed, since such a person could hardly possess any Christian convictions about how the church might be reunited. He would not even share with someone inside the church that element of tradition which each denomination holds. The only way in which one could create the illusion of impartiality would be if one believed that one's own denomination was the true church and that all other bodies were more or less outside the church. In that case there would be no issue of 'reunion', since strictly speaking the church had never been divided. It would merely be a question of how best to persuade the apostates to return.

We write, then, from the point of view of Anglicans. At first sight this might appear to be a very suitable point of view from which to consider the reunion of the church. Anglicanism claims to be both Catholic and Protestant. It has often been described as the *via media*, the middle way between Roman Catholicism and Protestantism. It has sometimes been described as the bridge church. But in actual experience the Church of England at least has not proved to

be a brilliant example of a bridge between Catholicism and Protestantism, at any rate as far as concerns reunion schemes. Indeed,
looking at the history of the last fifty years, the Church of England
might better be described as a ridge church, the hard unscaleable
ridge that prevents the successful climbing of the peak. A brief
review of the attitude of the Church of England towards reunion
schemes should bear this out.

In 1947, after twenty-eight years of negotiation the four Southern
Indian dioceses of the Church of India, Pakistan, Burma and
Ceylon (i.e. the Anglican Church in the sub-continent) entered
into corporate union with the Methodist Church in South India,
the South India United Church (itself a union of Presbyterians and
Congregationalists), and the Basel Mission Church (European
Continental Reformed), to form the Church of South India. Episcopal government was accepted by the uniting churches and nine
new bishops were consecrated on the day of inauguration, but no
attempt was made to re-ordain or re-commission ministers who did
not already have episcopal ordination. The Lambeth Conference of
1930 had agreed that if union went ahead on those principles the
Anglican Communion should, and the Church of England would,
enter into full communion with the newly united church. The next
Lambeth Conference met in 1948 and proceeded to go back on
this undertaking. The Anglo-Catholic party in the Church of
England had made a great furore at the time of the inauguration of
CSI, claiming that the mere acceptance of episcopal government
was not enough: non-episcopally ordained ministers should be re-
commissioned by bishops and some agreement reached as to the
necessity of episcopacy for the existence of the church. The
bishops of Lambeth in 1948 were so much impressed by these
protests that they withheld recognition of CSI and laid it down that
any future union schemes to which Anglicans were parties should
include some arrangement whereby non-episcopally ordained ministers were re-commissioned or conditionally ordained by bishops.

This had two consequences in the area of reunion negotiations:
the first affected both North India and Pakistan. Here there had
been strong pressure for reunion, much strengthened by the example of South India. In 1970 a united church came into existence,
the Church of North India, and its counterparts the Church of
Pakistan, and when Bangladesh came into existence the Church of

Bangladesh. But here the union scheme involved a ceremony in which a commissioning was given by bishops, as well as by presbyters of the non-episcopal churches, to all ministers of the uniting churches. What is more, any minister in future coming from outside into the CNI must submit to this ceremony. From the theological point of view, this has the curious consequence that, whereas the Church of South India accepted the orders of all the uniting churches, the Church of North India recognized nobody's orders and appears to possess a ministry which exists in proud isolation from the rest of the world. But we must remember that CNI succeeded in uniting a wider range of traditions than did CSI, including both Baptists and Brethren though its actual membership is much smaller than is that of CSI.

A second consequence was that a reunion scheme proposed in England itself between the Church of England and the Methodist Church in England included an arrangement for mutual commissioning of ministers. This scheme at one time seemed to have good prospects of success. There are no serious points of doctrinal difference between Anglicans and Methodists; the Anglican-Methodist schism is not more than two hundred years old. Most Methodists have no objection on principle to an episcopally ordered church (they have one themselves in the USA), But the scheme collapsed in 1972. The necessary two thirds majority of each order (bishops, clergy, and laity) voting separately in the General Synod could not be obtained in the house of clergy, though it was achieved in the other two houses. The failure was the consequence of an ill-omened alliance between Anglo-Catholics who were not satisfied with the terms in which ministers were to be re-commissioned and Evangelicals who wanted Methodist orders accepted without any re-commissioning. An alternative scheme was hatched up by the leaders of these two elements, quite impractical in itself, but enough to sow doubts in the minds of some of the representatives of the clergy in the General Synod. By this time the Church of England had come to terms with the Church of South India. In 1955 both houses of Convocation agreed to recognize the orders of those episcopally ordained in the CSI and a measure of intercommunion was established. Indeed by the seventies the CSI had almost become the model of what a united church should be in the eyes of many Anglo-Catholics, and at the time of the failure of

the Anglican-Methodist scheme some Anglo-Catholics were in-
genuously arguing that a simple straightforward scheme such as
that followed by CSI was much preferable to dubious attempts to
devise a form of commissioning that would satisfy both Anglicans
and Methodists.

Between the failure of the Anglican-Methodist scheme and
today one other reunion scheme has been attempted in England.
This was known as covenanting: all churches involved in this
scheme were to covenant to come together into one organically
united church within a certain period. In the meantime episcopal
consecration would be conferred on certain chosen leaders of the
non-episcopal churches engaged in covenanting; a form of mutual
recognition of ministers by mutual laying on of hands would be
accepted by all the ministers of the covenanting churches, and
plans would be laid for bringing the covenanting churches into
closer union in a series of stages lasting over a period of years. This
scheme cast its net wider than had the last one. It included the
Church of England, the Methodist Church in England, large elements of the United Reformed Church (an already existing union
of Presbyterians and Congregationalists), the Moravian Church,
and the Disciples of Christ. But the elaborate nature of the arrange-
ments for covenanting offered from the first too large a target for
ill-disposed critics. Perhaps too much was conceded to each successive criticism, so that the scheme underwent a series of last-
minute modifications. At any rate in 1982 this scheme met the
same fate as had the previous one; it gained a two-thirds majority of
the house of bishops and of the house of laity in the General Synod,
but failed to gain a two-thirds majority in the house of clergy. It is
probably true to say that another formidable difficulty was the
question of the status of women ministers in the united Free
Churches. Opponents of the ordination of women to the priesthood
in the Church of England saw in this scheme a dangerous acceptance, in principle at least, of the possibility of women being accepted as priests in the Church of England. It need hardly be
pointed out that this objection rules out in advance any attempt
whatever to unite the Church of England with the Free Churches.

It is not surprising that after this experience of failure to agree on
any scheme of reunion Free Churchmen in England conclude that
the Church of England, far from being a bridge church, is in fact

completely incapable of uniting with the Free Churches on any terms whatever except those of complete adoption of an entirely Anglican church polity and order. Again and again Free Churchmen have been encouraged by specious promises of success, of apparently sincere assurances of the passionate desire on the part of Anglicans for union with their Free Church brethren – only to find at the last minute that the clergy in the General Synod do not share this desire and have no intention of compromising any of the claims of the established church in the interests of reunion. To be fair, one should say that it is not the majority of the clergy even in the General Synod who obstruct plans for reunion, but a sufficiently large minority. It may safely be conjectured that most of those clergy who do so obstruct the course of reunion are not very well read in modern theology or biblical criticism, and would probably profess a view of church order and of the origin of the ordained ministry very like that held by Bishop Charles Gore fifty years ago. Thus it would hardly be unreasonable to conclude that the Church of England is inhibited from uniting with any of the Free Churches by those who hold a theory of the origin of the ministry that no respectable modern scholar would defend. But such, unfortunately, is the situation.

It is still the case that the Church of England is immensely influential among the other members of the Anglican Communion. It is rare indeed for another Anglican province to take the initiative, whether theological or otherwise. We can, however, point to two examples of this in recent years. One we have already referred to: the Church of India, Pakistan, Burmah and Ceylon permitted four of its dioceses (Madras, Tirunelveli, Travancore, and Dornakal) to enter the Church of South India in 1947. Admittedly it did this under the conviction, based on what Lambeth 1930 had said, that this step had the approval of the rest of the Anglican Communion. The other example is more remarkable: several Anglican provinces have ordained women to the priesthood (the Episcopal Church of the USA; the Church of the Province of New Zealand; the Anglican Church of Canada; the Church of the Province of Kenya; the Diocese of Hong Kong and Macao). It seems unlikely that the Church of England itself will be able to hold out forever against the pressure to sanction the ordination of women in England also. However, though this would remove one great obstacle to the reunion of the Church of England with the Free Churches, it would not in itself resolve the problem.

We may draw a number of conclusions from the melancholy record of the last forty years about the prospects for reunion as far as Anglicans are concerned. We set out five conclusions as follows:

1. Reunion between the Church of England and the Roman Catholic Church, at least the entire Roman Catholic Church, seems extremely improbable in the foreseeable future. This is not only because Rome has never actually disavowed its claims to universal jurisdiction by divine right; nor only because it is by no means easy to see how the theologians could get round the very explicit statements of *Apostolicae Curae* without saying that Leo XIII was mistaken, which it seems most unlikely that they would be permitted to do. Actual theological differences, even conceivably differences about the nature of the Pope's supremacy, might in the present ecumenical climate be resolved. When theologians get together they often find that genuine agreement is not impossible. The difficulty of reunion between the Roman Catholic Church and the Church of England seems rather to be one of organization and structure. How could one huge community, making up half the Christians on this planet, ever circumvent the difficulties involved in recognizing the Church of England at one stroke? Highly centralized though the Church of Rome is, it seems impossible that any Pope, no matter how influential, could carry with him all the members of his church, many of whom will never have heard of the Church of England, and most of whom know nothing about it. This is true even without taking into consideration the difficulties on the side of the Church of England. There is still some truth in Hensley Henson's dictum that the sole remaining relic of religious belief in the minds of many Englishmen is a prejudice against the Pope.

It is possible, however, that some form of union between Roman Catholics and Anglicans might be achieved somewhere outside these islands. Other parts of the world are not cursed with our history of mutual persecution. African bishops and clergy, for example, on both sides of the divide do not necessarily perceive such a very insuperable difference between Roman Catholics and Anglicans. In the northern area of Mozambique, an inaccessible region, there already exists a situation of mutual intercommunion between the two churches: 'In this remote diocese both Anglican and Roman Catholic priests serve the same congregations and Christians of both denominations are baptised and confirmed together, and receive communion together.'[1] This is indeed an area where there is a hostile Marxist government in power. But what has been done in time of emergency need not be repudiated when the emergency is over. It may well be that Marxism is God's scourge by which the timid denominations will be compelled to come together. Something like this has already happened in China, though, as is so often the case where there is a repressive Communist régime, it is impossible to say with certainty how far we are hearing the genuine sentiments of church leaders and how far a mere echo of official party policy. At any rate the remnants of the small Anglican church in China have thrown in their lot with all the other Protestants, and most of the Roman Catholic Church seems to have broken off any relationship with Rome. This does not mean that there is any sign of official rapprochement between the pan-protestant church and the independent Roman Catholic church. It is possible that any such move would be frowned upon by the government. But one could without difficulty imagine a development taking place whereby the survivors of the Anglican Church, in a less stringent climate perhaps, made moves towards a relationship with the independent Roman Catholic church. Elements of the Roman Catholic Church that repudiate obedience to Rome tend to gravitate towards intercommunion with the Anglican Communion. This has happened in Holland, the USA, and the Philippines. Such developments might set a precedent for wider union.

2. If there is to be another successful scheme of reunion between Anglicans and Reformed or Lutheran Christians (and at least three such schemes have been proposed and failed outside these islands, to wit in Sri Lanka, Nigeria, and Canada), by far the best arrangement would consist in not attempting to re-commission or re-ordain some or all of the ministers of the uniting churches at the outset. The Church of South India method of requiring the clergy of the uniting churches nothing more than a pledge of obedience to the authority of the united church is simpler, more honest, and theologically much preferable. After all, even on the strictest interpretation of the necessity of episcopacy, who loses by such an arrangement? No ex-Anglican need be compelled to accept the

ministrations of a non-episcopally ordained minister. The members of the former non-episcopal churches simply continue to enjoy the services of the ministers they have always had. These ministers are gradually in the course of time replaced by episcopally ordained ministers acceptable to everyone in the united church. The standard objection to this arrangement is that if Anglicans consent to enter a united church some of whose ministers are not episcopally ordained they are compromising themselves. In fact, the only people in whose eyes we would be seriously compromised would perhaps be Roman Catholics and Orthodox, who do officially hold that without episcopal orders the sacraments cannot be validly celebrated. But, since the Roman Catholics officially maintained that our orders are invalid anyway, it hardly seems worth while avoiding being compromised in the interests of maintaining the purity of a ministry whose validity they do not accept. As for the Orthodox, though they normally appear intransigent about orders, they have a very useful principle called 'economy' which consists in claiming that in the interests of some higher good of the church what would normally be regarded as defective can in certain circumstances be accepted as sufficient. We might hope that such a principle might be applied in the situation which we have been envisaging.

3. We must admit that it is doubtful whether the Church of England as at present constituted is capable of uniting with anyone. Henry VIII could order the Convocations to renounce the obedience of the Pope, and his setting up of an independent Church of England was eventually accepted by two thirds of Englishmen. Today we have a democractic system of government of the church with a built-in system of checks such that it is always possible for a sufficiently large minority of the representatives of the clergy to block any move of any significance in any direction. During the last fifty years Anglo-Catholics have rejected almost every possible form of reunion with the Free Churches short of an arrangement whereby the Free Churches simply return to the Church of England on the Church of England's terms. Anglo-Catholics do so, as we have seen, under the influence of a theory of the origin of the ministry which is indefensible on scholarly grounds. But this does not prevent it being widely held. It is impossible to ensure that every representative of the clergy elected to General Synod should bring his reading up to date. Some are elected precisely because

they are not up to date. The same is true of course in a lesser degree of those Evangelicals who try to read directly out of the New Testament rules for church order, such as, for instance the rule that women should not be ordained. In any case most informed Free Churchmen must by now be thoroughly disillusioned with the Church of England as a negotiating body. It does not know its own mind; it goes back on its apparent commitments; as a church it is ecumenically discredited. Church of England leaders and theologians should cease from devising promising schemes for reunion with the Free Churches. Free Churchmen have surely had enough.

4. The movement towards the reunion of the church will not cease. It will go ahead at the grass roots. First laity, and then clergy, will pay less and less attention to church rules and denominational divisions. This is already beginning to happen. Young people, those of them who are loyal members of the Church of England, do not normally feel themselves bound not to take communion with Free Churchmen. There is much more going to and fro between the denominations among committed Christians than there was thirty years ago. This is not only on the part of those Evangelicals who always tend to ignore church rules and are accustomed to frequenting any minister who agrees with their outlook. This movement is even to be found among Roman Catholics. Many lay Roman Catholics have no scruples about communicating at Anglican altars, though the rules of their church strictly forbid such a thing. Indeed the free acceptance of the reality of Free Church as well as of Roman Catholic orders is often found nowadays among clergy of the Church of England of all schools of churchmanship. It is much more common today, for instance, for a Methodist minister to be accepted as virtually a member of a team ministry in an area where Anglicans and Methodists are working closely together. Such acceptance of Free Church orders is now quite common among all Church of England clergy except those of old-fashioned Anglo-Catholic convictions. There are even a few Roman Catholic priests who, with great courage, for they are far more vulnerable to episcopal discipline than are Church of England clergy, occasionally communicate with Anglicans.

We foresee, then, a gradual osmosis of all the main-line traditions in these islands at the grass roots. This will be a messy and often illogical process, but we Anglicans have brought it upon ourselves by our obstinate refusal in the Church of England to unite with any Free Churchmen on any terms except those which we should not expect them to accept. At least gradually increasing union by osmosis is preferable to our present disgraceful condition of disunion.

5. After even the most harmonious scheme of union there will always be groups of intransigents left who refuse to accept the will of the majority. If such people are on the Catholic side they tend to represent themselves as martyrs for the cause of the Catholic Church in the face of schism and heresy. If they are Protestant non-co-operators they simply form themselves into independent congregations, a state of affairs by no means uncongenial to their ecclesiology. It is useless trying to avoid the necessity of allowing for such 'rump' churches. If the union is a success, rump churches will probably die out during the ensuing generation. We could point to one such rump church in a large city in South India. This consisted of one congregation belonging to a certain tradition which refused to join the united church in 1947. A few years later it found itself unable to maintain a reasonably qualified minister and was relying entirely for its services (including sacramental services) on the good-will of the ministers of the church it had refused to join. Not surprisingly, within a very short time after that it had acceded to the union.

4. The Form of the Ministry

As we approach the subject of the form of the ministry today, certain propositions must first be laid down. The first is that there can be no talk of any contemporary form of ministry claiming institution by Christ or his apostles in such a way that it bears dominical authority in a line of succession of ministers ordaining each other independently of the rest of the church. Historical scholarship has laid the conventional doctrine of apostolic succession to rest, and the sooner this is accepted by all thinking Christians the better for the prospects of Christian unity and good understanding between Christians of different traditions. The same applies to the old and cherished idea that some denominations today possess, unlike others, a 'scriptural' ministry, that is a form of ministry which is authorized in scripture as official or valid or universal or original, whether this be presbyterian or episcopal or any other. A careful examination of the New Testament yields no satisfactory evidence for such a conclusion. The New Testament witnesses to the very beginnings, fragmentary, gradual, not fully formed, of an official ministry of some sort, but that is all that we can say. The pages preceding this one have tried to make this clear. The ministry as we know it stems from the action of the early church, and has the authority of the church, and if it bears the authority of Christ, as it does, this is because the whole church, as a priestly, commissioned, evangelizing body, bears the authority of Christ. The minister, whatever office he or she holds, represents Christ in the church and not Christ independently of the church. The official ministry is a development, as the canon of the New Testament, the creeds and the liturgy are developments. This does not mean that the Bible is irrelevant to the form of the ministry. It tells us what is to be ministered – the gospel – and how it is to be maintained, i.e. in what spirit and with what intentions and purposes. But on the form of the ministry it throws no certain light.

Next, we must distinguish the subject of the efficacy of ministry and sacraments from that of the form of the ministry. It must be obvious to any impartial observer that almost all forms of Christian ministry produce among those to whom the ministry is directed the fruits of the Holy Spirit, the signs of a good Christian life, holiness, charity, self-sacrifice, an attractive and lovely character. This is not, of course, an automatic process, but we can confidently say that in every denomination such fruits of the Spirit appear among some of their members. This can only be because the Holy Spirit chooses to use their ministry and their sacraments. There may be some exceptions to this rule, sects where hatred and bitterness or sheer folly appear to have driven out all other possibilities, or churches so corrupt and remote from the Christian tradition that they seem to have forgotten the Holy Spirit. But they are few and in these cases it is not the form of the ministry that is at fault, but something else. In these circumstances, to employ the category of validity or invalidity to describe ministry and sacraments of any denomination is meaningless. It seems likely that the Holy Spirit does not recognize such a category, and neither should we. If we can see the Holy Spirit at work in any body of Christians, this means that they are in Christ, for we must not separate the Spirit and Christ, though we may observe that different individuals, and perhaps different communities, have different ways, perhaps even different degrees, of responding to Christ.

Thirdly, all forms of ministry inevitably show some signs of their origin in human society. For instance, episcopacy might be said to suggest an aristocratic society, the Kirk Session a bourgeois society and the Pentecostal ministry a proletarian society. This is an unavoidable phenomenon of all terrestrial things, and applies to the Bible as much as to the ministry. Similarly, all forms of ministry can suffer abuse and become corrupt. Episcopacy can become tyranny, presbyterianism can succumb to narrow-minded doctrinaire bigotry and congregationalism or Methodist ministry can turn into the rule of the uninstructed mob. We should not judge any form of ministry by its worst examples.

In short, the form of the church's ministry is neither optional nor sacrosanct. Because no form is directly authorized by the New Testament, this does not mean that any and every form of ministry will suffice, any more than any list of books of the New Testament or any form of creed will suffice. One particular form of ministry did develop and establish itself universally. On the other hand, no form of ministry is so securely authenticated that it must be immediately accepted as that which is alone in accordance with the will of Christ.

If these preliminary observations are understood and accepted, we next proceed to point out that one form of ministry, and one alone, has in the course of history emerged as the standard, traditional, universal form, universal in that it was accepted universally for at least one thousand three hundred years and still is the form adopted by the great majority of Christians. We mean the form of episcopal government of the church. We do not commend in equivalent terms what has been often termed (and not least by Anglicans) the 'threefold ministry' of bishop, priest and deacon. We have already shown that those denominations who put forward the claims of this 'threefold ministry' ignore the fact that they have allowed the office of deacon to atrophy and become little more than a venerable historical relic. It becomes hypocritical to make claims for the universal authority of an office which has fallen almost into desuetude, for little more than a name. And we have also shown that the priest *par excellence*, he who represents the priesthood of

Christ expressed in the priesthood of all baptized persons, is the bishop and not primarily the 'priest' or presbyter. Among the traditional forms of ministry it is the bishop who is significant.

Episcopal government of the church can of course be abused. There are arrogant and legalist Roman Catholic bishops, pretentious and vain Anglican bishops, unscrupulous and power-seeking Orthodox bishops, But every form of ministry can be abused and has been abused. The office of bishops has suffered through history from having achieved too great a success. During its long career it has been manipulated and distorted for secular ends until at times it became almost unrecognizable as the original office of a father-in-God and chief pastor. Just because it has had a far longer history than other forms of ministry it has suffered more distortion.

But before the bishop began to be exploited by secular authorities and in recent times when he has freed himself of the embrace of the state, episcopal government has commended itself in a remarkable way. It seems to ensure protection against schism more than other forms of government. It is above all a personal, non-bureaucratic form of ministry. It does not suffer from the disadvantages of government by committee. It is flexible, capable of adjusting itself to very varied conditions, from that of the modern conurbation to that of the African bush or Indian village or Australian outback. The bishop can perhaps most effectively manifest the continuity and unity of the church, and though evangelical humility is not to be despised by Catholics, continuity should be important in the eyes of Protestants. Indeed any Protestant denomination which excercises care in ensuring regular ordination of ministers is in fact displaying a concern for continuity. Episcopal government need not be despotic, on the Roman Catholic model. Constitutional episcopacy, a form in which the bishop is controlled by the necessity of working with other clergy and laity and a synodical system, has been long practised in many places and can be said to have stood the test of time well. It is worth remarking that in several places non-episcopally governed churches – Methodists, Congregationalists and even Baptists – have voluntarily instituted ministries, such as superintendents and moderators, whose function and ethos is surprisingly like that of the traditional bishop. Sometimes, as among the Methodists in the USA, they are actually called bishops. One can say with reverence that the episcopal office at its best comes nearest to representing in imperfect human form the rule of Christ in his church.

We therefore would like to put to the readers whose churches have not adopted the episcopal form of government, in all charity and modesty, this question: if we allow that our episcopal ministry is not falsely decked out by a claim of apostolic succession, and enjoys no more (and no less) direct scriptural authority than their form of ministry, but is surely the traditional, universal form of ministry, why should they not adopt it? It is wholly unlikely that widespread re-union should take place under any other form of ministry than the episcopal. The practice and style of episcopal government can be enriched, deepened and made more effective by the contribution of Free Church traditions of ministry, as it appears to have been in the Church of South India and the Church of North India. Anglicans at least ought to want to see their episcopal ministry improved by the experience of the spirituality and the pastoral tradition of Methodists, Presbyterians, Congregationalists, Lutherans and Baptists. They should envisage themselves as the receivers and not merely the givers in united ministry. But that united ministry could only take an episcopal form.

'Priesthood' is a term which makes many Free Church hackles rise. It suggests priestcraft, claims to exclusive control of grace, sacerdotalism. Yet Anglicans have now for four hundred years been ordaining priests who can, in all honesty, be accused of none of these faults. The office of priest has suffered from the fact that in the Middle Ages a priest came to be defined solely in terms of his actions in the eucharist, solely by his alleged cultic capacity, his privilege and power of offering the sacrifice of Christ and turning bread and wine in the eucharist into the body and blood of Christ. This was a disastrous development which was rightly repudiated by all Reformed traditions in the sixteenth century, including the Anglican tradition. A priest is primarily one who represents God to men and men to God, not so as to exclude all other such representatives, not so as to control all forms of grace, but as his or her main purpose and work. This is how in effect the Anglican Church redefined the priest at the Reformation when it gave him authority to forgive or retain sins, to preach the Word and administer the sacraments, to be a watchman, steward and messenger of the Lord, but said nothing at all about offering sacrifices for the living and the dead nor turning bread and wine into the body and blood of Christ. No Anglican forms of eucharistic liturgy have ever suggested that the celebrant offers Christ.

Now, it would be very difficult, if not impossible, for Presbyterians, Methodists, and Lutherans at least, not to mention other denominations, to deny that their ministers represent God to men and men to God, both in their own eyes and in the eyes of their faithful laity. If they do not do so, then it is hard to see what their function is. In other words, most, if not all, non-episcopal traditions carry within their church a priestly principle, though they may not describe it as such. This is not surprising, because they are all faithful to the New Testament. The New Testament witnesses clearly to the heavenly priesthood of Christ, and to the whole body of the faithful as a priestly body. The minister is the official (though not exclusive) focus and representative of that priesthood, whether he is called minister or presbyter or (as among the Lutherans) priest.

Episcopal government and the principle of priesthood whereby the bishop, the priest *par excellence*, can delegate priesthood in a limited form to other priests, presbyters or ministers: these are the two crucial points for the Anglican form of ministry, which Anglicans cannot forego. All other forms of ministry are open to the widest possible flexibility that circumstances may demand. We do not think that this position should be found intransigent or unaccommodating by either Roman Catholics or Free Churchmen. It is at least founded upon a careful and honest survey of historical origins and a consistent theology. Can we call this a 'Catholic' ministry? Only in the sense that it is traditional and universal, not because this ministry confers a special kind of first-grade grace or validity unlike the second-grade, inferior, grace of other ministries. Christ is not divided. The Holy Spirit is not drunk in vintages of varying quality.

8

The Authority of the Church

1. Authority

We must begin by making a distinction. We must carefully distinguish between authority as office and authority as competence. We need both sorts of authority; we must have the authority of office; otherwise the state would not be able to function at all. But we cannot avoid the authority of competence; this is the authority which naturally belongs to those who are well versed in any particular subject. It is not an authority which is conferred, like the authority conferred in holy orders, but naturally arises and is recognized in those who are in fact experts in any sphere. We can illustrate it from the various grounds upon which the authority of our judicial courts can be challenged. When an IRA terrorist is arraigned before a court in Northern Ireland, he often declares 'I refuse to recognize the authority of this court'. He is here challenging the authority of office. But it sometimes occurs in other circumstances that someone who has been convicted of a crime (or more often his family and friends on his behalf) declares that the conviction is mistaken and should be reversed. In this case the authority that is being challenged is the authority of competence: it is claimed that the court was misinformed, or that it has mistakenly drawn the wrong conclusion from the evidence. Here what is challenged is not the official authority of the court. The complainants would acknowledge that the court was empowered to try the convicted person. What is challenged here is the authority of competence. This will prove to have a bearing on what we have to say later on.

The church certainly has authority. As soon as we have any information about how the early church functioned (in other words in the Pauline epistles) we find the local church claiming and exercising authority. Paul, in fact, though he claims the authority of a founding apostle, is anxious that the local church should exercise its own authority. But it is important to realize that this is the authority of the church, not merely of the ministry of the church. Jesus did not constitute a ministry for the church and grant it authority over the church. The twelve were not appointed officers of the church; they were the earliest church. Nor do we ever find an apostle handing on authority to anyone else in the New Testament. This is because it is the church that succeeds the earthly Christ as the bearer of the church's authority. It is the church that has to exercise Christ's priesthood in the world. The church is a priestly body, and every member of it shares in some degree in its priestly character and work. The ministry has no right to arrogate all authority to itself. The fact that the church delegates its authority to the ordained ministry does not mean that the other members of the church have no authority or no ministry at all. Authority resides in the priestly body at large and may not be permanently alienated into the hands of the ordained ministry.

How is the church's authority to be exercised? And above all is it to be exercised in a coercive way, so that those subject to the church's discipline, for instance, have to accept it whether they like it or not? In some sense it must be coercive. Those whom the church decides to cut off from its communion are not free to say 'I do not choose to be excommunicated' and so be permitted to continue as before. (We must of course concede that the church's judgment does not necessarily coincide with God's, and that the excommunicant may appear at God's right hand at the last judgment while those who condemned him are rejected.) The real question here is what sanction is to lie behind the authority of the church.

In the earliest times the sanction consisted simply in the free obedience of the members of the church. The excommunicated person was rejected by the other members, it was in that sense a voluntary process. The church authorities had no other way of enforcing their sentence. And we find that a very similar state of affairs prevails in some parts of the church in the third world today. One can see in South India a system of excommunication that depended on the sanction of voluntary obedience on the part of Christians working quite successfully. But with the advent of the

Constantinian era the authority of the church began to be backed by the authority of the state, so that quite soon we find church authorities appealing to the power of the state to enforce its decisions. In course of time this developed in the West into a state of affairs in which the authority of the church and of the state became quite indistinguishable. To be a member of the church was virtually to be a member of the state, and to be condemned by the church was in effect to be classed as a criminal.

Today we are living in a post-Constantinian era. As far as church authority is concerned, this looks like a return to a pre-Constantinian state of affairs, and in many ways it is so. In most countries the church's authority can only be enforced by voluntary means, though of course the church can have recourse to the secular courts in the same way that any voluntary society can. And the parallel with pre-Constantinian times holds valid in another respect also: in certain countries the state is in open opposition to the church and loses no opportunity to injure the church and weaken its authority. Where the church has not wholly freed itself from the state connection (as in Czechoslovakia or the Soviet Union for example), this can be extremely damaging to the church's life: incompetent or unscrupulous persons are appointed to high office in the church, and to be successful pastorally is to incur the attention of the police. In such circumstances the church's authority can only be vindicated by suffering. Sometimes the only way in which a bishop can vindicate his authority is by going to prison. Painful though this situation is, and easy though it be to write about it from outside, it must be said that this method of vindicating the authority of the church is entirely in accord with what we know of God's method. The cross is the supreme example of the vindication of the authority of God, and those who suffer because they are quite legitimately standing out for the free exercise of the authority of God are not only witnessing in the clearest way possible to the nature of God. They are also exercising that authority in a way which does in fact prove astonishingly effective.

Finally, we must consider that other kind of authority to which we referred above, the authority of competence. How is this kind of authority to be exercised in the church? Here we may very relevantly examine the Roman Catholic notion of the church's *magisterium*. According to official Roman Catholic teaching, Christ has vested in the ordained ministry of the church the right not only to rule the church, but also to declare what is and what is not correct doctrine. The *magisterium* is vested primarily in the Pope but also in the bishops and the priesthood of the church. They are, it is true, to be assisted in making their decisions by the theologians and the scholars of the church, whether they be bishops or not. But in the last resort the authority of their decisions does not consist in the fact that they are necessarily competent in the various disciplines which assist them in deciding on questions of doctrine and morals. Indeed in the case of the highest authority of all, the Bishop of Rome, it is expressly claimed that the correctness of his decisions does not rest on the depth of his learning or the extent to which he has consulted the other members of the church. He is in certain circumstances promised an infallibility which proceeds from his office alone, and is not dependent on his competence.

This concept of the *magisterium* seems to confuse the two aspects of authority. For those who are outside the Roman Catholic Church, and who are therefore free from the fascination exercised by the institution of the papacy, no pronouncement on a matter of faith or morals has any authority unless we have sufficient assurance that it comes from someone who is competent in the subject. Mere authority of office carries no guarantee of correctness of doctrine. We have had several very clear examples of this during the course of this century. Let us take one example. It is that of the Biblical Commission appointed by Pope Leo XIII in 1902 in order to resolve various questions about the authorship and authenticity of the Bible which were troubling certain well-informed members of the Roman Catholic Church. Here was an excellent test of the theory of the church's *magisterium*: the members of the Commission certainly represented the higher ranks of the *magisterium* very adequately. They were all cardinals; they had the assistance of a number of theologians and scholars who appeared to be well informed on biblical and historical topics if degrees conferred by church institutions were any guide. They were in the course of the years following the setting up of the institution requested to settle a number of burning questions about the Bible: was Moses the author of the Pentateuch? Was the text of the 'three heavenly witnesses' in I John 5.7–8 an original and authentic part of scripture? Could a Catholic safely hold that the latter half of the Book of

Isaiah was not written by Isaiah of Jerusalem but by an anonymous prophet of the Babylonian exile? To these and other questions the Biblical Commission gave clear and definite answers. No one could complain that they prevaricated or showed any doubt about their competence to resolve these difficulties. It might seem that the *magisterium* had been triumphantly vindicated, and indeed many Roman Catholics at the time pointed to the working of the Biblical Commission as an example of the superiority of the Roman system: the faithful were not left in any doubt as to what they should believe. There was, however, one difficulty about the answers provided by the august tribunal. They were almost invariably wrong, and competent Roman Catholic scholars knew at the time that they were wrong. Today, when the Roman Catholic Church has considerably modified its stance upon authority, every informed person admits that the answers were wrong. It is of little avail comforting oneself with the consideration that these answers were not at the time regarded as infallible. The fault lay, not in any lack of consultation, but in treating those who have only the authority of office as if this conferred upon them the authority of competence.

But we are still left with the question, how are questions of faith and morals to be decided in the church? Are we to leave the question in abeyance? Is it perfectly legitimate for any person, whether a member of the clergy or of the episcopate, to profess and teach any version of Christianity he chooses without let or hindrance from the church? We have made fun of our Roman Catholic friends for their addiction to a *magisterium* that is too often incompetent for its task. But they might very well round on us with some such question as we have just posed above. It seems indeed to be the case in the Church of England at least that anyone may profess and teach anything without any interference from the church. The church seems to have abrogated its authority in the sphere of doctrine and morals. This is not true perhaps of its positive statements, for there are various commissions of well-qualified persons to give help in the matter of doctrine, and the General Synod has made genuine efforts to make pronouncements about various important matters concerning morals. But no attempt has been made to exercise any control over what is taught by way of doctrine by those who at least appear to be authorized teachers of the church.

This is not a satisfactory state of affairs. There is no reason why we should not have a body of people officially recognized by the church, who will be sufficiently respected to be able to exercise a genuine authority of competence. They would, of course, in making pronouncements on matters of faith and morals, be required to state their reasons. One of the most unsatisfactory features of most doctrinal pronouncements made by the authorities of the Roman Catholic Church is that they do not give their reasons. These questions must be decided by reasoning and evidence, not be *ipse dixits*. But there is no reason why this should not be done. It should also follow that on occasion it will be necessary to stigmatize one or more members of the church who have published their views on questions of faith or morals as not being satisfactory guides to the subject, or as being in fact involved in heresy to so grave an extent that their very membership of the church is called into question. Whether the church should ever go so far as actually to excommunicate solely because of heresy may be doubted though there is much to be said for excommunication being used in some questions of behaviour. But we owe it to the great mass of the relatively uninstructed Christians to give them some guidance in questions of doctrine and even if need be to mark certain persons as unsafe or unsatisfactory guides in questions of doctrine or morals. If such pronouncements are ever made, they must not be treated as infallible or irrevocable. But until we in the Church of England take some such action as this we lay ourselves open to the charge that we do not care about safeguarding the Christian faith. We are in danger of finding ourselves in a situation where the liberty which we rightly value in a world where liberty has been so much restricted during the course of the century will have degenerated into indifference and even license.

We must now look briefly at how the question of authority has risen to crisis proportions in the church. For the greater part of its history the Christian church has been in a situation in which the vast majority of the laity were relatively docile as far as doctrinal knowledge was concerned because they were illiterate. All knowledge and expertise in church matters was in the hands of the ordained ministry. The Reformation in the West did not make a great deal of difference to this, first because higher education remained for a long time in the hands of the church, and that meant in the hands of the ordained ministry; and secondly because the proportion of illiterates in the church diminished only slowly. Even when universal education arrived it did not provide sufficient education to enable very many lay people to challenge the expertise of the clergy effectively. It is in many ways very convenient from the point of view of those who have to run the church to have a largely illiterate laity. An illiterate knows that he does not know. A well educated person is also usually easy to deal with because he or she can appreciate the true perspectives of the problems that church leaders have to deal with. The really awkward person is the semi-educated. They think that they know but their thinking is usually pretty crude. Every church perhaps has to go through a period during which the semi-educated can wreak considerable havoc in the church's government.

Today, however, in the West and increasingly in the third world also, this situation as far as concerns the clergy and the laity is altering very rapidly. In the first place the general level of education has advanced beyond the primary school. Millions of people are receiving a secondary education and thousands are receiving a university education. This is very much to be welcomed and is one of the really solid benefits of the second half of the twentieth century. Apart from anything else, this means that the clergy have to take more pains to make the Christian message comprehensible to the laity than they did before. If you are preaching to a congregation many of whom have as good an education as yourself, and some of whom have a much better one, you have to mind your p's and q's. The well educated ones will be able to detect nonsense or pious twaddle very easily.

But there is another consequence as well: today many laity are actually receiving an excellent training in theology and related disciplines at university level. The authors of this book have spent the last twenty years teaching biblical studies and theology to young men and women the great majority of whom have no intention of taking orders. But nearly all of them leave the university actually better qualified in theology than are most of the clergy under whom they will sit if they attend any church. And please note that more than half of them were women. Consequently in the future in the UK at least a growing proportion of the laity are likely to be as well qualified in theology and the study of the Bible as are most of the clergy, indeed better qualified than most of them. Increasingly clergy are likely in the future to be challenged on questions of faith and order, not as it has so often been in the past by half-educated laity who do not understand the true proportions of the problems of doctrine and morals which the church today must face, but by thoroughly well-educated laity who must be accorded as much authority in the sphere of theology, at least as far as concerns the authority of competence, as any cleric.

We should consider one other element in the situation. Most denominations nowadays have given themselves, or are in process of giving themselves, a constitution of a distinctly democratic nature. The Free Churches have done this from the first; the Anglican Church has now done it almost everywhere, even in England; and there is a strong movement inside the Roman Catholic Church for a more democratic modification of its structure. It cannot be said that this process of democratization has resulted in a mad rush of innovations in the church. On the contrary, sometimes a democratically constituted church seems to be more conservative than one with a more autocratic structure. But it certainly means that the day has passed when important decisions in the church could be made by a small ruling group and be meekly accepted by the laity.

It is clear therefore that there is a crisis of authority in the church in the sense that the structures of authority have to be adjusted to this newly emerging situation. We will end by making four suggestions which may throw some light on this problem:

1. We must accept the democratization of the ruling structures of the church. We are not so naive as to fail to realize that this movement towards democracy is largely due to the *Zeitgeist* and we do not imagine that our democratic structures will last for ever. But we must accept them, and if so it is as well to learn something from the experience of those who have had them for some time. From the experience of our own home church, the Anglican Church of Ireland, we would urge that we should not go too far in democratizing our machinery of government. When we first received independence in the Church of Ireland in 1870 we established a method of electing bishops that gave a very great influence to the representatives of the diocese that was to be filled. The consequence was that the local mediocrity, who offended no one, had a vast advantage over everyone else. Some years ago we altered this

arrangement so that quite often someone gets elected bishop who has a certain amount of originality. Again, a fully democratic system of election has not, it must be confessed, really benefitted the Church of South India. Owing to certain tendencies apparently indigenous to India, an appalling amount of canvassing goes on during an episcopal election, and it is to be feared that too often the successful candidate is the one who has organized his supporters most effectively. One could also point with some dismay to the not wholly successful functioning of the General Synod of the Church of England. The method of election to this body has resulted in an unhappy resurgence of party spirit and party organization which had previously appeared to be on the wane. In short, let it be democracy by all means, but a carefully considered democracy which contains inbuilt checks and safeguards against the various forms of corruption which can afflict democracy.

2. All denominations without exception must admit women into the highest levels of church life and organization. This undoubtedly means that women must be admitted to the priesthood, however unwelcome be the prospect of this to some clergy and laity. This will not in itself solve all our problems, but it will remove one of the worst examples of discrimination which exist in the church, and will rebut the accusation (at present only too much justified as regards some of the major denominations) that our standard of conduct towards women is lower than is that of the secular world.

3. We must revise our methods of teaching both faith and morals. We are not referring to paedogogics. We mean that we must treat all the members of God's people as responsible adults as far as the teaching of the church is concerned. Gone are the days when all that was necessary was for those in authority (i.e. clergy) to make an authoritative statement on some point of faith or morals without giving any reasons and expect the laity meekly to accept it. The reception of the encyclical *Humanae Vitae* surely demonstrates this. When authoritative statements on faith and morals are made, as no doubt they will have to be made in the future, they must be made by persons who have the authority of competence not the authority of office only, and they must be expressed in such a way that the reasons behind the statement are clearly discernible, the evidence for the conclusions clearly set forth, and the alternatives

reasonably discussed. Every church therefore urgently needs to set up a doctrinal and moral commission containing people of both sexes whose authority of competence is beyond dispute. This is the body whose statements will carry conviction, rather than a body largely composed of people whose authority is purely that of office. We must find a middle way between the *ipse dixit* method of old-fashioned autocratic churches and the 'every man his own theologian' approach which is often associated with Protestantism.

4. We have one last suggestion to make. Could not church union help in this matter of authority? It may seem Utopian to make such a suggestion in a country where union schemes have so lamentably failed to come to fruition. But the various denominations need the help of each other now as never before. Even if we cannot endure the prospect of organic reunion, can we not consult one another as churches (or rather as separated elements in the one church) on matters of our common faith? It is unlikely that any one denomination is in itself so well equipped with experts in every aspect of the theology and biblical studies that it can afford to ignore the help which the others could give.

2. Authority and Doctrine

Of course the church has authority to determine doctrine. Who else could possibly claim such authority? Could any individual layman or priest or bishop? Manifestly not. Neither Anglicans nor Orthodox look favourably on Paisleys or Lefèvbres. Could any individual church or province of the church determine doctrine? Again we must say no; no church standing alone nor province of churches standing alone has the authority to determine doctrine. Only the whole church, the consensus of all true Christians, or some body which adequately expresses that consensus, could have authority to determine doctrine. Finally, has any Pope on his own authority, *ex sese* (if that is what the First Vatican Council meant by those words), the right and capacity to determine doctrine? We cannot be sure that the Roman Catholic answer to this question is an unqualified Yes; but can be confident that the Orthodox and Anglican answer is an unequivocal No. The addition of the *filioque* clause to the Western version of the Nicene Creed in 1012 should

alone be enough to convince us that this method of determining
doctrine is unsatisfactory.

The traditional method whereby the church has exercised this
right has been through the work of councils, above all Ecumenical
or General Councils. We cannot allow that the council described
by St Luke in the fifteenth chapter of the book of Acts can seriously
be regarded as a General Council. We are too uncertain about its
details to permit confidence on that point, and scholars have not yet
succeeded in reconciling the Letter of Paul to the Galatians with
the data given in Acts. The fact is that conciliar activity in the
church developed gradually, as so many other features of the life of
the ancient church developed gradually – creed, liturgy, ministry,
New Testament canon. It was possibly during the second century
that the custom grew up of calling local councils of bishops. We
have information about a few councils in the third century, though
no *Acta* of any. Immediately after the Diocletian Persecution in the
fourth century there was a flurry of councils, as the church tried to
tidy up the havoc caused by the persecution. But even in 325 the
project for holding a General Council of all available bishops was a
wholly new one, and must have seemed daring to many.

This first General Council can hardly be described as a success.
It failed to solve the crisis caused by the Arian Controversy and was
followed by nearly sixty years of conflict during which many councils met, only a few of which had lasting results. But the Council of
Nicaea set the pattern for determining doctrine. General Councils
met not only at the end of the fourth century, but in the fifth, the
sixth, the seventh and the eighth centuries; the last one formally
recognized by the Orthodox as a General Council assembled in the
year 787. The Western church continued to hold councils which
it regarded as General throughout the Middle Ages. The Papal
Schism at the end of the fourteenth and beginning of the fifteenth
centuries was finally ended by a General Council held in spite of
rather than with the consent of the Pope or Popes, and when
Luther nailed his famous thesis to the door of the Schlosskirche at
Wittenberg a council which the Pope at least regarded as General
had only recently dispersed. The church of the Counter-Reformation
continued to hold councils which it deemed General, the Council
of Trent, the First and Second Vatican Councils. By Roman
Catholic reckoning the score is now twenty-one.

Has the Ecumenical Council proved a satisfactory way whereby the church can determine doctrine, and are there any alternative ways? We may first point out that in the ancient church at any rate every General Council was followed by excommunications and schisms. In some cases the schisms were large and lasting, especially those caused by the Council of Ephesus in 431 and the Council of Chalcedon in 451. Considerable disagreement between the Eastern and the Western church resulted from the General Council of 553. The next General Council actually branded a Pope as heretical and the council of 787 did not in fact end the Iconoclastic Controversy. Further, we know enough about several of the General Councils to recognize that the atmosphere prevailing and the methods used at them were far from proper. We can recall the disgust and contempt which filled the soul of Gregory of Nazianzus at Constantinople and we must not forget the communal slogan-chanting and howling down of opponents which took place at Chalcedon. The Council of Constance may have ended the Papal Schism, but it burnt John Hus, and the bright hope which it raised that the church might be reformed by General Councils was extinguished during the next fifty years. The Second Vatican Council is perhaps too recent for us to draw conclusions from it, but the accounts of the First Vatican Council in 1870 which scholars are now able to examine freely do not suggest that it was an ideal or even a particularly efficient way of determining doctrine, and we certainly cannot applaud the doctrinal definition which emerged from it.

One more point must be made about General Councils. The last council unequivocally recognized as General by all Anglicans took place 1527 years ago. The last Council recognized by the Orthodox as General took place almost 1200 years ago. Somehow Anglicans have managed to exist as a communion without the benefit of any later General Councils, and Orthodox also appear to have survived sufficiently well without General Councils for a very long time. We conjecture that if we insist upon General Councils as the church's only way of determining doctrine we play into the hands of J.H. Newman. The Roman Catholic Church certainly has not neglected the duty of holding General Councils, if duty there be. It is manifestly incorrect to say that there have been no serious controversies since 451 or since 787. It is obviously wrong to suggest that the

Anglicans since 1534 and the Orthodox since 787 have had no occasion to determine doctrine. How have these bodies then determined doctrine?

Before we answer that question, however, we should ask another one which is not irrelevant to that. In this context, what do we mean by authority? In one sense scripture is an authority, in another it is tradition. The church must clearly consult both before it determines doctrine, and these two authorities constitute a limitation of the church's authority to make doctrinal decisions. But more pertinently, are there not other authorities which the church must take account of before it determines doctrine? If the leaders of the Roman Church in the early seventeenth century had been properly observant of expert scientific authority they would not have burnt Bruno and silenced Galileo. If Bishop Wilberforce at his famous meeting with T.H. Huxley had realized the necessity of respecting the authority of the expert he would not have made a classic fool of himself on the subject of the origin of the human species. To take a hypothetical case: if tomorrow the Pope, the Patriarch of Constantinople and Archbishop of Canterbury were to make a joint statement to the effect that St Paul wrote the Pastoral Epistles, this would not in the least affect the question of their authorship. That is a matter for the experts.

It is a truism to say that it is impossible to know whether a doctrinal decision of a council is valid, lasting and true until it has been accepted, indeed assimilated by the whole church. On this principle the Orthodox rightly reject the decisions of the Council of Ferrara-Florence and the Anglicans reject, e.g., the decisions of the Lateran Council of 1215. The Anglican argument in the latter case must rest on two supports: (1) that the Eastern church was not consulted about these decisions and never accepted them; (2) that centuries afterwards the Anglican Church rejected the decision about transubstantiation. If we accept the first argument we might have to face the retort that it was in the circumstances impossible to consult the Eastern church, in which case of course we must acknowledge that it was at that point impossible to hold a General Council. If we accept the second argument, we must allow that there is a certain provisional nature about the decisions of apparently full councils if they can legitimately be rejected more than three hundred years later and the council branded as not General and as in error. In either case the value of holding large, full councils which aspire to be ecumenical is seriously called in question.

Let us now at last return to the question which we asked earlier: are there any alternative ways for the church to determine doctrine apart from the clumsy, infrequent, uncertain and indeed almost disused method of calling a General Council? We are not well enough acquainted with the history of the Orthodox Church to be able to answer this question for them with any confidence. There was a controversy about Palamism in the fourteenth century and there was at least a tendency among some Orthodox churches to be influenced by tridentine Catholicism in the eighteenth century, from which they have since recovered. It would be interesting to know how the outcome of both situations was achieved.

But we can look at the manner in which doctrinal controversies and movements have been handled by the Anglican Church in order to give us some material for answering this question. The Arminian Controversy in the seventeenth century was scarcely serious enough to qualify for inclusion here. But the Deist Controversy in the eighteenth century was a serious one. Deism had a very wide influence on thinking people, both clergy and laity. The nearest that the Anglican Communion came to taking formal action against Deists was when Clayton, bishop of Clogher in Ireland, was prosecuted in the Irish House of Lords for the Socinian heresy. As he died before the legal process could be completed, this is hardly a test case. Deism in fact died out through the lapse of time and the rise of other philosophies and interests in the next century. No official action, conciliar or other, was effectively taken against it. The nineteenth century, however, saw the Church of England and several other parts of the Anglican Communion racked by controversy caused by the Tractarian Movement, a movement which we would today call the Anglo-Catholic Movement. This controversy certainly involved doctrine, the doctrine of ministry, the doctrine of the sacraments, the doctrine of the authority of the church and in particular of the bishop. No conciliar action was taken in connection with this controversy. No official body met to pronounce upon the rights and wrongs of the case. There was, however, one manner in which the Church of England and with it many other provinces of the Anglican Communion made a doctrinal decision, and it was a manner peculiarly characteristic of Anglicanism. The *Book of*

Common Prayer was changed. Everywhere new forms of worship have appeared, and these forms have certainly expressed a different doctrine from that expressed by the old Prayer Book of 1662. It is not that the doctrine is novel in the sense of heretical or erratic, but the Christian faith has been differently presented. The compilers of these new forms have drawn on contemporary scholarship and theology, but also on patristic sources and the Bible itself, in order to give to the forms a new expression of the old faith. Here certainly the church has determined doctrine. One reason why it has been possible for these new forms to be accepted and widely used is that the controversy aroused by the Tractarian Movement has largely, though not entirely, died down.

Another source of controversy, or at least of doctrinal confusion, within Anglicanism has been the rise of historical criticism. This is a new method of examining historical documents, but more, a quite new attitude towards and understanding of our exploration of the past, which had its roots in the Renaissance and the Enlightenment but which first came prominently into view in the middle of the nineteenth century. It started an historical revolution which is still with us now and is not yet finished. It involved the necessity of a drastic and far-reaching revision of the attitude of Christians towards the Bible and towards all the documents and monuments of the Christian faith. It is probably the most searching and testing intellectual and moral challenge which Christianity has ever been compelled to face.

The Church of England, like other communions of the Reformed tradition, at first reacted against this new and apparently threatening phenomenon with predictable violence. Efforts were made to prosecute its champions and disciples in the ecclesiastical courts, to brand them as heretical, to deprive them of their posts, and so on. Virtually all these efforts failed, partly because it was found that the ecclesiastical machinery would not work effectively and partly because a genuine spirit of liberalism in the church found these efforts distasteful. Gradually the church began to set itself the task of coming to terms with, of discovering how to live with, of in some measure assimilating this new learning with all its implications for the re-assessment of Christian doctrine. It entailed taking a great deal more notice of the deliverances of the experts, and becoming accustomed to accepting much more uncertainty than before, and tolerating in many areas provisional rather than permanent conclusions. But that was the price which had to be paid if this revolution in historical study was not to be excluded by prejudice or reduced by narrow-minded views to a harmless minimum. For thoughtful, honest people there was no alternative. There were consequently no councils, no Confessions, no excommunications and no schisms. We have not become perfectly acclimatized to this revolution yet; far from it. But we are coping with it by a process of gradual testing and assimilation which is taking place within the church at almost every level. It has certainly meant doctrinal change, but not a change registered, declared or accomplished by a council nor by any official church authority.

Now contrast with this way of coping with a new intellectual movement the methods used by the Roman Catholic Church. Precisely the same intellectual pressure began to affect the Roman Church towards the end of the nineteenth century and during the first two decades of the twentieth. It took the form of what is called Catholic Modernism. When the authorities of that church became aware of the existence of this movement, they dealt with it in ways which could, we suppose, be called traditional, except that a good deal more rigour and severity was used than had in the recent past been conventional. They suppressed Modernist authors, forbidding them to publish; they degraded or threatened with degradation anyone suspected of Modernist views, sometimes suspending their powers of celebrating Mass if they were priests (as they usually were), sometimes sending or driving them into a kind of exile, as Duchesne was driven into Egypt and Teilhard de Chardin to China. They did not hesitate to use the extreme weapon of deprivation of priest's orders and excommunication. The Pope himself, Pius X, issued a violently condemnatory Encyclical, *Pascendi Gregis*, and instituted throughout the Roman Catholic Church a system of delation or encouragement of informers and imposed on anyone who was likely to teach in any capacity an anti-Modernist oath. The result was that Modernism for the moment disappeared. Its leaders were driven out of the church or permanently silenced; some died of a broken heart. Only von Hügel escaped the net because he was a layman, and a socially influential layman; and even in his case the anti-Modernist campaign can be said to have caused him gradually to abandon the movement.

Authority apparently triumphed, having successfully operated all the machinery of suppression. But the triumph was only apparent. Fifty years after Pius X's encyclical free thought reappeared within the Roman Catholic Church. All the questions which the Modernists, impelled by their acquaintance with historical criticism, had asked in vain were now reopened. The methods, conclusions and implications of historical criticism were now revived and openly canvassed. The pressure for Catholic scholars to take their place with their Protestant colleagues in the field of open enquiry and research unhindered by ecclesiastical authority, unmenaced by official censure, no longer vulnerable to the impertinent intervention of ignorant superiors, was irresistible, and the Curia gave way to it. George Tyrrell might well use of Hans Küng the prophetic words of Dido as she foretold the coming of Hannibal who would avenge the wrong inflicted on her by Aeneas:

exoriare aliquis nostris ex ossibus ultor.
'some avenger will arise from our bones.'

It may well be that the precise answers given by the Modernists to the searching questions which they addressed to the church of their day are not the answers which we would give now. They were, after all, pioneers working under great difficulty. But their moral courage and their intellectual integrity and the fundamental justice of their cause have been abundantly vindicated. The grave of George Tyrrell in Storrington churchyard is today the goal of a steady stream of visitors.

We may well ask which of these two methods of dealing with the necessity of determining doctrine represented by the advent of historical criticism is the better, the better, we mean, in the eyes of God. Should we prefer the Roman way in which the authority of the hierarchy as the exclusive teaching organ of the church is called in to suppress the daring, venturesome, questioning individual who sees the necessity of doctrinal change and prophetically calls for it? This is certainly tidy, traditional, logical and for a certain time completely effective. Or should we opt for the untidy, inconclusive, incoherent, largely tolerant Anglican method of letting the new movement of thought with all its disturbing implications and consequences take its course and trusting that God, who may not be as tidy as man, will guide the church, the ordinary faithful as well as the theologians, into a gradual understanding and sifting of truth? At first sight this may seem a disastrous method, but in the long run it has enormous advantages, the two most obvious of which are that nobody is excommunicated, nobody is crushed by injustice, and that the inevitable impact of the new movement of thought is met early and gradually instead of being fiercely resisted at first and then later suddenly surrendered to.

We do not deny that there have been occasions in the past when councils, either General or local, were the right way for determining the doctrine of the church. The Council of Constantinople which drew up the final form of the Creed of Nicaea was one. Those assemblies which in the sixteenth century produced confessions which made it clear where particular Reformed communions stood seem to have been necessary. And we can hardly deny that the Creed of the Council of Trent was a necessary and useful document round which the forces of the Counter-Reformation were able to gather. In our own time the Barmen Declaration against Hitler's attempt to corrupt the Lutheran church in Germany was, we must concede, the right and proper result of a consensus among German Protestants. And we do not deny that there may be occasions in the future when councils, either General or local, may be precisely the right response to the needs of the moment. For all we know, the proposed General Council of the Orthodox Church if it takes place in the near future, as some hope it will, may prove to be one of these.

But it is worth while considering the Lambeth Conference, that confluence of quintessential Anglicanism. It passes no binding resolution. It makes no attempts to coerce anyone. It has never been known to excommunicate a single soul. It is a conference for consultation, for review and prospect, for interchange of ideas. It is quite possible, even likely, that as a result of any meeting of this Conference, as has happened at previous Conferences, doctrine will be determined in various parts of the Anglican communion. And certainly the bishops will strive to reach a consensus on the subjects under debate, though they know that they may not succeed in obtaining one on all subjects. Perhaps the Lambeth Conference may stand as a symbol, if not actually an example, of the kind of preferable alternative to conciliar action for determining doctrine which we have been groping after.

In the twentieth century, when every kind of traditional authority is being questioned, and when everything is still fluid in the fields of theology, of philosophy and of historical research, how far can any ecclesiastical person or ecclesiastical institution presume to say to anybody, 'you shall believe this, because I pronounce it to be true, without further thought or discussion'? We are not making a plea for sheer anarchic individualism. We are rather suggesting that for all churches today the model to imitate in determining doctrine should be that of consensus achieved by gradual persuasion rather than that of dogma imposed by conciliar (and far less by papal) fiat. This method of determination seems to us more realistic, more effective and more in accordance with the will of God declared in Christ.

We have already rejected the notion that the Bishop of Rome is, or ever could be, infallible. Moreover we have suggested that it is quite sufficient to speak of the indefectibility of the church. But it is not enough to reject an idea. We ought to make an attempt to put something better in its place.

The Pope, we have said, is not infallible, nor ever could be. This is not only because Popes have often made mistakes in their attempts to lead the church into the truth, but even more because the very notion of infallibility is misleading and illusory. Those who defend the infallibility of the Pope or of ecumenical councils almost always mean in fact the infallibility of theological propositions put forth by Popes or councils. But in the sphere of theology and morals there are no infallible propositions. This is because language itself is not designed to express propositions in formulae that will last for ever. 'Propositions always fall short of reality.'[1] When propositions are translated from one language to another something of the original meaning is always lost. Try, for instance, translating into English exactly what is conveyed by this line in Virgil's Latin: *sunt lacrimae rerum et mentem mortalia tangunt.* Also, in the course of time language alters its meaning. Some terms become unusable through misuse. Good examples in English are 'humanism', 'evangelical', 'gay'. Thus infallible propositions are impossible. But how else in infallibility to be conveyed?

Perhaps it might be claimed that there are infallible people, or people who in certain circumstances cannot mislead. Infallibility has in the course of Christian history been claimed for three classes of entities, for Popes, for ecumenical councils, and for the words of the Bible. But the objections to infallibility mentioned above apply just as much to all three classes, and that for two reasons: all three classes have in actual fact erred, and the infallibility must in the last resort be expressed in propositions, whether of Popes or of councils, or of the Bible itself. No well-informed historian will deny that ecumenical councils have erred; and only the most fanatical literalist will claim that the Bible contains no errors at all of any kind. Nor can we cast the mantle of infallibility over any theologians of the past, whether we consider Augustine or John of Damascus, or Thomas Aquinas, or John Calvin. If we are honest we must therefore repudiate the notion that there is to be found in the church some sort of an organ of infallibility.

Indefectibility means that God will not permit the whole church to go permanently and dangerously astray in its understanding of the gospel. We can certainly claim that so far in the course of nearly two thousand years of its history this has not yet happened to the church. When we assert that this can never happen, we are indeed making a statement of faith. But it is no more precarious than is the statement of our faith in the hope of the life to come. Both statements are based on God's promise, not on any reliance on some human institution. We must add that it is the church as a whole that is indefectible, not any one part, or organ, or office, or individual in it. If we review the whole of Christian history this belief in the indefectibility of the church should be strengthened. It is true that large parts of the church have gone astray. We think of the corruption of the church in the Middle Ages in the West. But this corruption was checked and the truth of the gospel recovered by means of the Reformation, traumatic and destructive though it was in many ways. In our own day we have seen the Roman Catholic Church being recalled to the truth of the gospel, a movement which cannot be reversed despite the fact that the present Pope seems to be very much of a traditionalist in theology. It is also true that large parts of the church can actually disappear and be lost: witness the disappearance of the numerous and flourishing church in North Africa as a result of the conquest of Islam in the eighth century. Parts of the church can fall into a state of advanced corruption: this seems to be the case with the indigenous Coptic Church in Ethiopia today. Other parts of the church may be gravely weakened in numbers and influence. This is certainly true of the modern church in Western Europe. But the church as a whole does not fail. It renews itself or finds scope for extension in other parts of the world. The Spirit works according to his own designs. We cannot anticipate him but we can trust him.

Together with the notion of the infallibility of the Pope there has grown up in the Roman Catholic Church a belief in the existence of a *magisterium*, the teaching office of the church. According to Roman Catholic official this office is entrusted only to the hierarchy headed by the Pope. Laity have no part in it. This idea is a very modern one: it only came into prominence in the last century. It is indeed one which we could well do without. There is no divinely appointed teaching body in the church. The bishops are not the exclusive successors of the apostles. The only reason that the clergy gained such an exclusive grip upon the teaching of the church in the West was that for almost five hundred years the clergy were the only people in Western Europe who were literate. In the East this disastrous eclipse of culture never took place. Consequently we find that in the Eastern Orthodox Church to this very day there are eminent theologians who are laymen.

If we study the history of the church we shall find that decisive influence in the development of the church's thinking, far from being confined to any one body of officials, was very often provided by individuals, not all of whom were bishops, and very often in the teeth of the opposition of the official leadership. There was Athanasius in the fourth century, who for some time almost alone defended the use of the term *homoousios* for the divine Son, a usage which was later accepted as orthodox. There was Sophronius in the first half of the seventh century who was only a monk when he first raised his voice against the Monothelitism (now recognized as a heresy) that was being propagated by both Emperor and Pope. In the Western church we think of the immense influence exercised by such people as Augustine in the fifth and Thomas Aquinas in the thirteenth century, neither of whom owed their influence to their position in the hierarchy. Or we could point to Anselm, who in his *Cur Deus Homo?* published in 1096 repudiated the widely prevalent belief that God had paid a ransom to the devil for our salvation. Anselm's junior contemporary Bernard of Clairvaux is another instance of someone who did not qualify as a front rank teacher according to later Roman Catholic categories, and yet who wielded extraordinary influence in matters theological and spiritual, even directing Popes as to how they should manage the affairs of the church. Consider again what a huge contribution to the course of Christian doctrine has been made by Luther and Calvin, neither of whom had very much official standing in the hierarchy. Almost in our own day Karl Barth provides an example of how Protestantism has been called back from the sterile paths into which a great deal of nineteenth-century theology had strayed. But when Barth issued his first trumpet call in the shape of the first edition of his commentary on the Epistle to the Romans he was only a country pastor in the Reformed Church of Switzerland. If we want to confine ourselves to Anglicanism, we could take the example of R.C. Moberly, an Oxford professor of Moral Theology who in two books published at the end of the nineteenth century achieved two remarkable results: he opposed the doctrine of penal substitution which had been Protestant orthodoxy up to the middle of the century; and he gave to Anglicans a doctrine of the ministry which in essentials has stood the test of modern enquiry.

There is no official, divinely appointed teaching office in the church; but God has never left it without those who have guided it into the truth.

But does the bishop not have a teaching office? Yes, in as far as he has been ordained to preach the word of God and to oversee the flock, he does have a duty to expound and teach the meaning of the gospel. Unfortunately in both the Roman Catholic Church and in the Anglican Communion (and not least in the Church of England) this duty has in our days become much more difficult to carry out effectively. In the Roman Church this is partly because, until recently at least, the bishop was not expected to think out his theology for himself. His role was more that of a policeman, to see that everyone kept the rules, just as the theologian's role was to find out plausible justification in scripture and history for whatever the *magisterium* declared to be doctrine to be believed by the faithful. In Anglicanism the difficulty is that the bishop has so many administrative duties that his teaching obligation is too often ignored. Moreover, study of the Bible and of theology is today an increasingly technical affair. Every bishop cannot be expected to be as well informed as are academic theologians or biblical scholars. But every bishop should at least keep himself *au fait* with what is happening in the world of biblical scholarship and theological thought. We have had in the recent past, and we still have today bishops who have been leaders of theological thought and scholars in their own right. In the last century the great examples of J.B. Lightfoot and B.F. Westcott are widely familiar. But more recently there have been philosophers such as William Temple and historians such as John Moorman. On a smaller scale, there was recently a suffragan bishop in the Church of England, now unfortunately departed this life, who delivered a set of six lectures on theology in public in a large industrial city during the winter months which were attended by a thousand people every night. And in the rural Church in South India the great pioneer bishop Samuel Vendanayakam Azariah wrote simple handbooks for his village congregations teaching them the elements of Christian living.

A priest also has a teaching ministry on a smaller scale. But nowadays this ministry in the parish is not confined to the priest. Since the gift of teaching is not one exclusively attached to ordination or office, it can be undertaken by laymen and laywomen, and is being increasingly exercised by them. The test of the Christian teacher is not 'is he ordained?' but 'is he or she qualified in the necessary studies?' Today's priest will, if he is wise, exercise his teaching ministry by the help of such suitable colleagues and helpers as he can find among his flock.

Our last word on the question of infallibility and indefectibility must be that the ultimate decision is our own personal one. We cannot use anyone else as a surrogate here. And none of us is infallible.

Formally speaking, the final authority for determining doctrine in the Church of England is a sufficiently large majority of votes cast in each House of the General Synod. But the thought that this should really be the ultimate method of decision concerning doctrine without further possibility of appeal is enough to make any responsible Anglican theologian shudder. If General Councils can err and have erred, then local synods can err even more egregiously. We do not mean that local synods are invariably wrong, but that they are subject, like all assemblies of imperfect men and women, to be swayed by passion, by prejudice, by fashion and by misinformation. If the General Synod of the Church of England makes a wrong decision, it is the duty of every faithful member of that church to accept the decision if it is a matter of law and practice, though perhaps under protest; and if it is a matter of doctrine to tolerate it without leaving the church or creating a schism, in the hope, perhaps in the confidence, that the wrong decision will eventually be righted. But nobody is bound to *believe* a doctrine which his or her conscience pronounces to be wrong.

Throughout history there have been many examples of ecclesiastical bodies possessing apparently high authority which have yet made wrong decisions. In the year 359/360 a General Council of the whole church, meeting in pieces at various places, approved of a creed which less than twenty years later the great majority of Christians repudiated. In the fifteenth century the General Council of Ferrara-Florence, meeting at intervals between 1438 and 1445, agreed upon terms of reunion between the Western and the Eastern Orthodox Churches which were very soon repudiated by the mass of the Orthodox faithful. The book *Essays and Reviews* published in 1860 was condemned by the Convocations of both Canterbury and York for ventilating views most of which would now be accepted by all intelligent Christians. We have already referred to the serious mistakes made by the Biblical Commission set up by Pope Leo XIII in 1902.

'Time makes ancient good uncouth.' The lapse of years, the hindsight granted to posterity, the perspective of history, enable us to see clearly what were when they first emerged difficult and complex issues. In relation to Christian doctrine, this means that the court of final appeal is the agreement or common mind of the great majority of believing men and women expressing itself over a long period. In traditional language this is called the *consensus fidelium*. The Eastern Orthodox Church wisely teaches that there is no tribunal, no authority, higher than this, and that here most decisively the Holy Spirit speaks. We can see plenty of examples of the *consensus fidelium* working in history. The ancient and medieval church saw nothing wrong in slavery; we repudiate it as incompatible with Christianity. The mediaeval church and the post-Reformation church up to the beginning of the eighteenth century thought it right to put people to death for professing religious opinions which the majority thought wrong and dangerous. We would regard this practice as horribly sinful. The doctrine that God inflicts everlasting punishment in hell on people because they hold wrong religious beliefs was believed very widely in all Christian churches up to the nineteenth century. Today it is not seriously believed by more than a small handful. The *consensus fidelium* appears to have banished the use of the Athanasian Creed in public worship in the Anglican Communion and in the Church of Scotland to have brought about the collapse of ecclesiastical courts for regulating the morals of believers and in the Church of Rome it bids fair to make official doctrine about birth control a dead letter.

But we must remember two points about the *consensus fidelium*. This process has nothing to do with head-counting. Head-counting may be a good method of arriving at decisions in democracies, but it is a disastrous way of forming doctrine. That is the first point. The second is that the operation of this consent of the faithful is a long-term affair. We must not identify the decisions of synods nor even of councils, not temporary enthusiastic movements, with it. A week may be a long time in politics; a century is a short time in church history. The Holy Spirit acts not only in his own way, but in his own time.

Before the advent of biblical criticism the most common means by which the clergy upset the laity was by preaching from the pulpit extreme or even lunatic theological opinions. But since the middle of the last century the laity have been much more often upset by hearing the views of clergymen who are abreast with modern developments in biblical scholarship or who are aware of modern theories accepted by the great majority of educated people, such as for example the theory of the evolution of the human species from the higher primates.

Two extremes are to be avoided here. On the one hand we have the type of clergyman who glories in being up to date and who very often proudly describes himself as a heretic. Frequently his heresy merely proves the shallowness of his understanding of the particular problem he is expounding. But in any case no theologian should be happy to find himself advocating heresy. The heretic is not always right! Heresy is not a desirable end in itself. On the contrary, the devout Christian will wish to agree with Christian tradition as far as intellectual honesty allows him. But the other extreme is more common today: this is the type of preacher who regards what he calls 'upsetting the people' as the worst of all possible crimes, and who therefore deliberately avoids ever challenging traditional views, even when he is well aware that they are wrong and intellectually indefensible. There is an opinion widely diffused among people in this country, very often non-church-goers or non-believers, that there are certain things which a clergyman ought to believe, whether they are credible or not. Thus when some prominent cleric has thrown doubt on the historicity of the Virgin Birth, or on the inerrancy of the Bible, outsiders sometimes accuse him of dishonesty or at least hypocrisy. He is paid to believe and defend such tenets. If he does not do so he is somehow not playing the game.

Behind this lies an unacknowledged assumption that Christianity is quite irrational and intellectually indefensible. If one is going to believe in it one ought to accept a wide range of incredible beliefs, because that is what constitutes Christianity. People who are determined to make use of their reason cannot be believing Christians.

This is nonsense. Like every other system of belief, Christianity must adjust itself to new knowledge. This does not mean that it is a putty-like thing, the mere reflection of the *Zeitgeist*. Every Christian has a duty to think out his faith by means of such light and knowledge as he possesses. The more highly educated a Christian is, the more he should acknowledge this obligation. The real *trahison des clercs* is when those who are highly educated refuse to use their education in order to illuminate their faith.

This does not assist the well educated clergyman or lay reader who is aware of the main conclusions of biblical criticism, and of the points where traditional belief and modern knowledge clash, but who has to expound the Christian faith every week to a congregation most of whose members have very little realization of the problems which biblical criticism and modern knowledge pose for the Christian. One thing must be asserted, however: there is nothing to be gained by hiding such problems from the flock. Thus we should confidently teach, for example, that Isaiah 40–55 was written in Babylon in the sixth century BC, not in Jerusalem in the eighth century; that the Book of Daniel gives us not history but story; that the Book of Jonah is a parable not an historical record. We should not be afraid to describe the Fourth Gospel as offering a

highly theological picture of Jesus differing at many points from the
Jesus of history as far as we can recover him. All this does not need
to be done in a polemical, obtrusive, or challenging manner, but
just as it comes up in the course of the lectionary or the church's
year. Gradually over a period of time one's congregation will begin
to see the point, will begin to ask relevant questions, and even to do
some study for themselves. So when some church leader makes a
statement about Christian belief or the Bible that seems to be
shocking or destructive, the impact will be lessened. Either the
congregation will realize, however dimly, that he is struggling to
meet some of the difficulties to which we have referred above. Or if
he is wrong, they will realize why he is wrong. At least they will
not condemn him solely because he is not speaking according to
tradition.

3. Preaching the Word of God

One of the most important functions of the ministry is to preach the
word of God. We shall deal later on with the apparent anomaly that
preaching the word is not confined to the ordained ministry as is
presiding at the eucharist.

In the New Testament the theme of preaching the word is much
more prominent than is either baptism or the eucharist. Jesus sends
out his disciples to preach the message of the kingdom. In Paul's
thought preaching the gospel is constitutive for the apostolic office
and for the apostolic community. In Hebrews the word of God is
described as 'sharper than any two-edged sword' (Heb. 4.12). In
the deutero-Pauline Ephesians the word of God is identified with
'the sword of the Spirit' and is part of the Christian's panoply (Eph.
6.17.). In Acts the preaching of the word is the chief activity of all
the main characters in the history. In I Peter 1.23 Christians are
described as having been born again by means of the word of God
that lives and abides. In Rev. 1.9 we are told that the author is in the
island of Patmos 'because of the word of God and the witness of
Jesus'.

As soon as we learn anything about the worship of the early
church after the period of the New Testament, we find that a
sermon or homily was an invariable part of the Sunday eucharistic
celebration. Very soon we begin to have examples of sermons given

on special occasions by Christian leaders. One of the earliest is the Easter homily of Melito of Sardis (ob. *c*. 190). Later on we have ample homiletic literature from all the great theologians of the church such as John Chrysostom and Augustine. The tradition of composing, uttering, and publishing sermons never dies out through the Dark Ages and the medieval period. But the Dark Ages in the West witnessed a disastrous break-down in educational facilities, and very often the local parish priest was not sufficiently well educated to be able to preach. Thus the sermon ceased to be an invariable part of the Sunday eucharist. Not that preaching died out. A conscientious and well educated priest would preach every Sunday. After the beginning of the thirteenth century the duty of preaching was often assumed by the friars. Indeed there are many complaints from the fourteenth century onward that the friars were monopolizing the preaching function in the parishes. Like many other features of the church in the West, however, by the year 1500 preaching had reached a low ebb.

The Reformation brought a great revival of preaching the word. The primary accusation that Luther made against the church of his day was that it had forgotten the gospel message or overlaid it with extraneous material. He therefore laid great emphasis on preaching. This is equally true of the churches that stemmed from Calvin's reform, the Reformed tradition proper. Here preaching became the main occupation of the minister. Except on the comparatively rare occasions on which the eucharist was celebrated, Reformed worship, one might almost say, *was* preaching. This tradition has continued right up to the present day: in most services of the Presbyterian, Methodist, Congregationalist, and Baptist traditions the sermon is the most important element. Only the other day an obituary appeared in *The Times* of a distinguished minister of the United Reformed Church in which it was claimed that his main activity in life had been preaching.

In Anglicanism from the sixteenth to the nineteenth century also preaching was regarded as one of the most important functions of the priest. Sermons of two hours' duration were by no means uncommon. Since the Reformation did not bring with it an automatic improvement in clerical education, it was at first considered perfectly legitimate that the parish priest should read a homily instead of preaching on a Sunday and a book of homilies was officially provided. Up till quite recent times sermons (sometimes a weekly sermon provided by an agency) were regarded as marketable commodities, and there was a brisk trade in sermons for the use of clergy who were too ignorant, too lazy, or too modest to compose their own.

The Oxford Movement, with its strong emphasis on the eucharist as the main Sunday service, meant that the sermon was rather downgraded among those affected by Tractarian ideas. Until quite recently one might expect an Anglo-Catholic clergyman to be less than enthusiastic about preaching and even rather inclined to look down on his Evangelical colleagues, and of course on all Free Church ministers, because they prized the sermon highly. But two factors have altered this. The first is the influence of the neo-orthodoxy of Karl Barth. For Barth preaching the word of God was the supreme duty of the minister. It is the preaching of the word that constitutes the church. This is a Reformation insight fully accepted by the Church of England. Article XIX in the Thirty-Nine Articles declares that 'the visible Church of Christ is a congregation of faithful men, in which the pure word of God is preached and the sacraments be duly administered'. The other cause for a renewal of preaching in Anglicanism is the effect of the Second Vatican Council. This council represented, among other things, an acceptance by the Church of Rome of the Reformation emphasis on the Bible and on preaching. Preaching sermons had never ceased in that church. Indeed they may be said to have had greater significance in that they were almost the only part of the mass that was uttered in the vernacular. But there was little or no idea of preaching the word of God, and very often the 'homily' consisted entirely of moral exhortation. Vatican II, however, sparked off a revival of biblical preaching in the Roman Catholic Church. Today if you enter a Roman Catholic church on a Sunday on the continent you are as likely to hear a sermon carefully based on the Bible, expounding the word of God, as you are if you enter a reformed church. Preaching the word in a responsible way is therefore a necessary ingredient in authentic Christian worship.

It is obvious that preaching the word is not something to be taken in hand without serious consideration. Preaching does not mean saying anything or everything. In a Christian context it means preaching the word of God or preaching the gospel. There are therefore two major parameters or boundary lines within which anyone must work who wishes to preach the word of God. The word must be

(*a*) related to the message of Christianity as recorded and witnessed in the Bible,

(*b*) relevant and adapted to the situation of the hearers.

Anyone who preaches while ignoring these limitations does not preach the word of God, whatever else he or she may do.

But once we have identified these parameters, we find ourselves faced by two problems, the second really a part of the first, but sufficiently important to be distinguished by its own technical term. These problems are *hermeneutics* and *demythologizing*. Both these terms were originally coined by German scholars, who combine with an acute understanding of the problem a strong penchant for inventing technical terms. Let us therefore briefly examine the problem of hermeneutics, and we shall find ourselves presently immersed in the problem of demythologizing.

Hermeneutics is simply the discipline of expounding any written text, but of course in this case the text is the Christian scriptures, the Old Testament as well as the New. In order, then, to be able to preach the word of God, we must understand the Bible, we must be able to expound it, that is, explain what it means and of course apply it to the situation of our hearers. But the Bible is very far from being a monochrome work. It is written over a period of a thousand years in very varying circumstances, using a very great variety of literary forms. This varied context we must try to understand, if the evidence permits us to do so. In some cases the context is uncertain: for instance, no one can say with any confidence in what circumstances the Book of Job was written. However, we can identify four questions which the preacher must try to answer before he can adequately expound *any* passage in the Bible, no matter how apparently straightforward:

1. What do the words actually mean? (Have we got an adequate translation?)
2. In what circumstances was the passage written? (Provenance, historical background.)
3. Who wrote it and with what purpose?
4. What does it mean to us?

As we have indicated above, these questions cannot always be fully answered, but at least the effort must be made. They must not be ignored.

We have not, however, finished with detailing the problem of hermeneutics when we have outlined these four questions. In the first place, the nature of the material means that question 4 can pose special problems of its own. But before looking at that we must observe that in two areas of the Bible very important ancillary questions arise. One set of ancillary problems is connected with the relation of the Old Testament to the New. When we deal as Christians with any passage in the Old Testament, we must ask ourselves how it is related to the New Testament. The relation is not always a simple one of promise and fulfilment. Sometimes the Old Testament passage is actually negated by the New Testament. For example, in I Samuel 15 Saul is rebuked in God's name because he did not slaughter all the Amalekites, men women and children, for a sin committed long before any of them was born. What we learn in the New Testament about the nature of God must convince us that Samuel, in rebuking Saul because of this, could not have been speaking the genuine word of God, however sincerely he believed he was. Sometimes, again, we may have to say that some passage in the Old Testament has no relation to the New Testament. We may not take for granted that the whole of the Old Testament is related to the New Testament. The Old Testament has a life and spirit of its own, not all of which finds its fulfilment in the New Testament. Thus, the Song of Solomon has no authentic relation to the New Testament. A relation can only be invented by an arbitrary use of allegory.

A further complication arises here. When we read the New Testament we find that New Teastament writers frequently quote the Old Testament, often claiming that the words of the Old Testament are fulfilled in some event of the New Testament, or by the saving events of the New Testament as a whole. Thus for example in Matt. 2.15 it is claimed that the flight to Egypt (and presumably the return) was a fulfilment of Hos. 11.1. If we look at Hos. 11.1 in its context, we can see no such connection: Hosea is referring to the exodus event. Only if we are willing to regard the infant Jesus as representing the true Israel, can we make any sense of Matthew's claim. And even if we are willing to do this, there is nothing very significant about Egypt in the context of Jesus' infancy. Hence we often encounter considerable embarrassment when we try to expound those places in the New Testament where a fulfilment of Old Testament prophecy is claimed. Our way of understanding the Old Testament is not always the way in which New Testament writers understand it.

The other area of complication is connected with the person and teaching of Jesus. The difficulty is this: often the evangelists seem to present Jesus, especially when he is teaching, as if he was addressing their situation and not the situation with which he was in historical reality confronted. The great example of this is the Fourth Gospel. The author of this Gospel has so completely adapted the person and words of Jesus to the circumstances in which he (the evangelist) was working, that very often it is impossible to reconstruct the original event or utterance. But the same difficulty on a smaller scale meets us in the Synoptic Gospels. The synoptic writers also tend to present a picture of the Jesus of history that is at least coloured by the features of the Jesus of faith. For example, Matt. 26.53 represents Jesus as saying at the time of his arrest: 'Do you think that I cannot appeal to my Father, and he will at once send me more than twelve legions of angels? But how then should the scriptures be fulfilled, that it must be so?' This looks very like a later theological reflection designed to meet the objection that if Jesus really had been the Son of God he could have freed himself from his opponents by miraculous means. When therefore we are expounding Jesus' teaching, we would do well to bear in mind two questions:

(*a*) What did Jesus mean by it?
(*b*) How does the evangelist mean it?

We may not always be able to answer (a) very adequately.

Finally, there is the problem of demythologizing. This problem is connected with the fourth of our original basic qustions: 'What does it mean for us?' Of course this question has always been with the church, but it was Rudolf Bultmann who posed it most acutely in our epoch. What he meant by demythologizing was that many of the presuppositions of the New Testament writers (and he was thinking of the New Testament in particular) consist of concepts and beliefs which we cannot accept today. He called them 'myths'. The ancients believed in a three-storied universe, a heaven above, a middle earth, and an underworld. Again most of them seem to have believed in the existence and influence of demons, invisible spirits on the side of evil who could invade and possess human beings and animals. Connected with this is the belief which Paul and his school evidently held in the existence of superhuman powers which Paul called 'the rulers of this world' (I Cor. 2.6) and his disciple called 'principalities ... powers ... the world rulers of this present darkness ... the spiritual hosts of wickedness in the heavenly places' (Eph. 6.12). Most of these cultural presuppositions we cannot today share, because of our educational background and the very great changes that have taken place in the fundamentals of European thought since the first century AD. The problem before us is obvious: what are we to make of these beliefs? Can we find equivalents in our own *Weltanschauung*? We are under no obligation to accept the very radical solution of this problem advocated by Bultmann, but we cannot deny that the problem exists.

By way of illustration we give three instances of the unhappy consequences of ignoring the fundamental questions which hermeneutics poses to the thinking Christian. All are drawn from real life.

1. A Jewish rabbi, expounding Num. 12, commended Moses for his freedom from racialism because he married a Cushite (Ethiopian), and the rabbi contrasted the narrow-mindedness of Aaron and Miriam, who opposed the marriage. Quite apart from the question of historicity, this was an unwarranted importation of a modern problem into an ancient situation.

2. In Mark 10.18 Jesus, on being addressed as 'Good Teacher', replies 'Why do you call me good? No one is good but God alone'. An Anglican vicar preaching on this text suggested that Jesus was ambiguously hinting at his own divinity. He meant his hearers to reason: 'Only God is good; but Jesus is good; therefore Jesus is God'. This is an example of illegitimately reading into the situation in which Jesus spoke those words a belief about Jesus' relation to God which only arose some time after his resurrection.

3. More than fifty years ago a Cambridge professor of theology, setting out his philosophy of religion in what became a well-known book, claimed that he found support for his own evolutionary interpretation of Christianity in the teaching of St Paul, referring to

such passages as Eph. 1.9–10; 3.9–12. This particular scholar was a theologian rather than a New Testament expert, but he might very well have known that in all his letters right up to Romans Paul manifests a firm belief in the imminence of the *parousia* quite incompatible with the evolutionary view which this scholar attributed to him. Only by assuming Pauline authorship of Ephesians was his argument valid. But Pauline authorship of Ephesians was denied by the great majority of competent scholars outside England. Only the rather amateur and out-of-date way in which too much New Testament scholarship was then conducted in some of the English universities can account for so distinguished a theologian putting forward so absurd a theory.

Our discussion of the problems involved in preaching the word of God might well make it seem an almost impossible task today. But this is not the case. The Bible is not an out-moded or out-dated collection of ancient documents. It can and does still speak to modern men of all cultures and all classes. This is because it is concerned with people who genuinely themselves heard the word of God in their generation and acted on it. Some of them actually saw and heard the Word made flesh. We can enter into and share their experiences and thereby hear the word of God ourselves and do it. But we must be aware of the circumstances in which the word was originally uttered and do our best to avoid those obstacles which we put between ourselves and the word if we ignore the context in which it was uttered, and behave as if we had unmediated access to God's utterance.

We end by looking at two objections which could be made against our exposition of what preaching the word of God means:

(*a*) 'Surely preaching the word, in whatever form, must become monotonous. May we not assume that the average congregation knows the content of the word of God already?' The same objection could be made about the celebration of the eucharist: in our eucharistic service we are remembering the same series of events every Sunday. But we are not justified in saying that the repetition of the eucharist must be monotonous. It is the living God whom we encounter there, and there is nothing monotonous about him. Preaching is therefore in its own mode a form of *anamnēsis*. It is an entering into, and in some degree experiencing for ourselves, the salvation which God offers us in Christ. The Reformers liked to claim that the sacrament was the word made visible; and it is true that in a properly run Christian community word and sacrament supplement and balance each other. Neither will be monotonous if both are properly observed.

(*b*) 'You have maintained that the president of the eucharist should be a properly ordained minister. But you do not make this a condition for preaching the word. If both word and sacrament are churchly ordinances surely you ought to restrict the preaching of the word to those who are ordained.' This is a point worth considering: a hundred and fifty years ago this objection would have been accepted as valid by the vast majority of Anglicans. Today, with the growth of an educated laity and the reduction in the numbers of clergy relative even to the number of church-goers the sight of a lay man or woman in the pulpit is quite normal in the Anglican Communion and the Free Churches, though it is still very rare indeed in the Roman Catholic Church. We should point out that normally only those licensed to preach are allowed in Anglican pulpits. In this sense therefore preaching the word is restricted to those who have been at least commissioned to do so. The fact that sometimes those who have not been commissioned are allowed to preach the word does not destroy the consistency of our position. We do not maintain that the eucharist *can* only take place if an ordained minister presides, but merely that it should be required as a condition. Similarly we are not so foolish as to maintain that only those commissioned are capable of preaching the word, but merely that preaching the word should normally be restricted to those who have a commission to do so. In our discussion of the relation of the ordained ministry to the eucharist we have emphasized that a state of affairs in which any group of Christians should be encouraged to celebrate the eucharist among themselves would be most undesirable (and we compared this with the consequences of indiscriminate baptism by any member of the church). In the same way, a church in which anybody, or even any Christian, was welcome to preach the word at the Sunday service would be a church in great danger of losing the gospel altogether. (And if it is objected that this is exactly the state of affairs in the Society of Friends, we must regretfully conclude that they have to some extent lost the word of God as we understand it.) God's word is not anybody's word. The church has a right to be protected from heretics, cranks, and fanatics.

We should also observe that preaching the word, unlike celebrating the eucharist, is not a community action. It can only be done by one person at a time. There is therefore no danger in this respect that it should lapse into a mere act of private devotion, as we suggested might happen to the eucharist if laity were encouraged to preside at it. But preaching the word is not a purely subjective matter either. There is an objective element in it, in the sense that the preacher is not free to express his or her private feelings, opinions, or emotions. He is not even relaying his own subjective experience, though his experience may very well be relevant to his preaching. He is accountable to his Lord for what he preaches and there is an objective rule of faith by which his faithfulness can be judged. A state of affairs in which preaching has degenerated into a purely subjective expression of the preacher's own ideas is closely comparable to a state of affairs in which the eucharist has degenerated into an individualistic rite in which I meet my Saviour and enjoy my religious emotion without any necessary reference to any of my fellow Christians. It would perhaps be not unjust to say that the church in the West fell into this error during the first half of the twentieth century. A combination of the Liturgical Movement and the theology of Karl Barth may have saved us from this peril today.

9

The Holy Spirit and the Church

1. How do you Know that you Have the Spirit?

'Have you received the Holy Spirit?' This question is actually asked in Acts 19.2. Paul encounters 'certain disciples' in Ephesus. He says to them 'When you believed did you receive the Holy Spirit?' They reply that they had not even heard that there was a Holy Spirit. It then transpires that they had only received John's baptism. Thereupon they are baptized into the name of the Lord Jesus. Then Paul lays his hands upon them and they receive the Holy Spirit. The sign of this is that they begin to speak with tongues and to prophesy.

Luke does not mean this incident to indicate standard practice in the church of his day. But it suggests that in the apostolic church the reception of the Spirit was an event which a Christian might expect to be indicated by clear signs. How far Paul himself used the imposition of hands as part of Christian initiation we do not know. There is no evidence of any such rite in any of the churches to whom Paul writes his letters. But there is plenty of evidence that in Paul's churches the presence of the Spirit was indicated by verifiable signs. People prophesied or spoke with tongues or interpreted others who spoke with tongues. In I Cor. 14.6 and 26 Paul gives an account of the various Spirit-inspired activities that could be expected in Christian worship. They consist of 'a revelation, a piece of knowledge, a prophecy, a teaching'; and in v. 26 he adds 'a psalm', 'a tongue', and 'an interpretation'. It is not easy to distinguish between the first three of these. 'A revelation' could mean direct guidance by God as to what was to be done. Thus in Gal. 2.2 Paul describes how he went up to Jerusalem 'as a result of a revelation'. But it could also mean the revelation of some heavenly secret. In II Cor. 12.7 Paul associates 'revelations' with the experience which he had undergone of being transported to the third heaven and hearing unutterable words. What is 'a piece of knowledge' (literally 'a *gnosis*')? Perhaps it has some connection with the understanding of the central mystery of the cross. In I Cor. 2 Paul uses the same verb 'to know' to refer to the apprehension of this mystery. 'A prophecy' might mean an interpretation of scripture. But in Acts 11.28; 21.10 we find a Christian prophet Agabos making predictions about the future, so that is what the word may mean in I Cor. 14.6. A 'teaching' here has probably to do with catechetics and will indicate a piece of teaching suitable for those preparing for baptism. The 'psalm' might mean one of the psalms of David but more probably refers to some early Christian hymn such as we find quoted in Eph. 5.14. 'Speaking with tongues' and 'interpreting' need no explanation. They are frequently referred to in I Cor. 13 and 14 and in Acts.

What all this activity of the Spirit signifies is that the early days of Christianity were marked by an outburst of ecstatic phenomena such as have often accompanied religious revivals ever since. They are not to be regarded as essential elements in Christian experience. Indeed Paul himself emphasizes this. He consistently refuses to make any capital out of the remarkable experience of rapture and revelation which he recounts in II Cor. 12. And we can see him in I Cor. 12 and 13 deliberately underlining the importance of the major gifts (I Cor. 13.13). These are the famous trio faith, hope and love. Of course we know Paul's conclusion: the greatest of these is love. As well as this we have in Gal. 5.22–23 a list of the qualities which go to make up 'the fruit of the Spirit': love, joy, peace, long-suffering, goodness, decency, faith, gentleness, self-control. Not one of these necessarily implies an unusual or ecstatic phenomenon.

We conclude therefore that as Paul's experience of the life of the church increased he realized more and more clearly that the Spirit is primarily, basically, and normally manifested in a Christian lifestyle. Ecstatic phenomena, which Paul certainly does not undervalue, are indeed gifts of God, but they are not a necessary or invariable sign that one has received the Spirit.

John, who wrote a full generation later, has no doubt on this score. In the discourses about the Paraclete which we read in John 14–16 many impressive promises are made about what the Spirit is to enable the disciples to do, but nothing is said about speaking with tongues or indeed about any ecstatic phenomena at all. When Jesus endows the disciples with the Spirit in John 20.22 no ecstatic phenomena follow. This seems to be John's version of Pentecost. If so, it is quite a muted event. The Spirit enables us to live the Christian life, and the sign that we have the Spirit is simply the living of the Christian life itself.

In view of this perhaps we should look again at our original question: 'How do you know that you have the Spirit?' We may well ask, why do you want to know whether you have the Spirit? The desire for some specific sign or signs that guarantee possession of the Spirit is not a healthy one. The Spirit blows where he wills. We cannot docket him, or patent him, or standardize him, or ration him, or computerize him. He is not amenable to scientific study. Possessing the Spirit means nothing more nor less than that God is at work in you. If God is at work in you you are not the person who should be concerned to know it, or notice it, or estimate it. That is the part of others. Anyone who opens himself or herself to God receives the Spirit. The Christian life is life in the Spirit. This life begins with baptism and continues as long as we live – unless we choose to abandon it:

> Return, O Holy Dove, return,
> Sweet messenger of rest.
> I hate the sins that made thee mourn
> And drove thee from my breast.

So wrote William Cowper. We possess the Holy Spirit if we have undergone Christian initiation, if we are striving to live the Christian life, if we are attending Christian worship and partaking in the sacrament of the eucharist. There are no other essential signs of possession of the Spirit, no matter how many ecstatic graces may be available for Christians by the mercy of God. Only sin can deprive us of the Spirit, and forgiveness is always accompanied by the presence of the Spirit. 'How do I know that I have the Spirit?' You could not ask that question if you did not already possess him. If you begin worrying as to whether you have the Spirit or not, you have not yet understood who he is.

In the New Testament there is frequent mention of Christian prophets. These were, as far as we can discover, individuals who made striking remarks showing insight into the circumstances facing the church of their area, or who predicted correctly what would happen in the immediate future (see Acts 11.27–30; 13.1–3; 21.10–14). It is to be noted however, that even in the New Testament prophets did not always prophesy with exact correctness; Agabus' famine took place, but not throughout the whole world, and his prediction that the Jews would hand Paul over to the Roman authorities was not exactly fulfilled. Moreover the true prophets of the Old Testament emerge from a penumbra of false or ambiguous prophets. These early Christian prophets are known to have continued as a phenomenon in the primitive church for some time. The *Didache* mentions them. It is often thought that the movement at the end of the second century called Montanism arose as a kind of protest at the disappearance of prophecy in the early church. But in fact fairly soon the practice of prophesying in this way fell into abeyance.

Whenever there has been a movement towards returning to the teaching of the New Testament in the church, the practice of prophesying has cropped up again, as has the practice of speaking with tongues. The early members of the Society of the Friends often prophesied thus. Those Christian groups which devote themselves to particularly intense religious emotion often revive this practice; it is widespread in Pentecostal and charismatic circles today. Whether this sort of prophecy is of any real benefit to the church is doubtful. The messages of these prophets are not usually of a particularly impressive sort, and their predictions, if they make them, often remain disappointingly unfulfilled. The 'gift of prophecy' too often gives rise in the prophet to an arrogant and dogmatic attitude towards his or her unprophetic, unilluminated brothers and sisters.

But to dismiss those people who mistakenly imagine that they can in an archaistic manner revive precisely the conditions of the primitive church is not to dismiss the whole subject of prophecy. The example of the prophets of the Old Testament, who were for the most part men sent by God to recall God's people to obedience to him, and who were approved by posterity as such, should remind us of this. The prophets whom we should look for are not the plants forced in the hot-house of sectarian religious experience, but those great men and women who, usually swimming against the current of the age, have spoken unwelcome but forceful truths to the church, such people as St Francis, Martin Luther, John Wesley, Josephine Butler, Sören Kierkegaard, Simone Weil, Feodor Dostoevsky, Reinhold Niebuhr, Teilhard de Chardin, and Alexander Solzhenitsyn. The trouble is that it is usually only in retrospect that these prophets are recognized and honoured, as it was with most of the prophets of the Old Testament. But at least we can cultivate an attitude of self-critical expectancy so that we shall have some chance of recognizing the prophet when he or she appears. All we can be sure is that the prophet will appear from a quite unexpected quarter and in an unexpected guise.

'It seemed good to the Holy Spirit and to us', said the apostles at the Council of Jerusalem (Acts 15.28). Since then many Christians have claimed the direct inspiration of the Holy Spirit, from irregular prophetic figures like George Fox to Popes making allegedly infallible pronouncements. The Christian must believe that, as he has been baptized and drunk of the Spirit and is in Christ, so he is under the guidance of the Holy Spirit. He should indeed expect the guidance of the Holy Spirit. But how can be recognize it?

It must first be realized that all Christian religious activities are done in the Holy Spirit or they are not religious activities at all. The Holy Spirit is much nearer to us, much more intimately concerned in our life in the church and in our individual spiritual lives than we usually realize. The Holy Spirit is in fact God in whom we experience God, God in whom we return to God. We cannot invoke God through Christ except in the Holy Spirit; we cannot pray except in him. He is directly and immediately God whom we experience. God the Holy Spirit is not *identical* with our prayers and religious experience (worship, meditation, 'all holy desires, all good counsels, and all just works'); he is the guide and medium of them. But we are still left with the question: how can we recognize his guidance?

We must be aware that it is very easy to deceive ourselves in the matter of divine guidance. The human heart is almost infinitely deceitful. The less sophisticated we are, the simpler we find it to identify some strong, self-interested motive with the guidance of the Holy Spirit, as when John Wesley in Georgia in the early days of his ministry imagined himself guided to excommunicate the girl who had repelled his advances. The more sophisticated we are, the more adept we are at devising ingenious reasons which disguise our baser motives. Academics as a class are the most pusillanimous of mankind because they are best at inventing apparently good reasons for avoiding unpleasant duties: when Hitler began to destroy the freedom of all the classes of the population in Germany in the 1930s, the academics surrendered as quietly and abjectly as any. It is difficult for us to know our true inner selves, our real motives, the real springs of our character and actions. This is one reason why it is not easy for us to discern the action of the Holy Spirit in our hearts and wills and minds.

One way which we must at all costs avoid is to say, 'When such and such happens, or in such and such conditions, then we shall always know that the Holy Spirit is guiding us'. This is to tempt or to exploit God; man is always liable to try to tempt or exploit God. This applies as much to the church which lays down conditions in which it is certain that the Holy Spirit will speak inerrantly as it does to the people who are sure, as the adherents of the Oxford Group used to declare themselves sure, that when they have their quiet time, or when they invoke God in a certain way, then whatever thoughts come into their hands can be identified with the guidance of the Holy Spirit. This is to deify the unconscious.

Perhaps the best sign of the Holy Spirit, in important matters at least, is if a particular course of action or choice comes repeatedly and steadily into your mind. This can only be calculated after some period of honest prayer and honest consideration. We should never act on impulse or under the influence of some wave of emotion, and imagine this to be the guidance of the Holy Spirit. It is also necessary to ascertain as far as possible whether our minds are deeply engaged in the course of action which we contemplate when we ask for the Holy Spirit's guidance. We should at least pay him the compliment of believing that he acts through the highest powers of our minds, our judgment and our deliberative powers, as well as through our subconscious selves (as he no doubt does also).

Even when we have made a decision in the Holy Spirit, we still make it and act on it only in faith. We never have in this life any right to say with complete confidence 'The Spirit is speaking directly through me. I can speak with unqualified divine authority'. In this life we walk by faith not by sight. It is important to understand that God the Holy Spirit communicates with us through our human faculties, not by by-passing them or freezing them or employing them as an instrument free from human imperfections. Unmediated knowledge of God independent of our human faculties of knowing and perceiving is not given in this life. There are in fact no true oracles and God does not favour oracular means of communicating with men and women. Grace perfects nature perhaps, but does not destroy it or supersede it.

But when we have done our best to seek the guidance of the Holy Spirit, using all the assistance available to us, the reading of the Bible, the advice of our friends, our prayers and meditations and deliberations, and have come to a clear decision, we can and should proceed to act on that decision with cheerful faith, not tinged by anxiety, saying to ourselves, 'It seemed good to the Holy Spirit and to us'.

2. The Spirit and the Church

The church certainly receives the guidance of the Holy Spirit, but it is not a simple task to say how or under what conditions that guidance has been given or may be expected in the future.

There is always a tendency for the ordained ministry to claim that it has a monopoly of the Spirit, or at least that it can arrange for the Spirit to be given to the faithful. The ordained ministry has often claimed that it, and it alone, has the right to decide what is a sign of the Spirit's presence and what is a delusion of Satan. This last claim is made more plausible by the undoubted fact that in many circumstances somebody must decide whether some new phenomenon in the church's life is a manifestation of the Spirit or not, and the ordained ministry is the obvious candidate for this task. Moreover the presence of the Spirit is closely connected with the two great sacraments, and these sacraments are normally administered or at least supervised by the ordained ministry. The ordained ministry has on many occasions claimed the right to withhold the sacraments if it thinks fit. Ambrose, Bishop of Milan in the fourth century, refused communion to the Emperor Theodosius because of a massacre for which he was held responsible. Many a medieval Pope cheerfully excommunicated political opponents. Because they were restricted by the trammels of the establishment, the English bishops in the late eighteenth century refused to ordain John Wesley's ministers in America. Modern Roman Catholic bishops in

Northern Ireland have refused to confirm children whose parents have sent them to non-Roman Catholic Schools. Whether any or all of these actions was justifiable or not, they suggest that the official ministry of the church has always evinced a tendency to attempt to monopolize, control, or at least ration the Spirit in the church.

The Spirit on the other hand has shown that he is not to be restricted to institutional channels. This is not to say that he abandons the institution, but that he is ready to manifest himself by means of non-institutional, or anti-institutional means. This can be illustrated again and again in the church's history. In the ninth century it was surely the Spirit who spoke through Gottschalk when he protested (unfortunately in vain) against his having to continue to be a monk because his parents had made him an oblate in Fulda when he was a child. When the church in France had become desperately corrupt during the Dark Ages, the action of the Spirit can be discerned in the way in which Irish monks, acting on their own initiative and without episcopal permission, revived the life of the monasteries and thus of the church as a whole. The Spirit certainly raised up Francis of Assisi in the thirteenth century when the church in Italy had been taken over by the rich and powerful and had forgotten the poor and outcast. It is true that Francis' movement was officially recognized by a far-seeing Pope, but Francis died a disappointed man, nursing the suspicion that his ideals were being compromised. It was the Spirit who was behind the movements of protest represented by the Spiritual Franciscans, the Waldensians, and the Lollards. They were protesting against a rich and venal higher clergy and an increasingly secularized papacy. We can surely trace the presence of the Spirit in the preaching of the early Quakers, George Fox and William Penn, when they witnessed against an established church that was too much the tool of the powers that be and a Calvinism that presented a repulsive and sub-Christian picture of God. We can detect the influence of the Spirit in the Wesleyan movement which arose at a time when the Church of England had grown torpid and complacent. The Spirit was assuredly on the side of Fr Robert Dolling when he faced the courtier-bishop Randall Davidson in Winchester in 1896. Dolling had spent ten years working with astonishing success in an appalling slum in Portsmouth and was rewarded by being compelled to resign the parish because a bishop who had spent virtually all his ministry among the rich and powerful disapproved of some of Dolling's ritual. It was the Spirit who was among the black congregation in Azusa Street Church Los Angeles in 1906 when what we now call the Pentecostal Movement began. It is the Spirit who has inspired so many confessors and martyrs in the Orthodox (and other) churches of Russia and Eastern Europe that this century may well be characterized by later historians as the century of martyrs. It is the Spirit who is responsible for the Liturgical Movement that has transformed the eucharistic worship of the entire Western church during the last thirty years. Above all, it is the Spirit whose activity can be seen in the *aggiornamento*, that wonderful development in the Roman Catholic Church that has already removed so many of the abuses of which the Reformers complained in the sixteenth century.

Was the Spirit not also responsible for the Reformation? Yes, of course he was. One might well point to the Reformation as the supreme example of how the Spirit will break the church's structures when the church grows corrupt. The Western institutionalized church had been warned often enough that reform was necessary and the official leaders had refused to listen. A hundred years earlier a great chance for reform had been missed in the Conciliar Movement. The Western church had an opportunity to reform and reduce the scope of the papacy. But the opportunity was lost and the papacy was allowed to go on its own way to revolution. However, the fact that the Reformation was undoubtedly the work of the Spirit does not mean that any reformed church is assured of the Spirit's assistance. The Reformers' maxim *ecclesia semper reformanda* has been justified in the course of history. The church must always be reforming itself. If it does not do so the Spirit will chastize it and correct it by instigating protest movements which very often in course of time become themselves institutionalized structures in need of reformation. This does not mean that the church can ever dispense with structures or that the Spirit refuses to use institutions. The one feature of the Spirit which is common to all these movements is that his presence in the official structures is not guaranteed. The Spirit blows where he wills. It is often by means of the neglected and despised that the Spirit corrects and disciplines the church.

The Reformation was the work of the Spirit. But the unreformed part of the church was not left without the Spirit's aid. On the contrary, just when the reformed part was settling down to what was eventually to become the routine of the eighteenth century, the Spirit manifested himself through a remarkable series of thinkers and saints in the French Church: Blaise Pascal, Vincent de Paul, Francis de Sales, John Eudes, Jean de Cassaude, Jean Grou. It almost seems as if when a national church becomes dangerously tied by the bonds of the state the Holy Spirit raises up saints and witnesses to compensate. Add to this the fact that it was the unreformed church in the throes of the Counter-Reformation that began that noble series of attempts to evangelize Asia and the Far East, whereas the churches of the Reformation only became conscious of their missionary obligation two hundred years later.

We may sum up the activity of the Spirit in the church by saying that the Spirit completely ignores our denominational divisions, does not guarantee either doctrinal orthodoxy or traditional structures, and often chooses the underprivileged and despised as instruments of reform in the church.

How far can the church be sure of the Spirit's guidance in questions of faith and morals? Once again we find ourselves in an area where great claims have been made by at least one part of the church. The nineteenth century was a period of great difficulty for the Roman Catholic Church in Europe. Ever since the Reformation successive Popes had come to rely on the support of the Catholic monarchies of Europe, Spain, France, Austria, Naples. During the nineteenth century these apparent sources of support were successively withdrawn and the church was left to face a situation in which new knowledge in a number of important areas was beginning to pose serious question-marks against fundamental doctrines. The Roman Catholic Church reacted by rallying round the papacy and by instituting a process of increased centralization. Both the life and the thought of the church were to be brought under stricter control. No concession was to be made to modern thought. This movement reached a fresh stage in 1870 with the declaration by the First Vatican Council of the infallibility of the Pope. This infallibility, it is true, was carefully defined. The Pope was only infallible 'when he speaks *ex cathedra*, that is when – fulfilling the office of Pastor and Teacher of all Christians – on his supreme apostolical authority, he defines a doctrine concerning faith or morals to be held by the Universal Church'. It was believed by the members of the council who assented to this definition that such a declaration of the Pope's infallibility would assure to Catholics the existence of an authority who could always be relied on to give them guaranteed guidance in matters of faith and morals.

This hope must prove delusive for the following reasons:

(*a*) The infallibility here referred to must be an infallibility expressed in written language. The decree refers to the Pope defining a doctrine to be held by the church. This ties the Roman Catholic Church down to a belief in infallible formulae. We have already discussed in Chapter 8 the difficulty involved by this. Perhaps the doctrine of infallibility may be modified by saying that it is not the words that are infallible but the meaning expressed by them. The question then arises, who is to decide what that meaning is? Anyway, even if the meaning has been agreed on, a new formula will be required to express this meaning. Together with the idea of an infallible Bible, the concept of an infallible Pope, however attractive at first sight it may seem to those who long for guaranteed guidance, proves on closer inspection to be dangerously elusive.

(*b*) The more carefully the conditions are defined under which infallible utterances can be made (and Vatican I defined them pretty strictly), the easier it becomes to argue that any given utterance of a Pope does not fulfil these conditions. This game of using the conditions of infallibility in order to avoid attributing infallibility to utterances of Popes in the past that are now admitted to be mistaken is one which has been extensively played by Roman Catholic apologists ever since the definition was made. The question always arises: how do we know that this particular utterance fulfils the conditions of infallibility? The answer too often given amounts in effect to saying that any utterance may be regarded as a candidate for infallibility until it is proved wrong. Nor is it any good a Pope making an utterance and then deciding that it is infallible. How do we know that the claim to infallibility is infallible? The Pope cannot authenticate his own infallibility.

(*c*) The purpose of the doctrine of the infallibility of the Pope is presumably to assure the faithful that the Bishop of Rome has always been and always will be a reliable guide in matters of faith and morals. But no honest and well-informed historian can deny that during the long history of the papacy some Popes have misled and misinformed the faithful on matters of importance to the faith. In about AD 635 Honorius I committed himself officially to the doctrine of Monothelitism. This doctrine was condemned as heretical at the Council of Constantinople in 681, and Honorius was proclaimed a heretic. This condemnation and proclamation was accepted by the Church of Rome. Again in 1439 Eugenius IV, in response to a request for guidance from the Armenians, declared that the rite known as the *porrectio instrumentorum* formed the essential 'matter' of the sacrament of orders. It is now universally admitted that this rite is of comparatively late origin and formed no part of the service of ordination until some time in the Middle Ages. These are two glaring examples of a Pope misleading the faithful in a matter of importance to the faith. Many others could be quoted. Even if it were argued by a determined defender of the decree of 1870 that these two pronouncements somehow did not fulfil the necessary conditions for infallibility, it cannot be denied that on these two occasions a Pope, under no external constraint, misled the faithful on important questions of faith. There is no advantage to the faithful in a Pope who may sometimes be infallible but who may equally sometimes mislead. A Pope capable of making infallible utterances implies a papacy that never errs. But no historian can deny that the Pope has sometimes erred. There is no guarantee that this could not happen again.

In fact it may be conjectured that papal infallibility is not a doctrine which future Roman Catholic theologians and historians will want to defend. It is not for Anglicans to press them too hard on this point. Some of them are already showing signs of wishing to modify the doctrine. Anglicans should be content to maintain the indefectibility of the church: the Holy Spirit will not permit the entire church to go permanently astray. He will by some means or other (and we have no right to prescribe the means) raise up witness to the truth. The church, like the individual Christian, must be prepared to live by faith. Living by faith is incompatible with any doctrine of infallibility.

It is scarcely necessary to say that sacraments are only effective if the Holy Spirit makes them so. Without the Spirit the Bible is no more than a collection of ancient literature, sacraments are empty gestures, clergy pretentious frauds. Because baptism is baptism into the Holy Spirit, it is a profoundly important rite of initiation in which God in Christ himself brings the baptized person into the way of salvation. It is only because we celebrate the eucharist in the Spirit that we can claim that Christ is present and that by communicating we are united with his body and his blood. That is why it is desirable to include in eucharist liturgies an explicit invocation of the Holy Spirit (*epiclēsis*), though the temptation which sometimes assails the Orthodox to say that all liturgies which omit an explicit *epiclēsis* are invalid must be resisted. Clergy can only receive authority from God because the service of ordination involves the action of the Holy Spirit himself.

But sacraments are not taps for turning the Holy Spirit on and off, means for manipulating the Spirit. The poet Gerard Manley Hopkins in one of his less happy flights of fancy once said in a sermon that the church with its seven sacraments was like a cow with seven udders. We do not simply milk the church for the Holy Spirit. Sacraments do not operate automatically, mechanically nor magically. There are circumstances in which the operation of sacraments do not receive the power of the Holy Spirit. Where the sacrament is used for some false ulterior end, either for superstitious purposes or as a test for qualifying for political office, or when baptism is regarded as a mere formality, akin to innoculation, then we cannot confidently say that the Holy Spirit acts in the sacrament.

Sacraments, like all proper Christian activity, are celebrated in faith, on the assumption that a right attitude of obedience exists in the celebrant and in those who receive them. The individual will not receive what the sacrament confers if he approaches it without faith. But neither the intention nor the moral character of the celebrant or minister affects the sacrament's efficacy. What matters is the intention of the church as expressed in the rite. Sacraments, too, must be administered according to the tradition which controls the conditions of the rite. If, for instance, some Chritians were wantonly and gratuitously to begin baptizing in milk instead of in water or to celebrate the eucharist in rice and tea instead of in bread and wine, then they could have no assurance of the activity of the Holy Spirit. But God is not capricious. If we approach him with honest faith, honestly desiring his presence and activity in our lives, then we can be sure that he meets us in the sacraments of the church.

One of the factors quite properly regarded as affecting the validity of a sacrament is that of intention. Does the intention of the celebrant affect the efficacy of the sacrament, or how are we to judge whether the sacrament has been administered with the right intention? If a properly ordained priest were to celebrate a deliberate mockery of the eucharist in order to amuse non-believers, would this be valid? If a nearly senile bishop were to ordain people priests so inexpertly that he had to be prompted at every other sentence, would these people be validly ordained? The Roman Catholic Church formally holds that the intention of the minister affects the efficacy of a sacrament. This seems a dangerously subjective rule. How can we determine the intentions of individuals? It seems to place a question-mark over the whole process of ordination. In the first case the priest, if he were an unusually unscrupulous individual, might genuinely be intending to consecrate the body and blood of Christ in order to amuse his friends, in which case the sacrament, according to this rule, would be valid. In the second case, nobody could be sure of the intention of a near-senile bishop, or whether he maintained any steady intention at all during the rite, and nobody could say whether he had succeeded in validly ordaining his men.

The Anglican doctrine of intention has always been that what matters is the intention of the church in the administration of any sacrament, and that the question to determine is whether the minister is carrying out the intention of the church, whatever his private thoughts may be. This is in most cases easily ascertainable by examining the circumstances in which the sacrament was administered and the words of the liturgy used. Thus in the case of a mock-eucharist it would be clear, that whatever the liturgy used, the church would not intend to hold a eucharist privately, in order to amuse individuals, and so the doctrine of intention rules out the validity of the rite. In the second case, however faltering the performance of the bishop, he clearly is implementing the intention of the church to ordain, and so the ordination holds good.

God will also meet us in the church's worship. From the first there has been only one main weekly act of worship observed by the entire Christian church. This is the eucharist. For fifteen centuries the eucharist, celebrated in one form or another, was the main service on Sunday for all Christians. It had no rival. It did not apparently occur to anyone that there could be any other normative act of regular Christian worship for Christians. But by the year 1500 the way in which the eucharist was celebrated in the Western church at least had reached an advanced stage of corruption. We have no space to describe this process of gradual corruption in detail, but the deterioration can be briefly described as showing itself in three ways:

(a) the rite was celebrated in Latin, a language which most of the worshippers did not understand.

(b) the communion of the people, the sharing in the bread and the wine, had almost ceased except on great feasts, and even then no one but the clergy were allowed to partake of the cup.

(c) the rite had become concentrated on the necessity for getting rid of our sins; other essential elements, such as thanksgiving, had become obscured or omitted.

(d) the emphasis was rather on the act of elevation than on the communion.

The Reformers attempted to remedy this state of affairs. Their intention was to bring the eucharist back to what it had been in the primitive church. It must be said that in this attempt all of them without exception failed. This was partly because the necessary information as to how the early church celebrated the eucharist simply was not available to them. But it was also caused by the fact that they were mesmerised by the errors of the late medieval period into taking up positions that were too often mirror images of these errors. Thus, they rightly insisted that non-communicating celebration must cease; the people ought to communicate in both kinds whenever the eucharist was celebrated. This the people were not prepared to do; they would not advance beyond the once or twice yearly communion to which they were used. Consequently the Reformers decreed that the eucharist should only be celebrated at such times as a large number of communicants might be expected. so the eucharist in all reformed churches ceased to be the main service on a Sunday and became an occasional event, for most Protestants not to be celebrated more than four times a year.

We can hardly blame the Reformers for this. But we must regret that they did not succeed in re-orientating the eucharist so that it was not so completely concerned with getting rid of our sins. On the contrary, they tended to emphasize the penitential element, so that Cranmer's eucharistic service of the *Book of Common Prayer* of 1552 is positively guilt-ridden in its insistence on reminding us of our sinfulness throughout the rite. The element of thanksgiving, which had been central and regulative in the early service, was almost entirely obscured. By the year 1600 most Protestant celebrations of the eucharist, on the rare occasions on which they occurred, amounted to little more than the repetition of the narrative of the institution accompanied by extensive penitential exercises.

Within the last thirty years all this has changed. The liturgical renewal which has affected the entire Western church, Roman Catholic, Anglican, Lutheran, Reformed, Radical Protestant, has meant a rediscovery of the way in which the early church celebrated this rite, a return to a pattern in which the thanksgiving prayer is central and communion of the people weekly is normal practice, and also an insistence that the service should be celebrated in the language of the people. The Protestant churches generally (in which category we do not here include Anglicanism) have not yet succeeded in restoring anything like weekly communion as the norm. The old tradition that the Lord's Supper was for the uncodevout is still too strong. But when they do celebrate it they all have at least the possibility now of following something like the primitive pattern. We have no space to describe this renewal in detail, but we must briefly indicate the significance of the eucharist for the church's life.

The eucharist is more than a means by which Christians may hope to get rid of their sins. It is a memorial of all God's mighty acts in Christ, his creation of the world by the word, his incarnation in Jesus Christ, the birth, life, teaching, sufferings, death, and resurrection of Jesus Christ (including the institution of the eucharist), the giving of the Holy Spirit to the church. In the eucharist the local congregation on behalf of the church as a whole offers itself to God by means of its offering of the bread and the wine. Then, in the person of the celebrant, it gives thanks to God over the gifts and prays that it may receive the benefits of Christ's redemption. In response to this prayer Christ is present in the Spirit by means of the consecrated elements to those who approach in faith. So the eucharist is the essential link between Christian faith and life. The

New Testament writers, and their successors in the early church, insist that the Christian has only one sacrifice to offer, the sacrifice of himself, and that his life is his sacrifice. Thus the eucharist does not constitute a new or separate or distinctive sacrifice. It is the place where the sacrifice that is the Christian life is made explicit and public and concentrated by being associated with the one great sacrifice of Christ. This process of offering the life is sanctified by the thanksgiving in which we declare the mighty acts of God and reaffirm our faith. Thus faith and life are linked in worship. This link has enormous potential implications for the relation of Christianity to society, for it is not only our individual lives that we are offering but also the life of our society of which we are indissolubly members. But this is an area which is still largely unexplored by Christian thinkers. We live in an age when the impact of society upon the individual is being more strongly realized and closely investigated than ever before. It must follow that future Christian theologians will exploit this most promising field of research.

At any rate Anglicans, in common with the Roman Catholic Church and with some other reformed churches, especially perhaps the Lutherans, are now returning to the early pattern of worship according to which the normal Sunday service is a eucharist at which all the faithful communicate in both kinds. When one considers that a very large part of the Western church has carried through in one generation a reform which implies the repudiation of fifteen hundred years of tradition, one cannot but be astonished that it has all taken place so quietly. Compared with this reform the Reformation of the sixteenth century was a dolls' tea party.

Perhaps it would be appropriate to round off this section by a consideration of the alternatives to the communicating eucharist as the main Sunday service. They seem to be five in number:

1. *A non-communicating eucharist.* This means a celebration of the eucharist at which only the celebrants communicate. The faithful merely look on. This certainly has the support of tradition, for it was the practice of the Western and Eastern church for a thousand years and still is the practice of the Eastern church today. But it largely frustrates the purpose of the eucharist. Christ did not give us the eucharist to be looked at and not shared in. Non-communicating attendance was originally an anomaly against which

church leaders protested. It is still an anomaly today. This practice turns the eucharist into an exhibition, a drama of which the congregation are spectators, a mystery performed by priests. Whatever the dangers inherent in weekly communion, they are dangers which the early church accepted, and they should not be made by us today a reason for discouraging the practice.

2. *The Lutheran 'dry mass'.* In some Lutheran churches, especially the Scandinavian, the normal Sunday service takes the form of a celebration of the mass, duly purged of its objectionable elements, right up to the point where the canon of the mass begins. There the service ends with an intercessory section. Of course a sermon will have been preached at the appropriate point. In Sweden the effect of a 'dry mass' is made all the more striking by the fact that the minister wears full eucharistic vestments even though he is not celebrating the eucharist. This form of service (as indeed the one referred to above) has the advantage that the Church's Year is observed, since the collect and scripture lections for the week are read. But, to an outsider at least, it seems strangely incomplete: the minister gives all the appearance of intending to celebrate the eucharist, and then breaks off just as he reaches the essential part.

3. *The Anglican services of Morning and Evening Prayer.* This is what Cranmer devised when it became plain that the people would not accept the practice of weekly communion. He compiled two daily services from the materials provided by the monastic daily office of the medieval church. It must be confessed that he produced a masterpiece. The two services have the same structure: both the Old Testament and the New Testament are read in order. Psalmody, that priceless legacy from the early church, is retained. The penitential element is not over-emphasized, as it is in Cranmer's eucharistic rite. Both services constitute beautifully balanced acts of worship. Evensong is infinitely the best rite for an evening service on Sunday. The only real objection to Morning Prayer is that it is a substitute for the eucharist, and if for any reason it is impossible to celebrate the eucharist on a Sunday morning Morning Prayer is certainly the best substitute. Modern revision has extended the range of canticles available, a useful reform.

4. *The 'free' service of worship.* This is the order followed by most Presbyterian, Methodist, Congregationalist, Baptist, and Free

Evangelical churches on the average Sunday. It consists in an alternation of free prayer led by the minister with scripture readings and hymns. It is deliberately designed to make the sermon the centre and climax of the service. In the hands of a master it can be very effective, but most ministers are not masters, and it can, and too often does, fall lower than any of the first three alternatives. Its merit is that it gives that flexibility in intercession which is necessary if prayer is to be made relevant. But this is attained at the cost of allowing the faithful no part in the service except the singing of hymns. It puts a very heavy burden on the individual minister and it almost totally excludes the use of the Psalms. We must regretfully conclude that of all the alternatives to the communicating eucharist this is probably the least satisfactory.

5. *The totally unstructured service of the Society of Friends.* This represents a courageous and almost heaven-storming attempt to rely wholly upon the guidance of the Holy Spirit. The company sits in silence unless and until some person present is moved to make a contribution, whether by prayer or by singing or by exhortation. Consequently this form of service can be deeply moving or appallingly banal. It is a form best suited to spiritual athletes who know the value of silence and can use it. It probably works better with a relatively small group. As an ingredient in Christian worship it is much to be desired. As the weekly diet of ordinary Christians it is precarious.

3. The Immediate Future of the Church

If one attempts to pierce the veil of the future in order to predict the life of the church, one cannot in all honesty foresee a revival of Christian belief and practice on a large scale in Europe, though there is no reason to be pessimistic about the growth of the church in other parts of the world. The church in Europe is suffering from a long-term nemesis for its centuries-old involvement with the ruling classes which has permanently alienated it from those classes of people who used to be under-dogs without political privileges and who have now almost completely excluded it from their outlook and culture. And the church has not yet come to terms with the intellectual revolution which the development of European thought since the Renaissance has brought about. These two forces have reduced the strength and influence of the church in Europe in a dramatic manner. There is no reason to suppose that they will not continue to act, or that ways will soon be found to reverse the tendencies and to overcome the problems which they present. The church has lost the social and intellectual leadership of Europe which it possessed from the fifth to the fifteenth centuries of our era.

On the other hand, there is no reason to expect the complete disappearance of the church in Europe. The chief reason for this is that as a religion Christianity has no serious rival in Europe. It is not likely that Islam will takes its place, even though there are today millions more Moslems in Europe than there were a hundred years ago. The only serious rival as a religion is Marxism. But it ought now to be evident that Marxism cannot compete with Christianity as a religion designed to satisfy the needs of the human spirit for security, wholeness and moral integrity, however successful it may be as a political creed. In fact, Marxism has only succeeded in capturing the allegiance of large numbers of people where it has been backed by terror, and, in spite of all the persuasion, compulsion and persecution applied, Christianity has survived and gives every sign of persistence in every Marxist state, with the infamous exception of Albania. Christianity then has an indefinite future as the bearer of an international religious culture (though in a vestigial state) and as a minority movement in Europe.

It seems likely that certain existing conditions within the church will continue for a long time and probably intensify. The shortage of full-time clergy is not in the least likely to diminish. The shortage of full-time male *celibate* clergy (in accordance with the rule of the Church of Rome) is likely to reach crisis proportions soon, so that the future of that church's insistence on celibacy in its clergy is very uncertain; we might almost say that this rule of celibacy is doomed. Not only are there far more careers open to well-educated young men then there were a hundred years ago, careers promising much more pay and a more attractive career structure than the ministry, but the capacity of any denomination to pay a large number of full-time clergy (and, outside the Church of Rome, married clergy) is severely limited. There is no reason to think that any denomination will experience a huge access of affluence or an enormous surge of suitable candidates offering themselves for the ministry (indeed the latter event, if it happened, would require the former to finance them).

This means that every denomination will be increasingly compelled to depend upon a varied, flexible and part-time ministry. This necessity has already compelled most of the non-Roman Catholic churches to institute part-time ministries, that is to ordain people who earn their living in some secular occupation but who also perform ministerial duties of one sort or another in their spare time. In the Church of England they go by the rather invidious name of non-stipendiary ministry; the most important point about them apparently is that they are not paid. But 'part-time' ministry is a more suitable name. The same necessity has produced a vast increase in the number of 'lay' men and women working in some capacity as ministers of the church. Some denominations have always been more inclined to employ the ministry of 'lay' people. In the Church of England so-called 'lay' people now regularly take non-eucharistic services, and even in the eucharist lead intercessions, administer the elements, read lessons and preach. Outside the rites of the church, 'lay' men and women quite often visit the sick and the whole, teach not only children in Sunday School but adults in the courses and study groups and, of course, are largely responsible for the financial administration of the parish. In the Church of Rome the same tendency is manifesting itself in a much timider and more conservative way. That church – much to its loss – has not yet brought itself to hand over the finances of the parish to the people; cardinals and archbishops can still become involved in financial scandals.

It is most likely that this process of diversification will continue and increase. It will have two effects. It will make all churchpeople generally more ready to accept the ministry of women, and in particular the priesthood of women, as they become accustomed to women as well as men performing a variety of functions in the church and in the parish. And it will cause the line of distinction between 'lay' people and clergy, which in some places has become very thin, to become even thinner. The Methodists have Lay Preachers (who in exceptional circumstances can celebrate the sacrament of Holy Communion) and the Anglicans Lay Readers, who usually do a lot more than reading the liturgy and are almost always expected to preach. The difference in function between a

Lay Reader who is licensed to take services, preach and administer Holy Communion, and a deacon in the Church of England is very small indeed. The difference between a male deacon and a female deaconess who has almost exactly the same functions and authority as a male deacon, is altogether invisible, though there are some clergy and some laity (among them some MPs) who can apparently see the invisible. This thinning of the veil between clergy and laity is not at all to be deplored if anyone accepts the principles which have been set forth in this book.

One result of the reduction of the exclusiveness of the clergy has been the democratic spirit which has invaded the government of the church (again with the exception of the Church of Rome). Laity are now accepted as administrators along with clergy in almost every part of the administrative structure of the church, and government by elected representatives of both laity and clergy, including the matter of choosing bishops, is now the general rule. In one respect this is to be welcomed, because it means a more open, representative order in the church's life. But it also contains dangers. The church may succumb wholly to the ideas, prejudices and limitations of the bourgeois, who can afford to take time off to help in administration, and distance itself even further from the working classes. It may stifle originality, and prophetic insight. It may encourage a hampering bureaucracy. It could lead to the clergy being dominated by and afraid of the laity. It could bring the values of the television commentator and the popular journalist into the debates and decisions of the church. We can, however, with confidence conclude that in the future the pattern of the parson as the sole source of religious authority and holy wisdom in the parish will be further eroded.

Most of these trends point to the necessity of the church taking local ministry more seriously than it has hitherto done. 'Local ministry' means choosing for ordination ministers in the local area and confining them to that area, instead of insisting that all clergy, once ordained, can minister anywhere in the church. The difference between a local and an universal ministry is greater than appears at first sight, and demands a capacity for bold experiment and a readiness to learn from errors. It is difficult to reconcile serious concern for local ministry with the present diocesan system of the Church of England, in which the bishop is by necessity anything but local. One set of statistics in the recent report on Urban Priority Areas, *Faith in the City*,[1] suggests that clergy in all types of parishes have little confidence in their bishops when they need moral support. Experiments with local ministry will be useless if local ministers, once ordained, are left without support because dioceses are far too large for bishops to give it.

As far as the future of theology is concerned, there are three movements which have been significant during the last twenty years: the charismatic movement, the revival of conservative evangelicism and the ecumenical movement. The first has had a widespread effect in loosening denominational allegiance and prejudice, for it has influenced almost all denominations. It has brought revival of faith to many people. It has served to remove some angularities, stuffiness and tendency to condescend among Anglicans and Roman Catholics. It has brought the Pentecostal tradition within Christianity from the periphery to the centre of attention. It has also in some cases introduced unnecessary division among Christians when the charismatics have distinguished themselves as holy, saved and genuine from other Christians who are not supposed to enjoy these advantages. It has done little for theology for it has tended to decry the intellectual element in religion. On the whole it is likely that the charismatic movement will blow itself out in the next few years, having served its purpose.

The tension between the conservative evangelicals and those Christians who strive to understand and assimilate the results of modern thought is likely to become a more prominent feature in the life of the church in the immediate future. This is a tension which extends to all denominations. It is one which must be taken seriously but for which there is at the moment no solution in sight. It is made the deeper and bitterer because the conservative evangelicals can point to remarkable success in pastoral work and are often activated by a selfless zeal, whereas the majority of lay people find it difficult to appreciate the point of view of those whom we may loosely call modernists, because comparatively few lay people (and not all clergy) are educated enough in history and theology to understand the points at issue. We are likely to see a continually widening gulf between the assumptions and beliefs of the ordinary churchgoer (and perhaps the ordinary minister or priest) and the outlook of those who are theologically educated. This is a situation which nobody can regard with complacency, but which nobody seems ready to take any steps to remedy. We do not here refer to the debate over the Alternative Service Book versus the Book of Common Prayer, because we are persuaded that it is of little importance; the *Book of Common Prayer* will sooner or later become a significant historical relic and nothing more.

The ecumenical movement shows no sign at all of decline. In its present phase interest tends to be concentrated less on large international gatherings of Christians which take place from time to time (important though they are) than on the conversations, inspired by the movement, which are being held between the representatives of individual denominations, such as Anglican/Orthodox, Roman Catholic/Anglican, Methodist/Roman Catholic, and which in several cases are resulting in the discovery of surprisingly large areas of agreement. Of course, it is one thing to encourage theologians to meet; it is quite another to draw up a scheme of re-union and to persuade everybody to agree to it. So far the only successful examples of the latter procedure have been, as we have already noted in this book, the Churches of South India and of North India, and there have been many failures. But alongside the convergence of the intellectuals there has been a remarkable convergence of ordinary Christians at the parish or congregational level. However difficult it may be to persuade the guardians of the structures of each denomination to modify their structures in order to bring about formal reunion, ordinary worshipping Christians of the great majority of churches are recognizing and treating each other as fellow-Christians in ever larger numbers. Common worship, common study of the Bible, common witness and common action in charitable and evangelizing activity are now of daily occurrence and likely to increase. It is impossible to doubt that this will have a good effect on the prospects of genuine church union in spite of the hesitations of the mandarins and the strong resistance of minority groups.

Finally, the existence of a world-wide church, the fact, for instance, that Christianity in almost all its manifestations is growing faster in Africa than in any other part of the world, is bound to have an effect on the church in Europe. In world-wide denominational and inter-denominational gatherings the voices of the new churches will become more and more powerful and will have the effect of reducing the prejudices and softening the attitudes of the older churches. They will be powerful in persuading the Roman Catholic church to accept a married priesthood. They may erode some of the resistance among Anglicans to the idea of woman priests. They will compel theologians in the West to distinguish between what is purely European and what is genuinely and permanently Christian in their faith and their theology. The Holy Spirit, who puts down the mighty from their seat and exalts the humble and meek, has always tended to work in ways that are unexpected. He probably has some surprises in store for the complacent conventional European Christian.

4. The Holy Spirit and the Future

'The Spirit and the Bride say "Come", and let anyone who listens say "Come" ... He who witnesses to these things says, "Yes, I am coming quickly" Amen. Come, Lord, Jesus' (Rev. 22.17,20). The New Testament ends on this note of intense expectation of the End, the winding-up of history, the passing away of this age and this order and this world, the bringing-in of final judgment and final salvation, all oriented towards the second appearance of Christ in glory. All this (and heaven too!) modern theologians describe by the formal but convenient word 'eschatology'. It is not by coincidence that the Holy Spirit appears in the eschatological passage quoted above, because in the New Testament the Holy Spirit is an eschatological figure and phenomenon, a sign that the Last Age and the Last Crisis have in some sense arrived. There is very little mention of the Holy Spirit in the Synoptic Gospels, and almost none in the teaching of Jesus. Careful enquirers may glean a few references but they are scanty and not particularly significant. But if we make a division between the Synoptic Gospels, which are intended among other aims to record what Jesus did and said in his earthly ministry, even though this record is filtered through the minds and affected by the interests of those who transmitted it in its oral stage, and the rest of the New Testament, from John's Gospel onwards, we find a very different state of affairs. These documents are all consciously written as it were from the other side of the passion and resurrection, looking back on these events in the light of the experience of the Christian community, and here the Spirit begins to appear at once. The Fourth Gospel at one point says explicitly that the Spirit during the earthly ministry of Jesus had not yet been given (John 7.39). But this evangelist ensures that Christ in his last great discourse shall promise the gift of the Spirit, and in the twentieth chapter Jesus formally confers the Spirit on the church (v. 22 and 23). And the rest of the New Testament, from Acts onwards, abounds with references to the Holy Spirit, just as it is full of expectation of the early return of Christ.

The Holy Spirit in the New Testament is indeed much more than a mere promise of final salvation and judgment, a mere trailer or presage of the End. Three times he is called the *arrabon*, the first instalment, of salvation (II Cor. 1.22; 5.5; Eph. 1.14). He is heaven anticipated, the end here proleptically, in advance, the guarantee that the new order is being introduced, God-at-the-end-of-the-world. The Fourth Gospel indicates that the Comforter for most intents and purposes *is* the Messiah returned. It gives us little eschatological language, because Jesus Christ present in the Spirit is the end. Instead of encouraging eschatological expectation, it presents us with Christ living in our midst in the Spirit, final Saviour and final Judge now, calling us now to understand and explore the significance of his person, instead of dizzying ourselves with apocalyptic yearnings and mysterious symbols. The Rabbis had taught that the Holy Spirit would be received, not in this present evil age, but in the next age, the age of the Messiah. The Christians declared that the next age had arrived and was overlapping this one. The proof of this was the presence among them of the Holy Spirit.

In later times the eschatological nature of the Holy Spirit was pushed into the background or forgotten. When the framers of the Nicene Creed of 381 described the Spirit as 'Lord and Giver of Life ... who with the Father and the Son together is worshipped and glorified', they were paying tribute to his eschatological significance, but in a dim and flattened way. But whenever in the later history of the church periods of crisis, of excitment, of turmoil have appeared, then people have returned to a consideration of the Spirit and have revived eschatological expectation. It was so with the Franciscan Movement of the thirteenth and fourteenth centuries. It was so at the Reformation in the sixteenth century. It has been so with the charismatic movement of our day.

But as well as signalling the arrival of the Last Age contempor-

aneously with the old one, the Holy Spirit is also intimately concerned with the church. It is he who gathers the faithful together
in Christ, who sustains them in persecution, guides them in per-
plexity, inspires prayer and worship, sustains the depth and mo-
mentum of the Christian life. The Holy Spirit is in fact God in
whom we return to God, God in whom we experience God, the life
and dynamic of the Christian church and the Christian tradition,
the true Vicar of Christ. He is not a tame force carefully bottled in
ecclesiastical institutions, available to be served out in rationed
doses according to the decision of the hierarchy or the ministry or
specially illuminated saints. He is the Lord of the church, not
subject to human control, and like the wind he blows wherever he
chooses. He is capable of causing explosions within the structures
of the church and bringing about discontinuities and surprises as
his wisdom determines. His judgments are unsearchable and his
ways past finding out. His sovereignty has been, it is hoped, adequately expressed in other parts of this work.

   The Holy Spirit and the church are brought together in an
eschatological context when we consider the relation of God to the
future. God as Holy Spirit is sovereign over time. It is not simply
that God exists in a timeless eternity where all succession is done
away in a single everlasting comprehensive present. The Old Testament is there to assure us that God is no Aristotelian deity, the
unmoved mover rapt in the eternal contemplation of himself while
the whole scheme of things operates at his impulsion. He moves,
intervenes actively in history, and most of all in the history of Jesus
Christ, however difficult it may be for philosophically trained minds
to conceive of this. God is not simply timeless, he is sovereign over
time. This means two things. First, it means that he is not limited
nor bound by time. The career of Jesus Christ is not a closed
incident. It is of eternal and perennial significance, while it is at the
same time something which, like all historical events, happened
once for all and will never be repeated. This once-for-all-ness
(what the Germans call *Einmaligkeit*) combined with eternal significance and application gives Christianity its peculiar character
and reveals to us something of the meaning and contemporary relevance of the apocalyptic and eschatological passages of the Bible.
By the power of the Holy Spirit we can here and now enter into the
life of Jesus Christ, who was an historical character as well as being

the eternal Son of God. In baptism we drink, are immersed in, the Holy Spirit and at the same time we are united in the body of Christ, in the flock of Christ, in the Temple of God. Hundreds and thousands of people visit Jerusalem every year. They eagerly suck up (often quite inaccurate) information about the sites there and spend their money or order to see a tomb of which the only importance is that Jesus is *not* there. They witness with apparent complacence the disgraceful competition of Christian denominations to claim portions of that empty place as their own. It would be well if they were first to read the fourth chapter of St John's Gospel with care. The earthly memorials of Jesus Christ are not the battered remains of archaeological sites in Israel, but the sacraments of the Christian church. In baptism we meet Jesus Christ. In the eucharist we enter again and again into his sacrificial life. Here time is overcome. Here the past becomes present. The inhabitants of Tierra del Fuego and New Zealand do not need to journey across the world to Jerusalem in order to find Christ. He is present, and the true Temple of God is present, wherever his people gather together in the Holy Spirit and call upon his name.

God's sovereignty over time, however, is not only concerned with the past and the present. It is also concerned with the future. To attempt to calculate when the end of the world will take place, using the words of the Bible as a kind of cryptogram capable of conveying to us some exact chronological information, is a peculiarly futile occupation, the study of fools and cranks rather than of rational men and women. But the expectation of an end to history, though it was not destined to come when the Christians of the primitive church thought it would, is part of the message of the New Testament. We cannot imagine what the end would be like. We can only speak of it in images and symbols which break to pieces before our eyes when we attempt to take them literally. The expectation of the end is a Christian myth, and here myth does not mean untrue story, like the myth of the Popish Plot in the reign of Charles II, but something which is so far beyond our conceiving of it that we can only speak of it in picture-language. The significance of the end for us is that it gives a meaning to history. History is not a meaningless succession of fortuitous events, not just one-damn-thing-after-another. Nor is it a cycle endlessly repeating itself to an exactly replicated series aeon after aeon, as some ancient Greeks thought.

It has a goal, a purpose, a consummation. And the whole human race is involved in that purpose. Human beings are not isolated atoms nor lonely individuals trapped in their own subjectivity. There is a solidarity of all men and women, whether black or white or yellow, whether advanced or primitive, and not only all human beings alive now, but the whole human race ever since it became *homo sapiens sapiens*, and all human beings of the future, whatever grotesque or unexpected forms they may take. God is the God of the future as well as of the past. The church guided by the Spirit is the first fruits and paradigm of humanity, but the Holy Spirit is concerned with the destiny of the whole of humanity.

The image for the church which was given prominence by the Second Vatican Council was that of a people on pilgrimage. It is a thoroughly biblical one and one well worth adopting by Christians today. It has seldom been better expressed than in the words of the eighteenth century hymn-writer John Newton:

> Round each habitation hovering
> See the cloud and fire appear
> For a glory and a covering
> Showing that the Lord is near.
> Thus they march, the Saviour leading,
> Fire by night and cloud by day,
> Daily on the manna feeding
> Which he gives them when they pray.

The church as it moves through history cannot see the goal clearly and walks by faith, not by sight. But because the Holy Spirit is guiding and leading, it does not travel aimlessly and it need not lack confidence and purpose.

There is a distinction, originating perhaps in the Middle Ages, between the church militant, the church expectant, and the church triumphant. The church militant is the church on earth at any given moment in history, carrying on its ceaseless warfare with the world, the flesh, and the devil. The church expectant is the group of those faithful Christians who have died and are in God's care but who have not yet attained full beatitude, since they are still being purged before they can stand in God's full presence. The church triumphant is made up of those who have attained the fullness of bliss and are therefore in heaven. This classification is precisely followed in

Dante's *Divina Commedia*. Those in the Inferno have no communication with God and never mention his name except to curse it. Those in Purgatory are full of hope and speak often of God, but are still enduring punishment and cleansing. Those in Paradise enjoy the full benefit of God's presence.

We must not be too dogmatic on this subject: there is no justification in scripture for a belief in purgatory. Such a belief can only be based on our experience on earth: it is hard to imagine how, no matter how faithful we have been in this life, we could on death be immediately purged of all sinfulness so as to be ready to stand in God's unmediated presence. A period of repentance and self-rehabilitation after death seems a reasonable conjecture – but no more. Of course the pretension of the Bishop of Rome to be able to alleviate or curtail the time anyone must spend in Purgatory must be rejected. In any case all Christians must believe in the church triumphant, the number of those who, having served God faithfully on earth, are now with him after death. We should remind ourselves that the church triumphant contains by far the larger number of Christians. It is a dimension in our doctrine of the church that we should not forget. The Christian church is a body the great majority of whose members are not on earth.

This consciousness of the communion of the saints and of the existence of the church in heaven is much better preserved in the Catholic than in the Protestant tradition. The Reformers on the whole, reacting against the corruptions that had crept into the cult of the saints during the Middle Ages, paid insufficient attention to the eternal dimension of the church. Those who were elect to eternal life, they said, fell asleep in the Lord at death and remained asleep awaiting the general resurrection at the *parousia*. The Catholic side of the church, on the other hand, is very much aware of the existence of the saints. As has happened with too much else in the Christian tradition, the Roman Catholic Church has moved towards schematizing, regulating, and institutionalizing our relation to the church in heaven in a way which has not always been for the benefit of Christianity. Perhaps of all traditions in the church the Eastern Orthodox have best preserved that consciousness of the eternal dimension to which we have referred. They do not dogmatize about the condition of the faithful who have died, but enter any Orthodox church anywhere and you must be made aware that the Christian is part of a family most of whose members are not on earth. On all sides are icons of the saints and especially of the Blessed Virgin Mary. Their liturgy has frequent references to the heavenly host. Indeed, any eucharistic liturgy of any value must refer to them. Even Cranmer in his extremely austere rite of Holy Communion includes a mention of 'angels and archangels and all the company of heaven' with whom we join in praise of God.

The New Testament does not provide us with much information about the state of the faithful who have died. The imminent expectation of the *parousia* which runs through most of the New Testament naturally means that there was not much speculation on this topic. Christians who have died are frequently described as those who have 'fallen asleep' (see Matt. 27.52; John 11.11–12; Acts 7.60; 13.36; I Cor. 7.39; 11.30; 15.6,18,20,51; I Thess. 4.13–15; II Peter 3.4). This usage does not necessarily imply that the faithful departed are literally in a state of sleep. Paul twice refers to the possibility of his dying before the *parousia*, and therefore being 'with Christ'. See II Cor. 5.8; Phil. 1.23. His language does not at all suggest that he expects to be in a state of sleep till the *parousia*. The usage therefore simply means that for the faithful Christian death is not an absolute end and that it is not something to be dreaded.

There are, however, two places in the New Testament where there is rather more description of what awaits the Christian after death. The first is Heb. 12.18–24. 'But you have come to Mount Zion and to the city of the living God, the heavenly Jerusalem, and to innumerable angels in festal gathering, and to the assembly of the first-born who are enrolled in heaven, and to a judge who is God of all, and to the spirits of just men made perfect, and to Jesus, the mediator of a new covenant, and to the sprinkled blood that speaks more graciouly than the blood of Abel.' We must bear in mind that this may be a description of what follows the *parousia*. We cannot fail to be impressed by its tone of mingled rejoicing and solemnity. The author of Hebrews had no doubt but that we shall be able to know and recognize our fellow-Christians in the life to come.

The other place in the New Testament where we learn something of the nature of the life after death is the Book of Revelation. Here are depicted magnificent scenes of the heavenly worship. Angels appear frequently sent upon various missions. Those who have died as martyrs take a keen (perhaps a too keen) interest in what is happening on earth (see Rev. 6.9–11). St John the Divine certainly believed that the faithful who have died continue to pray for those on earth. Perhaps we should also mention Jesus' word from the cross in Luke 23.43, where he promises the penitent thief 'this day you will be with me in paradise'. We must not regard this as privileged information about the life to come. It expresses rather the immediacy and reality of the Christian hope.

The faithful departed continue to pray, we may be sure. We may pray *with* them. Indeed we do so every time we join in Christian public worship. May we also pray *to* them? Addressing petitions to the saints has been a Christian practice for many centuries. It was repudiated by the Reformers. There is no evidence in scripture to support it. How are we to view it? Certainly the practice of praying to the saints had undergone much corruption during the Middle Ages. But are we justified in rejecting it completely? It is still a well established custom in the Catholic tradition both in East and West. This practice finds its clearest expression in prayer addressed to the Blessed Virgin Mary, as she is regarded as closest to her son. On the occasion when the present Pope visited the shrine of Knock in the West of Ireland a Roman Catholic priest appearing on BBC television defended the practice of making petitions to the Blessed Virgin on the ground that she knew her son so well that she was better placed than anyone else to induce him to grant our petitions. It must be added that no one suggests the saints can grant petitions on their own initiative; they can only commend our prayers to Christ.

We must confess that as Christians who believe they inherit all that is best in the Catholic tradition we find it very difficult to justify the practice of praying to the saints. It seems to betray a lack of trust in God, a disbelief in what the incarnation is meant to assure us of, God's unfailing benevolence and love towards us. If our petitions are more likely to be granted if they are commended to Christ by the Blessed Virgin, must it not follow that somehow or other Christ has to be persuaded to listen to us or to be favourable towards us? But such an idea runs clean counter to the whole tenor of the New Testament. God in Christ has declared his favour towards us; he does not need to be persuaded to be favourable to us by the exertions of someone else. No doubt millions of Christians will continue to make their petitions to the saints. We should not refuse to be in communion with them because of this. But we may state our opinion that they are mistaken. They behave as if they do not really believe in the mercy of God.

We have said that we pray *with* the saints. We have rejected the idea of praying *to* them. May we pray *for* them? Or rather, may we pray for those who have died? Yes, certainly. It is true that there is no evidence in the New Testament that anyone in the primitive church actually did this (except the dubious example of I Cor. 15.29), but there is nothing inconsistant with the Christian revelation in praying for those who have died. Indeed, if one has had the experience of losing by death someone to whom one is deeply attached, it seems very difficult indeed not to pray for such a person. What else can one do for them, and what better can one do for them? The great and holy bond of prayer transcends the limits of this life and unites us with those who have died. Perhaps this truth is most vividly apprehensible at the eucharist. That is the place where the veil between this life and the next is thinnest.

The church triumphant has also traditionally been taken to be the church as it shall be when all history is ended, all wrong and injustice atoned for, all human striving absorbed into the eternal peace and harmony of God, Father, Son and Holy Spirit, and when, again in traditional language, the saints shall have entered their everlasting rest. As we struggle here, fighting against the world, the flesh and the devil, not only in others but in ourselves, we, the church militant, not yet wholly redeemed, can be cheered and comforted by the hope, not of the conventional pie in the sky, but of the eventual accomplishment of the strategy of God who is good and loving and infinitely resourceful, not only for his church but also for his whole human race.

Notes

1. The Doctrine of the Church: A Historical Survey

1. Charles Gore (ed.) *Lux Mundi*, John Murray 1899.
2. Charles Gore, *The Church and the Ministry*, rev. ed., SPCK 1936, p. 662.
3. Karl Barth, *Church Dogmatics*, T. & T. Clark 1962, IV/3ii, p. 683.
4. See K.L. Schmidt, article on 'ekklēsia' in *Theological Dictionary of the New Testament*, Eerdmans 1964ff., Vol. 3, 1965, p.553.
5. Ibid., pp. 519–22.
6. Ibid., p. 522.
7. Ibid., pp. 528–30.
8. Rudolf Bultmann, *Theology of the New Testament*, SCM Press, Vol. I, 1952, p. 308.
9. Hans Conzelmann, *An Outline of the Theology of the New Testament*, SCM Press 1968, p. 42.
10. H. Ridderbos, *Paul: An Outline of His Theology*, SPCK 1977, p. 328.
11. D.E.H. Whiteley, *The Theology of St Paul*, Blackwell 1969, p. 189
12. Alan Richardson, *Introduction to the Theology of the New Testament*, SCM Press 1958, pp. 286, 290.
13. Bultmann, op. cit., Vol. I, p. 33.
14. W.G. Kümmel, *Theology of the New Testament*, SCM Press 1974, p. 210.
15. Richardson, op. cit., p. 243.
16. This point is made by E. Mersch in *The Whole Christ*, Dobson Books 1949, p. 117.
17. E. Schweizer, article on 'sōma' in *Theological Dictionary of the New Testament*, Vol. 7, 1971, p. 1066.
18. Mersch, op. cit., p. 146.
19. Bultmann, op. cit., Vol. I, p. 192.
20. Ibid., p. 302.
21. Richardson, op. cit., p. 256.
22. So also Ridderbos, op. cit., p. 394.
23. Mersch, op. cit., note 16 above.
24. Lionel Thornton, *Common Life in the Body of Christ*, Dacre Press 1941, p. 298.
25. Richardson, op. cit., p. 256.
26. J.A.T. Robinson, *The Body*, SCM Press 1952.
27. Ridderbos, op. cit., pp. 366–78.
28. Ibid., p. 380.
29. Whiteley, op. cit., p. 198.
30. Ridderbos, op. cit., p. 378.

31. Schmidt, art, cit., pp. 512–13.
32. Stig Hanson, *The Unity of the Church in the New Testament*, Almqwist and Wicksells 1946.
33. Bultmann, op. cit., Vol. II, 1955, pp. 113–14.
34. Mersch, op. cit., p. 394.
35. Ibid.
36. Ibid., pp. 487–88
37. Ibid., p. 578.
38. Avery Dulles, *Models of the Church*, Gill & Macmillan 1976, p. 41.
39. *Lumen Gentium*, I, 8, in W. Abbott and J. Gallagher (eds), *The Documents of Vatican II*, Chapman and America Press 1966, p. 23.
40. II, 15; Abbott, p. 34.
41. II, 12; Abbott, p. 30.
42. III, 18; Abbott, p. 37.
43. III, 20; Abbott, p. 39.
44. III, 20; Abbott, p. 40.
45. III, 21; Abbott, p. 41.
46. III, 22; Abbott, p. 43.
47. III, 25; Abbott, p. 48.
48. III, 25; Abbott, p. 49.
49. III, 27; Abbott, p. 52.
50. IV, 37; Abbott, p. 64.
51. B. Leeming, *The Vatican Council and Christian Unity*, Darton, Longman & Todd 1966, p. 313.
52. Ibid., p. 412.
53. Ibid., p. 414.
54. *Decree on Ecumenism*, III, 15; Abbott, p. 359.
55. III, 22; Abbott, p. 364.
56. Charles Gore, *The Church and Ministry*, p. 400.
57. Ibid., p. 7.
58. Ibid., p. 10.
59. Ibid., p. 41.
60. Ibid., p. 62.
61. Ibid., p. 63.
62. Ibid., p. 99.
63. Ibid., p. 215.
64. Ibid., p. 267.
65. Ibid., p. 298.
66. Charles Gore, *The Reconstruction of Belief*, John Murray 1926, p. 660.

2. The Ecumenical Experience

1. Lesslie Newbigin, *The Household of God*, SCM Press 1953, pp. 21–22.
2. Ibid., p. 22.
3. See above p. 23.

3. An Ecclesiology for Today

1. Karl Barth, *Church Dogmatics*, IV/3ii, p. 729.
2. Ibid., p. 754.

3. Ibid., pp, 568, 767.
4. Newbigin, *Household of God*, p. 127.
5. Ibid., p. 132.
6. Barth, op. cit., p. 722.
7. Ibid., p. 666.
8. F.W. Dillistone, *The Structure of the Divine Society*, Lutterworth 1951, p. 207.
9. This analogy is well worked out by Newbigin, op. cit., p. 116.
10. Newbigin, op. cit., p. 108.
11. Ibid., p. 134
12. Ibid., p. 2.
13. Barth, op. cit., p. 527.
14. Ibid., p. 678.
15. Newbigin, op. cit., p. 74.
16. Ibid., p. 85.
17. Barth, op. cit., p. 784.
18. Ibid., p. 871.
19. Dulles, *Models of the Church*, p. 167.
20. Thornton, *Common Life*, p. 92.
21. See also below Chapter 5, section 3.
22. D.A. Binchy, *Church and State in Fascist Italy*, Oxford University Press 1941.
23. Jürgen Moltmann, *Trinity and the Kingdom of God*, SCM Press 1981.
24. See above p. 62.

4. Orthodoxy

1. G.W.H. Lampe, *God as Spirit*, Oxford University Press 1977; reissued SCM Press 1983.
2. A.T. and R.P.C. Hanson, *Reasonable Belief*, Oxford University Press 1980, pp. 171–87.
3. Ibid., pp. 59–106.
4. Ibid., pp. 107–27.

5. Development

1. Karl Rahner, *The Foundations of Christian Faith*, Darton, Longman & Todd 1978.
2. *Reasonable Belief*, pp. 39–44.

6. The Ordained Ministry

1. *Reasonable Belief*, Chapter VI.
2. Dulles, *Models of the Church*, p. 152.
3. Raymond E. Brown, *Priest and Bishop: Biblical Reflections*, Chapman 1971
4. Robert J. Daly, *The Origins of the Christian Doctrine of Sacrifice*, Darton, Longman & Todd 1978.
5. E. Schillebeeckx, *Ministry*, SCM Press 1980.
6. William Temple, *Christus Veritas*, Macmillan 1930, p. 163 note.
7. Dulles, op. cit., p. 35.
8. R.C. Moberly, *Ministerial Priesthood* (ed. A.T. Hanson), SPCK 1969.

7. Particular Problems

1. *Quarterly Intercession Paper*, No. 313.

8. The Authority of the Church

1. Hans Küng, *Infallible*, Collins 1961, p. 130.

9. The Holy Spirit and the Church

1. *Faith in the City*, Church House Publishing 1985, p. 387, 'Sources of Support for the Clergy'.

Suggestions for Further Reading

The Church in the New Testament

J.A.T. Robinson, *The Body*, SCM Press 1952.
Stig Hanson, *The Unity of the Church in the New Testament*, Almqvist and
  Wicksells 1946.
R.E. Brown, *Priest and Bishop*, Chapman 1971.
C.K. Barrett, *Church, Ministry, and Sacraments in the New Testament*,
  Paternoster Press 1985.
E. Schweizer, *Church Order in the New Testament*, ET, SCM Press 1961.
H. Conzelmann, *An Outline of the Theology of the New Testament*, ET, SCM
  Press 1969.
R. Bultmann, *Theology of the New Testament*, two vols. ET, SCM Press
  1952 and 1955.
H. Ridderbos, *Paul: an Outline of his Theology*, ET, SPCK 1977.
D.E.H. Whiteley, *The Theology of St Paul*, Blackwell 1964.
Articles in the *Theological Dictionary of the New Testament* ed. G. Kittel and
  G. Friedrich, Eerdmans:
  apostolos by K.H. Rengstorf, vol. 1, p. 405f. 1964.
  ekklēsia by K.L. Schmidt, vol. 3, p. 501f. 1965.
  sōma by E. Schweizer, vol. 7, p. 1024f. 1971.
C.K. Barrett, *The Pastoral Epistles*, Clarendon Press 1968.
A.T. Hanson, *The Pastoral Epistles*, Marshall, Morgan & Scott 1982.

The first two books discuss the nature of the church in the New Testament. Robinson's theory made a great impression when it was published but has failed to convince the experts. Barrett, Schweizer, and Conzelmann should be read if you want to know what up to date New Testament scholars believe about the origin of the ministry. Bultmann was the great New Testament authority of the last generation. Ridderbos and Whiteley show how far he can be followed. Read the *Theological Dictionary of the New Testament* for expert information on key words. Thornton's book was of great importance when it came out and still has much to teach us. The commentaries on the Pastorals are a fair indication of what scholars believe about them.

Ecumenism

Lima Report: *Baptism, Eucharist, and Ministry*, WCC, Geneva 1982.
ARCIC Report: *The Final Report*, CTS/SPCK 1982.
B. Leeming, *The Vatican Council and Christian Unity*, Darton, Longman &
    Todd 1966.
H. Vorgrimler (ed.), *Commentary on the Documents of Vatican II*, ET, Burns
    & Oates 1967–69.
Modern Eucharistic Agreement, SPCK 1973.
Modern Ecumenical Documents on the Ministry, SPCK 1975.
S. Neill and R. Rouse, *History of the Ecumenical Movement*, SPCK
    1954–70.

All these are documents necessary for understanding both what the ecumenical movement has achieved and for appreciating the extent to which
different denominations are finding agreement between each other on
doctrinal subjects today.

Definition of the Church

A. Dulles, *Models of the Church*, Gill & Macmillan, Dublin 1976.
H. Küng, *The Church*, ET, Burns and Oates 1976.
L. Newbigin, *The Reunion of the Church*, SCM Press 1948.
    The Household of God, SCM Press 1953.
    A South India Diary, SCM Press, revised ed., 1960.
F.W. Dillistone, *The Structure of the Divine Society*, Lutterworth Press
    1981.
M. Santer (ed.), *Their Lord and Ours*, SPCK 1982.
Doctrine Commission of the Church of England, *Believing in the Church*,
    SPCK 1951.
S. Runciman, *The Great Church in Captivity*, Oxford University Press
    1968.
Joan Hussey, *The Orthodox Church in the Byzantine Empire*, Oxford Univer-
    sity Press 1986.
D. Obolensky, *The Byzantine Commonwealth*, Cardinal 1974.
Kallistos Ware, *The Orthodox Way*, Mowbrays 1979.

Dulles' book is an admirable account by an American Jesuit of the various
models of the church current among all denominations today. It is full of
ecumenical insights. Küng's work was written before he was disciplined. If
you read his other books on our lists as well, you will see why he was
disciplined. He is far from the traditional view of the papacy. Newbigin's
three books were written by someone who, brought up in the Presbyterian

tradition, became a bishop in the Church of South India. He is probably the most able exponent of the theology of the church in any tradition today. Dillistone offers us a thoughtful but not wholly satisfactory theology of the church from an Anglican Evangelical point of view. The book edited by Santer and the Doctrine Commission Report, like all such documents, are a mixture of excellent and less excellent. But they show us the mind of the Church of England today. The four books on the Orthodox Church between them give us a picture of an ancient and living church tradition which we ignore at our peril.

Orthodoxy and Development

J.H. Newman, *Essay on the Development of Christian Doctrine*, Pelican Classics 1973.

R.P.C. Hanson, *Tradition in the Early Church*, SCM Press 1962.
The Continuity of Christian Doctrine, Seabury Press 1981.

N. Lash, *Change in Focus*, Sheed & Ward 1973.

M. Wiles, *The Making of Christian Doctrine*, Cambridge University Press 1967.
The Remaking of Christine Doctrine, SCM Press 1974.

K. Rahner, *Theological Investigations I*, Essay on 'The Development of Dogma'.
Theological Investigations IV, Essay on 'Consideration of the Development of Dogma' Darton, Longman and Todd 1961–84.

G.H. Tavard, *Holy Writ or Holy Church*, Harper 1978.

S. Sykes, *The Identity of Christianity*, SPCK 1984.

F.F. Bruce, *Tradition Old and New*, Paternoster Press 1970.

A.R. Vidler, *The Modernist Movement in the Roman Catholic Church*, Cambridge University Press 1934.

R. Davidson and A.R.C. Leaney, *Biblical Criticism*, Pelican Guide to Modern Theology, vol. 3, 1970.

S. Neill, *The Interpretation of the New Testament 1861–1961*, Oxford University Press 1966.

H. Küng, *Infallible*, Collins 1961.

J. Sobrino, *Christology at the Crossroads*, ET, SCM Press 1975.

R.P.C. Hanson, *The Attractiveness of God*, ch. 6, SPCK 1973.

The books in the list down to Vidler's work are all concerned with the subject of tradition and development, beginning with Newman's classic work first published in 1845, which sparked off the modern debate on the question. Lash's book treats it in a very different manner from that which Wiles' *Remaking of Christian Doctrine* adopts. Rahner and Tavard give the contribution of two able Roman Catholic scholars. Sykes and Hanson represent Anglican approaches to the problem. *The Making of Christian Doctrine, Tradition in the Early Church*, and *Tradition Old and New* present the facts and points to be considered. The next two books (*Biblical Criticism* and Neill's book) throw light on the rise of biblical criticism and its results. The last three books deal with particular doctrines (infallibility, Liberation Theology, and the Holy Spirit).

Ministry

H. von Campenhausen, *Ecclesiastical Authority and Spiritual Power in the Church of the First Three Centuries*, ET, Collins 1968.

A.T. Hanson, *The Pioneer Ministry*, SPCK 1961.

(ed.), R.C. Moberly, *Ministerial Priesthood*, SPCK 1969.

R.P.C. Hanson, *Christian Priesthood Examined*, Lutterworth Press 1979.
Studies in Christian Antiquity, chs. 6, 7, 8, 10, 13, T. & T. Clark 1986.

E. Schillebeeckx, *Ministry*, ET, SCM Press 1980.
The Church with a Human Face, ET, SCM Press 1985.

FOAG Report, *The Priesthood of the Ordained Ministry*, Church of England Board for Mission and Unity 1986.

M.E. Thrall, *The Ordination of Women to the Priesthood*, SCM Press 1958.

Report of the Archbishops' Commission, *Women and Holy Orders*, Church Information Office 1966.

R.E.C. Browne, *The Ministry of the Word*, SCM Press 1958.

J.J. Hughes, *Absolutely Null and Utterly Void*, Sheed & Ward 1968.

Von Campenhausen's book is an authoritative account of the ordained ministry in the first three centuries. Moberly's work, published first in 1899, is the classical expression of the Anglican doctrine of the priesthood. *The Pioneer Ministry* is an attempt to present much the same doctrine in terms of our modern understanding of the New Testament. *Christian Priesthood Examined* shows how presbyters came to be called priests. The two books by Schillebeeckx and the book by Brown show us two good Roman Catholic scholars who are prepared to face the facts about the origin of the ministry. Dr M. Thrall has written an able vindication of the ordination of women to the priesthood. The Archbishops' Commission Report shows how far the Church of England was prepared to go twenty years ago. The FOAG Report is a careful expression of the Anglican doctrine of priesthood today. Hughes gives us an accurate and often amusing narrative of how the Bull, *Apostolicae Curae* came to be issued.

Index of Names

Index of Biblical References